Determination of $H\rho$ for magnetic field

Magnetic apparatus .042 cm apart
Mag field constant over 1.9 cm but taking into account average field, it corresponds to 8400 over a distance of 3.3 cms

$\therefore 2\rho d = (3.3)^2 \quad \therefore \rho = \frac{\ldots}{2} D$

Now β or more rays are all deviated for a magnetic field of 9600 units

~~ρ for that value $= \frac{(3.3)^2}{2 \times .042} = \frac{1090}{.0084} = 116$ cms~~

~~$\therefore H\rho = 9600 \times 116 = 1136000$~~

= ~~Now for E~~ Now value of d for that apparatus

$d = D + \frac{3.3}{1.65} = .3D$

$\therefore H\rho = 9600 \times 39 = \underline{378000}$

= Now for E-S apparatus $D = .055$ cms
Magnetic field constant over 4.5 cms
& completely deviated for a field of 6500 units

$2\rho d = (4.5)^2$

$\therefore d = D + \frac{4.5}{.9} = 6D$

$\rho = \frac{20.2}{6 \times .055} = 61$

$\therefore H\rho = 61 \times 6500$

$\therefore$ Mean value $H\rho = \underline{387,000}$

Rutherford and Physics
at the Turn
of the Century

Rutherford, ca. 1905, courtesy of Otto Hahn.

Rutherford and Physics at the Turn of the Century

edited by
Mario Bunge and William R. Shea

DAWSON
AND
SCIENCE HISTORY PUBLICATIONS
NEW YORK
1979

First published in the United States by
Neale Watson Academic Publications, Inc.
156 Fifth Avenue, New York, N.Y. 10010

© Neale Watson Academic Publications, Inc. 1979
Printed and manufactured in the U.S.A.

Published in Great Britain
by Wm. Dawson & Sons, Ltd.
Cannon House Folkestone,
Kent, England
ISBN 0-7129-0918-4

Library of Congress Cataloging in Publication Data
Main entry under title:

Rutherford and physics at the turn of the century.

   1. Physics—History—Addresses, essays, lectures.
2. Rutherford, Ernest Rutherford, baron, 1871–1937.
3. Physicists—Great Britain—Biography. I. Shea,
William R. II. Bunge, Mario Augusto.
QC7.5.R87   530′.09′041   78–13986
ISBN 0-88202-184-2

Acknowledgments

The editors gratefully acknowledge the generous
support of the Canada Council and McGill University
who, by sponsoring the Rutherford Symposium in
October 1977, made this volume possible. They also
wish to thank the Royal Society for the kind
permission to reprint Professor Norman Feather's
article which appeared in the *Proceedings of the
Royal Society*.

In memory of
Guglielmo Righini (1908–1978)

Contents

Preface

In 1903, Rutherford and Soddy published a paper on "Radioactive Change" in which they traced a series of products derived by successive discharges of an alpha particle from three elements, uranium, thorium, and radium, and concluded that radioactivity was in its nature essentially different from hitherto known physical operations. The last paragraph of this remarkable paper contains the following statement: "All these considerations point to the conclusion that the energy latent in the atom must be enormous compared to that rendered free in ordinary chemical change. Now the radio-elements differ in no way from the other elements in their chemical and physical behaviour. On the one hand they resemble chemically the inactive prototypes in the periodic system very closely, and on the other hand they possess no common chemical characteristics which could be associated with radioactivity. Hence there is no reason to assume that this enormous store of energy is possessed by the radio-elements alone....The maintenance of solar energy, for example, no longer presents any fundamental difficulty if the internal energy of the component elements is considered to be available, i.e., if processes of sub-atomic change are going on."

These predictions were fulfilled in 1937 by Hans Bethe when he worked out the cycle of atomic transformations that probably maintain the sun's energy, and in 1942 by Enrico Fermi when atomic energy was first released on a large scale at the University of Chicago. But in 1903, they seemed little more than a humorous remark. The well-known British scientist William W. Dampier in a letter to Rutherford referred to "Your playful suggestions that, could a proper detonator be found, it was just conceivable that a wave of atomic disintegration might be started through matter, which would indeed make this old world vanish in smoke." Elsewhere he mentions Rutherford's "joke" that "some fool in a laboratory might blow up the universe unawares." Three-quarters of a century later, when the possibility of procuring energy through atomic transmutation holds out, on the one hand, a promise of untold economic prosperity, and, on the other, a threat of universal destruction, Dampier's facetiousness sounds grim.

We live in an atomic age, and less than two decades since scientists put forward the bold idea that every atom had a very small electrically charged core in which practically all its matter was concentrated, hun-

1

dreds of thousands of men and women all over the world are devoting their lives to harnessing nuclear power. The governments of the developed and developing nations invest more money on the new science than they formerly spent on their armies and navies. The change has been so rapid and so complete that we are apt to forget how recent it is and how much it derives from the pioneering work of Rutherford and the scientists who shared his discoveries. The essays of Lawrence Badash, John L. Heilbron, Norman Feather, Thaddeus J. Trenn, and Stanley L. Jaki paint the living man at work and provide us with illuminating insights into his character, his methods, his qualities, and his influence. It is, however, difficult to appreciate a scientist's contribution without some understanding of the conditions in which he lived, and the essays by Erwin N. Hiebert, Neil Cameron, Stephen Brush, and Guglielmo Righini offer lucid and penetrating analyses of some of the most important institutional and intellectual aspects of science at the beginning of the twentieth century.

Rutherford was essentially an experimentalist with a tendency to mistrust any theory involving conceptions of which he could not form a clear mental image. When Sir Arthur Eddington remarked after a dinner party that possibly electrons were only mental concepts, Rutherford got up and exclaimed, "Not exist? Not exist? Why I can see them as plainly as I can see that spoon in front of me." He applied his own great intellectual gifts to devising simple experiments that were marvellously fruitful, and he was never deterred by lack of funds. His optimism in the power of the human mind is enshrined in words that are beginning to re-echo through departments of physics: "We've got no money so we've got to think."

William R. Shea

The State of Physics at the Turn of the Century

ERWIN N. HIEBERT

From McGill, in 1902, Rutherford wrote to his mother: "I am now busy writing up papers for publication and doing fresh work. I have to keep going, as there are always people on my track. I have to publish my present work as rapidly as possible in order to keep in the race."[1] A study of the history of physics around 1900 certainly gives one the impression that hitherto unexplored domains of natural phenomena were being identified and experimentally sought out and exploited. It is plausible to assume that for Rutherford, as for many other physicists of his day, it was just second nature to get into the act, "keep in the race," and get on with the new discoveries as briskly as possible.

It may be observed, further, that scientists, in general, and physicists, in particular, were remarkably vocal about discussing and analyzing the implications of the novel trends that the turn of the century ushered in for them. Physicists were presented with a new challenge to explore a wide spectrum of hitherto unrecognized experimental techniques to pry into the laws of nature, and notably at the molecular and atomic levels. Consequently, it is not surprising to discover that they undertook to evaluate the state of physics in relation to the strategy that might be required to rebuild the discipline on new foundations.

In this paper the objective has been to examine the state of physics at the turn of the century as seen from the point of view of physicists. To achieve this end it has been my intention, as much as possible, to refrain from engaging in an interpretation of events that is colored, in hindsight, by what we all know happened later on during our century. I have in mind the in-depth study of X-rays, radioactivity, black body radiation, quantum phenomena, atomic and molecular structure, spectra, and relativity. These new fields of inquiry stood out most prominently on the horizon at the time. Their complicated, puzzling, and far-reaching implications were pursued most effectively, triumphantly, and with great intensity, for at least three decades. I want to accentuate in this context that it has been my firm resolve to furnish a conspectus of physics around 1900 that does not take the history of twentieth-century physics as its sphere of action or horizon. The focus is rather singlemindedly on what professional physicists had to say

3

about the state of their own dicipline at the time, i.e., around 1900, plus or minus five years.

Fortunately, there is a great wealth of literature, written around 1900, that is devoted to reflection on the nature of the accomplishments of physics in the nineteenth century. This is frequently coupled with comments about the pressing and most significant unsolved problems of the day and various prognoses for the direction that physics might take for the future. In fact, there is far more readily accessible literature pertinent to this topic than I possibly could have examined with care for presentation on this historic occasion that marks the opening of the new Rutherford physics building here at McGill University.

We recognize, of course, that historians of science always are blessed with a great outpouring of reflections about the current state of affairs at chronologically conspicuous times such as the end of the century, mid-century, and other whole number increments thereof. Nineteen hundred, accordingly, is no exception. The literature on the subject could inundate the historian. The problem primarily, therefore, is one of choice of materials that are worth examining with care.

Our method will be to approach the literature on the subject in three different ways. First, we are interested in discovering what major trends and currents of opinion were thought to be shaping the direction in which the discipline of physics was moving around 1900. Second, we would like to know what physicists considered to be the anchor points of the discipline that had not been put in jeopardy by recent discoveries and trends, and that, therefore, not having been challenged, probably would be extended in the future with confidence and anticipation of new rewards. Third, we want to search out those comments and evaluations of the current discoveries and the expansion of the discipline that were thought by physicists to show the greatest promise for the advancement of physics, and that, in fact, were seen to suggest novel and revolutionary changes that either had not been clearly anticipated or not anticipated at all.

I have chosen this approach to my topic of the state of physics at the turn of the century because I thought that it would be appropriate to see if we can discover something significant about the self-image of the physicist around 1900. Accordingly, I have adopted these three themes around which to structure my comments: major trends, anchor points, and puzzling problems.

Growing Perceived Unity of the Physical Sciences

Never before, we are told by physicists, has there been a greater need for persons capable of encompassing the entire sweep of physical science and thought in a unified way that will take cognizance of the radical conceptual reformulation of physics indicated by the new discoveries. The complexity of recently disclosed phenomena are greeted with considerable bewilderment but with exhilaration and high expectations. In the background, of course, are the glorious theoretical conquests of the nineteenth century: mechanics, thermodynamics and electromagnetic theory. They occupy a prominent place in the physical sciences by virtue of the multiplicity of far-reaching deductions that can be drawn from a surprisingly small number of fundamental principles. It simply is taken for granted that the range and strength of potential coherence between these three major branches of natural science and the recent discoveries will contribute to the unity of physics and thicken the bonds of kinship with mathematics, astronomy, chemistry, and philosophy. I suspect that fields such as evolutionary cosmology, meteorology, and geophysics, notably, provided important stimuli for the new physics, but I have not examined them in this context.

Progress is a conspicuous keynote. It finds its affirmation not only in reference to the recognition of expansion in the knowledge of the nature of things, but also in expressions of self-confidence about the growth of refinement in the methods of scientific investigation. Declarations concerning the unity of the physical sciences frequently are correlated with the forceful suggestion that the correct methods of scientific investigation are on the verge of being mastered and that those methods will be applicable to all of the natural sciences. At least by implication, a strong scientific reductionism is silently and patiently at work.

It is apparent that physics is considered to occupy, among the sciences, a position of preeminence by virtue of its generality, fundamental nature, and theoretical pertinence for all the other sciences. One might argue that this was the case throughout history, but I see that it is a far more openly and brazenly advocated position around the turn of the century than earlier. What is the historical rationale for this? Can it be correlated with the rise, cultivation, perpetuation, and revival of Comtian or critical positivism? Can it be attributed to the unambiguous evidence for the continuous and successful exploitation and accelerated progress in all the traditional, i.e., nineteenth-century, branches of physics? Can it be attributed, mainly, to the high density of sensational discoveries following rapidly upon one another over a short period of time at the turn of the century?

While all of these components may be invoked to account for the alleged elite position of physics around 1900, there are a number of additional factors that merit our attention. The future of electrical technology, at the time, was seen to be very promising, indeed, although we recognize that much of what was known to be technically and economically feasible

was communicated at the level of grand exhibitions and public demonstrations. In any case, reflections on the state of science constitute a veritable hymn of praise for practical progress in electrical engineering:
motors and dynamos with shuttle-wound armatures, polyphase transmission, electric induction machinery, frequency transformers, the tele-
phone, the microphone, and wireless telegraphy. There is hardly a word
about the use of combustion engines for transportation, but the number
of articles devoted to the rosy future that was about to be ushered in by
electrical means of communication is impressive to say the least.

Implausible as it may seem on the face of things, in no other area can
a convincing case be made to demonstrate that physics around 1900 owed
its exalted status to practical accomplishments. Nor does there appear to
be much evidence that physics commanded great attention because of
what it had to contribute to the life-style of most persons in society—at
least not in comparison with disciplines such as chemistry or biology.

The practical importance and prominence of chemistry undoubtedly
was considerably more conspicuous than physics, at least at the level of
public awareness of various products and processes. In this connection we
may mention: mining and metallurgical practice (assaying, alloys), phar-
macy (drugs, anaesthetics), agriculture (nitrogen fixation, synthetic ferti-
lizers), military activities (explosives), textiles (mortising, dyeing), and
fermentation (brewing). There is no counterpart for this in physics at this
time. The same could be said about the biological sciences in reference to
sanitation, epidemiology, and public health. To be sure, I am referring
here to developments in the sciences from the standpoint of the practical
differences that their advancement generated, and not to the perceived
intellectual prowess of the discipline within the academic and scientific
communities in which these advances were spawned. By all accounts our
appraisal of the impact of physics on society in the twentieth century
must be the inverse of the situation I have just described, especially after
World War II.

Again, I suggest that if physics in 1900 was heralded as the queen of
the sciences, this cannot be accounted for by virtue of its advanced organizational or institutional structure. In all of these matters that touch
upon the development and refinement of a professional scientific discipline, physics achieved maturity relatively late when compared with the
professional status of several other natural sciences.

The issue that apparently characterizes the prestige of physics most
accurately among our physicist writers undoubtedly is connected with the
intellectual appeal to what is most fundamental and basic, and thus con-

tributory to discipline, subtlety, and sophistication. In that case, it will help to clarify what was meant by being more fundamental and more basic. From the point of view of the science of matter, for example, it could be maintained, that physics is fundamental by virtue of its preoccupation with views or theories on the structure of matter; whereas a secondary science would have the study of the structure of matter itself as its major objective. Of course, the dividing line between these two is not completely clear. In any case, the expressed difference would give meaning to the saying that a secondary science may have an aim of its own quite distinct from that of the primary sciences, despite being guided, as it were, by the primary science. Thus physics, it seems, was thought in 1900 to influence to a preeminent degree the thinking of scientists in all fields.

Physics of the Large and Small

Another trend that is prominent in the self-reflective literature of physicists around 1900 is the extension of physical principles to the very large and the very small. The power of analogical reasoning, in inferring the unknown and unobservable from the known, is seen to be operative for analysing problems connected both with the remote in space and with the ultimate constituents of matter. The strongest component in the rationale for analogical reasoning invariably is the striking success of mechanical models. Maxwell's approach is frequently cited in this connection.

In the physics of the very small, there seems to have been virtually a 180-degree shift of interest and confidence around 1900. It is seen conspicuously in the way that cautious and anti-atomistic pronouncements disappeared among both physicists and chemists shortly after 1895 when a number of spectacular scientific discoveries began to be announced. Let me mention some of these: the discovery of X-rays as connected with cathode rays (Röntgen, 1895); the demonstration that a cathode discharge carries negative charge with it (Perrin, 1895); the announcement of the discovery of the new chemical element argon as a monatomic gas that had no valency, no chemistry, and no place in the periodic table (Rayleigh, Ramsay, 1895); the discovery of the spontaneous disintegration of certain elements, i.e., radioactivity (Becquerel, 1896); the effect of a magnetic field on spectra, i.e., Zeeman's magneto-optic effect (1896); the Wilson cloud chamber experiments on the particle induced condensation of water vapor in gases (1897); the discovery of the electron as a particle of discrete mass and charge (J.J. Thomson, 1897); the confirmation that cathode rays are particles of high velocity (about one-third the velocity of light) and negatively charged (Wien, 1897–1898); the discovery of the corpuscular nature, charge and velocity of positive rays using combined electric and magnetic deflections (1898–1899); the discovery and isolation of radium and polonium from pitchblend (the Curies, 1898); and the detailed and impressive experimental investigations on radioactivity undertaken by Rutherford and his collaborator, Soddy, while at McGill in Montreal between 1898 and 1907.

In 1908, Jean Perrin announced his exponential law that describes the vertical distribution of colloidal solutions at equilibrium. This work so impressed the die-hard opponent of atomism, Ostwald, that in 1909, in the preface to the fourth edition of his *Grundriss der allgemeinen Chemie,* he made the straightforward confession that he had adopted the idea of the physical existence of atoms and had abandoned his anti-atomistic philosophy.

The encroachment of atomic-molecular ideas and the kinetic theory, however, is not only visible in reference to spectacular discoveries such as X-rays, radioactivity, and electron studies, but also extends to views on the ether, optics, thermodynamics, and electromagnetic studies. Robert Woodward, Columbia University Professor of Mechanics and Mathematical Physics, writes in 1904, "It would be too bold, perhaps, to assert that the trend of accumulating knowledge is toward an atomic unity of matter, but the day seems not far distant when there will be room for a new *Principia* and for a treatise that will accomplish for molecular systems what the *Mécanique Céleste* accomplished for the solar system." And then he adds: "If the progress of physics during the past century has been chiefly in the direction of atomic theory, the progress of chemistry has been still more so. Chemistry is, in fact, the science of atoms and molecules *par excellence.*"[2]

Citing the work of Faraday, Bunsen and Kirchhoff, Gibbs and Helmholtz, Woodward identifies the recent progress in molecular science with the gradual disappearance of the imaginary lines that have served to separate chemistry and physics. This line of reasoning is not at all uncommon in the physics literature: *viz.,* the appropriation to the discipline of physics of domains once thought to be the sole prerogative of chemistry. Thus chemistry is frequently identified as the physics of the atom. Earlier on, in the nineteenth century, essentially the same thing happened when heat and electricity—once the domain of chemistry—were added to physics or natural philosophy so-called.

Great strides, similarly, were taken in the extension of physical reasoning to the very large. The application of gravitational theory to all aspects of celestial phenomena was the monumental accomplishment of the eighteenth and nineteenth centuries; however, more pertinent for evaluating opinions in this direction at the turn of the century is the development of astrophysics as a major scientific discipline. I cannot discuss that here, but want to indicate that the phenomenal progress in astrophysics and spectroscopy toward the century's end, supplied a most important component in the argument of an essential material—and molecular—unity throughout all nature.

Scientific Speculation Sanctioned

Physicists at the turn of the century were becoming increasingly aware that unforeseen phenomena and new functional dependencies were being discovered that could not have been predicted on established theoretical grounds. Taking risks, accordingly, was something to be encouraged, especially in view of the strongly held belief that empirical findings sooner or later would reveal and automatically eliminate empty and harmless speculations. It need hardly be emphasized that the prevailing scientific sentiment was not conducive to one that would have encouraged physicists to engage in the occult, the mystical, and the obscure. Rather, the accent was on the positive stimulus and heuristic value of imaginative and interrogative assumptions that might generate experimentally feasible and theoretically fertile consequences.

At this stage of my studies I am prepared only to suggest—without having examined the situation in its details—that physicists around 1900 were caught up in a spirit of scientific speculation that would have been considered quite reckless ten years earlier. At least it is apparent to me that the majority of physicists around 1900 were far more willing to challenge the fixity of the traditional categories of physics than they had been a decade earlier, when mechanics, heat, light, electricity, and magnetism were lumped together theoretically under dynamics, thermodynamics, and electrodynamics.

Collaborative Investigations

By 1900 a number of fields of experimental enquiry were recognized to be well beyond the easy reach of individual investigators. Collaborative work was being especially stressed, for example, in spectral studies, the establishment of standard scientific units, and the study of matter under extremes of temperature and pressure. Access to adequate instrumentation for precision experiments, to be sure, had become a matter of high priority. Cooperative group projects had been and were being shaped in connection with the establishment of enterprising and well-funded national laboratories such as Berlin (1887–1890), London (1900), and Washington (1901).

With an increase in the number of investigators engaged in physical measurements in highly structured laboratories, experimental precision, at times, became an end in itself. Not only were analytical instruments being pushed to the limits of measurement, but special apparatus was designed to increase the accuracy of measurement irrespective of any explicitly formulated theoretical rationale for more precise information. I will not venture to say whether this new thrust toward precision measurements was furthered mainly by the personal satisfaction of scientific craftsmen, revelling in the wizardry of analytical instrumentation, or to the perpetuation of a world view committed to the extension, through refinement, of the basic constants of physics. The situation probably fostered both—wizardry and refinement of the known—and, undoubtedly, reveals that superior experimentalists were being reared in continually increasing numbers, even if no Newton, Lagrange, or Maxwell were visible on the horizon.

Conservation of Energy

Radioactive transformation studies, early on, suggested modifications in the doctrine of the conservation of mass. There was also some talk about violations of the principle of conservation of energy, but most investigators agreed that conservation of mass was far more likely to lose its place among the category of the most fundamental conceptions. On this question the contrast between Ernst Mach, Henri Poincaré, and Max Planck provides a case in point. For Mach the energy conservation principle, although deeply rooted in the experiential impossibility of a *perpetuum mobile*, was just another theoretical principle invented to simplify various complexes of related functional dependencies. He thought it not at all impossible, writing in 1892, that the principle would someday outlive its purpose and be replaced by other, more useful concepts.[3] Similarly, Poincaré regarded conservation of energy as no more than a useful convention. In 1906, Poincaré, having analyzed the doctrine of energy and thermodynamics, simply concluded: "Of the principle of conservation of energy there is nothing left but an enunciation. There is something which remains constant. In this form it ... is outside the bounds of experiment and reduced to a kind of tautology."[4]

Such views, it seems to me, were very much in the minority among physicists at the turn of the century. Planck's view, in fact, was far more representative, *viz.* that the principle of conservation of energy is an accurate representation of the really real world and, therefore, was destined to maintain its preeminent position in physics. Planck was quite adamant about this. I want to suggest, therefore, that physicists in general supposed that the new experimental discoveries and theoretical trends should and could be integrated into the discipline of physics with the help of strong support from the principle of conservation of energy. It often was cited at this time as a well-established and perennially fertile anchor point.

Periodic Table of Chemical Elements

By the turn of the century, the periodic table was almost universally recognized to be an enormous aid in organizing a very heterogeneous cluster of individual bits of empirical information about the chemical elements. Whereas chemists had been preoccupied with periodic relationships for almost three decades, physicists only realized the pertinence of periodicity in physics when they sought to develop theories for the structure of matter that would encompass recent discoveries and trends. The question of the nature of the internally structured atom was seen to depend upon the correlation of periodic relationships with both the chemical behavior of the elements and precision measurements of their physical properties. The discovery in 1896 of argon, as a completely unreactive monatomic gas, opened up a number of theoretically bothersome questions about atomic structure in relation to atomic weight, spectra, valency, and the kinetic theory of gases.

The experiments connected with the phenomenon of radioactivity, of course, brought the periodic table right to the doorstep of physics. By 1900 there was a growing consensus that periodicity was closely connected with electrically charged particles as ultimate constituents of matter. J.J. Thomson's work had shown that since electrons from different elements are identical, it was plausible to suppose that all matter was composed of electrons as the ultimate units. This was a position that was not borne out by Rutherford's investigations.

In physical chemistry—newly launched in 1887—physicists made a number of crucial, fundamental contributions toward the end of the nineteenth century and onwards. The relation of electrolytic dissociation to valency and periodicity had been recognized and used to advantage before any acceptable structure of matter theory was put forward. But around 1900 all of these issues were taken up anew with vigour and dispatch not only by chemists, but by an increasing number of physicists. The periodic table had become an important new anchor point around which physicists proceeded to build a physics of matter at the atomic-molecular level.

Electromagnetic Theory

Comments about the electromagnetic theory, in both frequency of discussion and enthusiastic recognition of its unchallenged status in physics, far outweigh anything I have said about conservation of energy or the periodic table. Electromagnetism, in both theory and application, was treated as the most conspicuously successful and unifying accomplishment of the nineteenth century. It was emphasized that post-Maxwellian expositions and enlargements of the theory had added nothing but glory to this chapter of physics. To name just the most outstanding exposés of Maxwell's theory of 1873 we have the monographs of Helmholtz (1874), Rayleigh (1881), Poynting (1884), Heaviside (1889), Hertz (1890), Lorentz (1890), Boltzmann (1890), Duhem (1902), and Abraham (1904).

In 1890 Hertz had written: "We cannot study this wonderful theory without at times feeling as if an independent life and a reason of its own dwelt in these mathematical formulae; as if they were wiser than we were, wiser even than their discoverer; as if they gave out more than had been put into them."[5] Commenting on Hertz's statement Boltzmann wrote: "I should like to add to these words of Hertz only this, that Maxwell's formulae are simple consequences from his mechanical models; and Hertz's enthusiastic praise is due in the first place, not to Maxwell's analysis, but to his acute penetration in the discovery of mechanical analogies."[6]

All of this is fine, but we also may recall that toward the end of the century physicists such as Larmor, Lorentz, Abraham and Kaufman essentially stood Maxwell's theory on its head. They argued that the power of Maxwell's theory to absorb the concept of matter as an electromagnetic phenomenon was fundamental although Maxwell had developed his equations with the help of analogical reasoning that was utterly mechanical.

Maxwell fully recognized the transitory role of his mechanical models, but it was surely an audacious theory that sought to explain matter and its laws of motion and detailed behavior in terms of the properties of the ether and electricity rather than the other way around. Physicists reflecting on trends in their own discipline recognized the dawn of a new era when it became clear that they were being called upon to grapple more seriously with the physics of the ether and the electron, than with the physics of matter in motion under the influence of forces. Accordingly, whether one examines the literature of theory or of practice, it is unambiguously evident that the electromagnetic theory was as firm an anchor point for future investigations as anything can be.

The Ether

When we come to consider the areas of investigation that were seen to contain the most pressing issues in need of elucidation and solution, we find that the ether problem is a matter of high priority. An understanding of the nature of the ether is seen to be an enigma, but also the focus of great potential promise for the future of physics.

First of all, it is evident that apparent failure has dominated all attempts to reconcile the law of gravitation with other rapidly developing branches of physics. Physicists claim to have gained virtually no insight into understanding the mechanism of gravitation. The most frequent solutions to this problem are assumed to be connected with views on the nature of the ether; but the ether, too, turns out to defy analysis. At the turn of the century, the assumption of the ether obviously continued to be invoked as an intellectual necessity—*viz.*, that forces can only be explained with reference to pressures exerted between the contiguous particles of an underlying medium. The most troublesome questions about the ether centered about its nature, function, the properties needed to fulfill that function, and its connection with mechanics, radiation, and the constitution of matter.

There was, nevertheless, one dominant, optimistic note: Some satisfaction and encouragement was gleaned from rehearsing the earlier even more confusing history of the various ethers that had been invoked to account for optical, thermal, chemical, and electromagnetic phenomena. To move from a pluralism of ethers to a single luminiferous ether represented some progress. The whole field of optics, as Maxwell had shown, could be treated as a branch of electromagnetics. Artificially produced electromagnetic waves, as Hertz had shown, were identical with light waves. The idea of one universal medium as a basis for all physical phe-

nomena was not altogether new to the theoretical physicist, but the unifi-
cation of optics and electricity did much to reinforce this conception. The
weakness of the ether hypothesis was that its existence was totally a matter
of inference; but the null result of the Michelson-Morley experiment was
not taken as seriously as modern physics books would have us believe.

The strength of the ether hypothesis was its apparent universal adapt-
ability. Helmholtz and Kelvin, notably, had explored the idea of the atom
as the vortex motion of a perfect fluid—the ether. It had been conjectured
that J.J. Thomson's corpuscles and Stoney's electrons were to be interpreted
as phenomena of the ether. There were physicists, too, who would have
been satisfied to reduce all of physical chemistry (with its atoms and ions)
and all of molecular physics to the mechanics of the ether. Even the theoretical difficulties associated with the transmutation of elements were softened by postulating that matter might be regarded as the product of certain
operations performed on the ether—to explain variations in mass, and, if
needs be, both the creation and disappearance of matter.

Such conjectures suggest another issue that may be formulated as a
question. Despite a plethora of clever hypotheses and numerous experimental attempts, why was there no positive evidence to decide whether
the luminiferous ether passes through matter or participates in the translation of matter? One plausible response was that the issue had been
wrongly posed and formulated, i.e., in terms of a corpuscular rather than
an undulatory theory. At one time the problem of the ether had been
formulated in connection with issues such as action-at-a-distance, gravitation, and aberration. By 1900 the ether idea had taken wings and existed as a problem on its own merits. It gradually had become woven into
the fabric of the theories of electromagnetism.

Indeed, the electromagnetic world view seemed to stand a good
chance of replacing the mechanical world view. Larmor argued that matter has an electrical base. J.J. Thomson was gathering evidence in favor of
the electromagnetic view and suggested that the primordial element of
matter was the electron. It was not, we must remember, until 1911 that
Rutherford published his nuclear theory of the atom based on the alpha
scattering experiments initiated by Geiger and Marsden. Lodge wrote in
1904: "Electricity under strain constitutes 'charge'; electricity in locomo-
tion constitutes a current and magnetism; electricity in vibration constitutes light. What electricity itself is we do not know, but it may perhaps
be a form or aspect of matter. So have taught for thirty years the disciples
of Clerk-Maxwell. Now we can go one step further and say, Matter is
composed of electricity, and nothing else,—a thesis which I wish to explain

and partially justify."[7] In essence physicists could take their pick: Matter is composed of electricity and nothing else; or, matter is composed of ether and nothing else. Still, the puzzle remained: What is electricity and what is ether?

Electron Theory

The overriding concern and most pressing topic of discussion at the turn of the century was that of electron theory. In the minds of physicists, the problems connected with the electron were closely tied to the conception of the ether. By 1900 the experimental and theoretical triumphs of electron physics were conspicuous. They extend from the work of Plücker and Hittorf in 1868 to that of Crookes (1879), Goldstein (1886), Hertz (1892), Lenard (1894), Perrin (1895), Röntgen (1895), Lorentz (1895), Becquerel (1896), Zeeman (1897), the Curies (1898), J.J. Thomson (1898), Walter Kaufmann (1898), and so on, to the brilliant theory of atomic disintegration of Rutherford and Soddy. The theory of the electron had become the trust and the mandate of the twentieth century. No physicist who neglected the physics of the electron would henceforth come to terms with the discipline.

The electron, it was conjectured, would occupy a prominent place in the restructuring of dynamics on an electromagnetic basis. Electron physics was invoked to explain the electrical conduction of metals, the index of refraction, optical dispersion, spectra, the Balmer formula, Rydberg's law of spectral groupings, the breakdown of atomic structure, phenomena associated with heat, light, and X-rays, magnetism, and diamagnetism.

The most beautifully clear, informative, and provocative account of the state of electron and ether physics at the turn of the century is given in a paper of 1904 by the 32-year-old Paul Langevin. He was well qualified by training to provide good critical insight on the state of the subject at the time. He had worked under J.J. Thomson when the Cavendish Laboratory first admitted foreign students and had received his doctorate in 1902 while working with the Curies in Paris.

In 1904 Langevin asserted that the discontinuous structure of electric charge was the most striking characteristic of recent progress in electricity. He felt that its consequences extended and illuminated the whole network of physics from electromagnetism to optics and radiant heat. We see that Langevin essentially identified the immovable ether with the electromagnetic medium, and the origin of electromagnetic radiation with the electron undergoing acceleration.

Langevin, in fact, believed that the idea of the electron was so fundamental that a vast new synthesis was conceivable of which the main lines but not the details had been specified. He remarks that there can be no electric charge without matter and no matter without electricity. The ether, he feels. is completely known from the electromagnetic and optical points of view; nevertheless, how the ether and matter are related is unknown. The electron, being a particle and carrying electricity, therefore, presents the ideal situation to explore the relationship between matter and the electric field.

How this is to be accomplished is the real puzzle. Langevin is not sure that the problem has been formulated correctly. He writes: "Perhaps there is a difficulty which belongs to the actual constitution of our minds, habituated by our secular evolution to think through matter, unable to form a concrete representation which is not material; also it seems scarcely reasonable to seek to construct a simple medium such as the ether by considering it to spring from a complex and various medium like matter. I believe it will be necessary to think *ether,* to conceive of it independently of all material representations, by means of those electromagnetic properties which put us in contact with it."[8]

To the extent that Langevin's views represent the opinions of a large segment of the physics community—and I am convinced that they do—it would seem that the whole world of the new physics at the turn of the century was dominated by electrical ideas "as the place of choice where the explorer feels that he can found a city before advancing into new territories."[9] This conviction is based on the realization, as Langevin puts it, that "already all views, not only of the ether, but of matter, source, and receiver of luminous waves, obtain an immediate interpretation which mechanics is powerless to give, and this mechanics itself appears today as a first approximation...but for which a more complete expression must be sought in the dynamics of the electron."[10]

Langevin's concluding appraisal about the relation of the physics of electrons to the other branches of physics is supremely optimistic. He certainly believes that physics finally is on the right track. He says: "Although still very recent, the conceptions of which I have sought to give a collected idea are about to penetrate to the very heart of the entire physics, and to act as a fertile germ in order to crystallize around it, in a new order, facts very far removed from one another."[11]

Problems connected with the electron and its relation to the ether, matter, and electromagnetic theory, clearly, reached a state of self-evident

visibility during the first decade of the twentieth century, despite old, unsolved puzzles and new, uncorrelated phenomena. Gravity stood completely and obstinately outside of the electromagnetic synthesis.
Gravitational forces simply were superimposed on electromagnetic forces.
If gravitational forces were known to be far too weak to account for the
cohesion of matter, however, how were they to be accounted for by electromagnetic forces? The nature of positive electrons, X-rays, and Goldstein's Kanalstrahlen were all obscure. No explanation of the radioactive
disintegration of the elements was forthcoming, although it had been suggested that accelerating electrons in the atom lost energy by radiation,
thus to diminish their velocity and reach a state of instability like a spinning top that falls. The chemical modifications associated with radioactivity had hardly been unexplored.

Radioactivity

The discovery of radioactivity initiated many questions that were
quite embarrassing to traditional physics and chemistry. For example, the
method of estimating the age of the earth from a consideration of its cooling
had been thought by most physicists to be sufficiently sound to challenge
figures presented by geologists and biologists. Radioactive studies suggested that the progress of physics in this domain now had to be abandoned. Within chemistry the discovery of radioactivity introduced so many
fascinating and puzzling phenomena and so many proposed explanations
that a whole new domain was added to the discipline, *viz.*, radiochemistry.

The study of spontaneous chemical reactions, properly speaking, always had belonged to chemical thermodynamics. Now spontaneous
atomic disintegration reactions brought into play the periodic table,
chemical dynamics (i.e., kinetics), transmutation, atomic structure, the
question about the source of nuclear energy, and much more evidence to
support the incredible complexity of the internally structured atom.
W.K. Clifford, reasoning from spectra, had put it right when he said "an
atom must be at least as complex as a grand piano."[12] The structure of
matter obviously was very intricate, but at least the facts about the structured atom gleaned from radioactive studies were seen to be harmonious
and beautiful, and indicative of steady and inevitable progress—experimentally, that is.

Between 1903 and 1904 monographs on the state of radioactive investigations were published by Marie Curie, Henri Becquerel, Ernest Rutherford, and Frederick Soddy. A concise and excellent summary of the most pressing problems facing investigators in radioactivity was given in an address by Rutherford in 1904, i.e., after six years of intensive research on the subject at McGill.

As Rutherford saw it, the problems facing investigators in the immediate future hinged upon determining the nature of the characteristic alpha, beta, and gamma emanations from radioactive substances. Rutherford obviously felt that the phenomena were very complex, but that the best clue would be provided by the electromagnetic theory, namely, predicted deflections in magnetic and electric fields. In this context he also treated questions about charge, mass, velocity, penetration, the ionization characteristics, and the mass alterations of the various emanations as a function of velocity. While he highly praises the experimental work of Becquerel and Kaufman, he treads lightly on questions of theoretical interpretation. He suggests various hypotheses to account for the known facts, but concludes: "The question is in a very unsatisfactory state, and requires further investigation."[13]

There simply are many unknowns in Rutherford's mind at this time. He puzzles about the difference between positive and negative electricity, about the unexplained nature of secondary rays produced by gamma rays, about the huge amounts of energy involved in emission, and about the conceivable external and internal sources of that energy. He spends considerable time discussing the major differences between radioactivity and ordinary chemical reactions. He is unable to resolve questions associated with the specific chemical changes involved in radioactive disintegrations. In paragraph upon paragraph Rutherford reports the fascinating new results encountered in the study of radioactivity, but invariably ends by saying "no adequate explanation has yet been put forward." It was all very novel, very fascinating, and very promising, but also very unintelligible. Obviously, much was at stake that was in need of theoretical elucidation.

The Second Law of Thermodynamics

Finally, we turn to an older more classical nineteenth-century problem that continued to present serious theoretical dilemmas. The second law of thermodynamics was not, in general, received at the turn of the century without substantial reservations. Barus wrote in 1900: "Clausius, indeed, succeeded in surmounting most of the objections, even those contained in theoretically delicate problems associated with radiation. Nevertheless, the confusion raised by the invocation of Maxwell's 'demon' has never been quite calmed; and while Boltzmann (1877, 1878), refers to the second law as a case of probability, Helmholtz (1882) admits that the law is an expression of our inability to deal with the individual atom. Irreversible processes are quite beyond the pale of thermodynamics. For these the famous inequality of Clausius is the only refuge. The value of an uncompensated transformation is always positive."[14] Our author recognizes that Boltzmann, Clausius, and Helmholtz all have invented mechanical systems which more or less fully conform to the second law. However, "Gibb's (1902) elementary principles of statistical mechanics seem...to contain the nearest approach to a logical justification of the second law," but his approach is "more than a dynamical illustration."[15]

Difficulties with theoretical interpretations apart, fruitful applications of the second law abound in physics and more conspicuously in physical chemistry in the works of investigators such as Duhem, Planck, van't Hoff, Helmholtz, and Gibbs. By 1905 the Nernst heat theorem, built as it was on second-law considerations, promised to offer the first practical solution to crucial questions in chemistry associated with equilibrium, process, spontaneity, and molecular stability. By contrast, chemical dynamics were in a primitive state. The literature around the turn of the century is richly decorated with vigorous critical discussions about the theoretical status of the second law, but there is little doubt about its fundamental permanence in physics. The details, we are told, will have to be hammered out critically. It was not an easy assignment.

Before leaving this discussion of the puzzling and pressing problems that dominated the reflections of physicists around 1900, a comment is in order about the status of radiation theory. In fact, topics such as black body radiation, the experimental activities going on at the Physikalisch-technische Reichsanstalt in Berlin, and Planck's quantum ideas receive surprisingly little comment. The results are reported in survey and review articles, but without much pretension or amplification. It was not until around 1913 that Bohr's work led scientists to focus on the quantum theory. Far greater emphasis was placed on spectral studies as such, on detection instruments to extend the spectrum into the far infra-red and ultra-violet, and on subjects such as anomalous dispersion. The Lorentz theory of 1892, according to which light is caused by vibrating electrons, and the prediction that splitting should occur in a magnetic field, were topics of great interest, especially when the Zeeman experiments of 1896 gave an e/m value in good agreement with J.J. Thomson's value of 1897.

In a rather incomplete, and therefore preliminary, way, I have now covered the main points that I wanted to make about the major trends, anchor points, and puzzling problems in physics around 1900. Let me, however, attempt to repeat and elucidate a number of the salient features of our problem, in order to achieve a more integrated representation of the self-image of the physicist that I am trying to capture. We began with Rutherford lamenting in 1902 that he was putting forth a great effort "in order to keep in the race." Almost everywhere that he and his contemporaries looked, they discovered that adequate explanations had not yet been put forward. At the turn of the century new phenomena and unsolved puzzles were generated in greater abundance than readily acceptable explanations, theoretical solutions, and syntheses. Rarely in the history of physics had one had the opportunity to look so far either into the past or the future.

It seems to me that there can be no doubt that whole new domains of physics (and chemistry) were being opened up at the turn of the century, and that this new thrust was initiated in connection with fundamental novelties that hinge on the discovery of the electron and its relation to the electric current, the discovery of cathode rays and their properties, the discovery of X-rays and radioactivity, and the establishment of various methods to deal with the atomicity of electric charge.

And so I wonder what it must have been like to be a scientist at the time, and to become convinced that what was then happening in physics would dominate the whole of physics more than all that had gone on before. One gets the impression on reading the reflective works of physicists around 1900 that, rightly or wrongly, they felt that way, *viz.*, that the events and implications contemporary with their times would soon dominate the whole of physics.

It has been my claim that at the turn of the century in physics, there was an extraordinarily high density of impressive new discoveries that generated new domains of inquiry within the discipline. They simultaneously initiated revolutionary theoretical attempts to embrace the new phenomena, but these received less publicity than the experimental work. The dominant trends that I was able to discern within the physics community at the time were, first, a growing perceived unity of the physical sciences. It is conceivable that this involved more wishful thinking—focused on coming to terms with a superabundance of apparently unrelated and unexplained phenomena—than reality. Some might want to argue that this was no more than the logical extension of nineteenth-century reductionism. In fact, late nineteenth-century critical positivists like Mach, Duhem, and Poincaré, who were often accused of being associated with such trends, were not reductionists at all, but rather maintained a radical pluralism that championed the autonomy of different principles within different scientific disciplines. They did subscribe to a monism of method—a position which is far removed from reductionism, as I understand it.

Second, I sensed among our turn-of-the-century physicists an expansion in mental awareness and an urgency to embrace in one world view the physics of the very large and the very small. Certainly, the proponents of the electromagnetic world view—who emphasized the role of an all-pervading ether that was coupled somehow with electron physics—thought that they had launched a research program that could compete with the mechanical (i.e., dynamical) world view based on the mechanics of matter in motion under the influence of forces—as modelled in gravitational theory.

There were two additional points that I wanted to stress as major trends in physics around 1900, *viz.,* a new relaxed attitude toward scientific speculation and the emphasis on collaborative investigations. I have not investigated these deeply enough to do more than recognize both their importance and the difficulty of providing convincing evidence to give them a prominent place in my analysis. The argument for increased collaborative investigations, plausible as it may seem, needs careful and comparative studies of what actually went on in the major laboratories and research institutes at the time. I have not done it.

Having differentiated a number of major trends in physics around 1900, I proceeded to search out those anchor points of nineteenth-century science that physicists were sure they would not want to, or perforce have to, abandon or even alter radically. In so choosing to bind their perspective to fundamentals which it was inconceivable to challenge, physicists felt that they were ready to construct a different, and if necessary radically new world view that would encompass the newly acquired discoveries and ideas without losing sight of all that had been accomplished since the scientific revolution of the seventeenth century.

As anchor points for the new physics I mentioned the principle of conservation of energy (no surprise), a new commitment to the importance of periodic relationships among the elements, and the near-worship of Maxwell's elegant, comprehensive, and theoretically powerful electromagnetic theory.

Finally, I said something about problems (or rather puzzles and enigmas) that essentially were theoretically unresolved and elusive, but widely recognized to be of great potential significance for the direction that physics would take. I simply want to mention them here again, in this context, as the problems of the ether, the electron, the radioactive disintegration of chemical elements, and the second law of thermodynamics.

I conclude by raising two historically significant questions that come to mind almost instinctively when one attempts to reconstruct the self-image of the physicist around 1900. The first of these may be formulated as follows: To what extent did the self-image of the physicist coincide with the image, or identity, of the physicist held by investigators in other disciplines—both in the sciences (natural and social) and in the humanities? Secondly, how did the self-image of the physicist around 1900 compare with the self-image of the physicist before and after, i.e., during the period of steady growth and expansion of physics in the nineteenth century, and during the so-called exponential growth of physics that more or less coincides with our own times?

Notes

1. Quoted from E.N. da C. Andrade, *Rutherford and the Nature of the Atom*, Garden City, 1964, p. 55.

2. Robert Simpson Woodward, "The Unity of Physical Science", *Congress of Arts and Science, Universal Exposition, St. Louis, 1904*, Boston, 1906, volume 4, p. 5–6.

3. Ernst Mach, "Zur Geschichte und Kritik des Carnot'schen Wärmegesetzes," *Sitzungsberichte der Kaiserlichen Akademie der Wissenschaften*, Wien, *101*, IIa (1892) p. 1611–1612.

4. Henri Poincaré, *Science and Hypothesis*, New York, 1952, p. 127.

5. Heinrich Hertz, "Ueber die Beziehungen zwischen Licht und Elektricität" (1899), *Schriften vermischten Inhalts*, Leipzig, 1895, p. 344.

6. Ludwig Boltzmann, "Ueber die Methoden der theoretischen Physik," *Populäre Schriften*, Leipzig, 1905, p. 8.

7. Oliver Lodge, "Electric Theory of Matter," *Harper's Monthly Magazine, 109* (1904), p. 383.

8. Paul Langevin, "The Relations of Physics of Electrons to other Branches of Science," *Congress of Arts and Science*, Boston, 1906, volume 4, p. 124.

9. *Ibid.*, p. 155

10. *Ibid.*, p. 156

11. *Ibid.*

12. Quoted in Oliver Lodge, *Atoms and Rays*, London, 1924, p. 74.

13. Ernest Rutherford, "Present Problems of Radioactivity," *Congress of Arts and Science*, Boston, 1906, p. 161.

14. Carl Barus, "The Progress of Physics in the Nineteenth Century," *Congress of Arts and Science*, Boston, 1906, p. 42.

15. *Ibid.*, p. 43

The Origins of Big Science:
Rutherford at McGill

LAWRENCE BADASH

The noted geophysicist, Sir Edward Bullard, once told me what it was like to be a research student in Rutherford's Cavendish Laboratory. In need of a length of one-inch diameter steel pipe, he went—with great misgivings—to Lincoln, that ogre of a laboratory steward, with his request. To his surprise, Lincoln was quite agreeable to this "drain" on the laboratory's supplies. He handed Bullard a hacksaw, pointed to an abandoned bicycle in the courtyard, and told him to saw off the bar.

Anecdotes of this sort are prevalent enough to convince one that Rutherford remained throughout his career an exponent of the "sealing wax and string" experimental philosophy. Surely, few have done so much with so little in the way of elaborate apparatus. Yet, I would like to suggest that Rutherford, while still a practitioner of "little science," nevertheless was a harbinger of today's "Big Science," and that we can find the seeds of this transition in his years at McGill.

Quite naturally, the quality and quantity of a person's scientific work stand foremost in evaluating his role. Discovery of thorium emanation, the transformation theory of radioactivity, deflection of alpha rays and their recognition as charged atomic particles, and detection of alpha ray scattering are among the highlights of Rutherford's contributions in Montreal. They were, in fact, impressive enough to win him the Nobel Prize. Yet, this does not go far enough in assessing his impact. Rutherford must be honored also for his institution-building skills. By this I do not mean that he designed, erected, or even directed a laboratory from 1898 to 1907; rather, he developed the infrastructure and environment in which science could be actively pursued. He determined the nature of scientific activity and the behavior of would-be scientists. Indeed, it is in this success that we most clearly see the roots of the transition from little science to Big Science. Contemporaries such as Henri Becquerel and the Curies also had important research contributions to their credit, but they did not establish dynamic "schools" of radioactivity about them. It is the reasons, institutional and personal, for Rutherford's accomplishment that bear examination.

When Rutherford was a boy, the laboratory was a place where students might be allowed to repeat classical experiments on expensive, finely crafted pieces of apparatus. Not long before, scientific instrument collections had been used more to illustrate lectures to students and others than to provide them with opportunities for educating their hands as well as their heads. During Rutherford's youth the style changed still further. The pace of science quickened. Those pursuing it became more professionally oriented, while the research front simultaneously receded into specialized expertise and the number of scientific amateurs dropped. New laboratories were built where research was more the goal than teaching. And the apparatus of science became less decorative and the object of loving craftsmanship, and more functional. This last change removed any inhibitions about altering an elegant instrument, and unused pieces were cannibalized for the next research needs. The professor might still wear a frock coat in the laboratory, but the work bench now represented the sealing wax and string approach, which was, in fact, quite appropriate for a faculty of middle-class origins which had replaced the wealthy bluebloods of previous generations.[1]

With scientific education expanding, its applications increasingly appreciated by society, its practitioners honored, its successes in the headlines of newspapers, and—despite a persistent rumor as the nineteenth century closed that all the great discoveries had been made—its future apparently an exciting one, science was regarded as a profession offering, if not riches, then both upward social mobility and intellectual gratification for those bright and energetic enough to pursue it. In the succeeding years the profession has been transformed—for many—from this exciting adventure into a nine-to-five job with a respectable salary, wherein one connects various pieces of catalogue-ordered apparatus to a computer, which prints out reams of data that Ph.D. candidates—or their working wives—then analyze. The professor, frequently an apparition in his own laboratory, through which he dashes on his way to deliver testimony before some legislative committee or to consult with industry or government on some weapon system, or even to appear on the Johnny Carson Show, directs his research team as a general deploys his troops. Like the military, the bills are mostly paid by the government, and much time is consumed documenting how that money was spent and making sure that every penny is spent, so that the next grant request can be for a larger sum. This deliberately overdrawn catalogue of contemporary science's less attractive features must be balanced by the very real accomplishments for which it deserves credit. Twentieth-century advances in nuclear physics, molecular biology, radio astronomy, geophysics, space sciences, and medicine would surely not have been as spectacular as they are had not massive amounts of money enabled highly organized research efforts to be mounted. I am providing not a value judgment, but a brief contrast in these comments, the better to enable us to see Rutherford's influence.

Stephen Leacock, the noted humorist and political scientist, who was a faculty colleague of Rutherford's at McGill, once wrote: "If I were founding a University I would found first a smoking room; then when I had a little more money in hand I would found a dormitory; then, after that, or probably with it, a decent reading room and a library. After that, if I still had more money that I couldn't use, I would hire a professor and get some textbooks."[2]

Fortunately, the McGill University authorities seem to have placed a higher priority than Leacock on attracting a faculty of high quality and on providing for their research needs. In fact, attuned to contemporary values, they wanted professors who would contribute to the advancement of knowledge, and in the late nineteenth century, they knew that J.J. Thomson's Cavendish Laboratory was the logical source within the British Empire for talented physicists. In 1893, on Thomson's recommendation, they hired his former student, H.L. Callendar, who had graduated from Cambridge University with honors, been a fellow of Trinity College, and at the time was physics professor at the Royal Holloway College.[3] His excellent thermal investigations, which he continued at McGill, earned him a fellowship in the Royal Society of London within a year after he arrived in Montreal. Such was the impression Callendar had made that no one expected to find a comparable replacement when he left for a chair at University College, London, in 1898. No one, that is, except J.J. Thomson, who told the visiting search committee of Principal William Peterson and physics professor John Cox that Rutherford was the best research student he had ever had.[4]

This was decisive, for in this post McGill was far more concerned with research than teaching.[5] Peterson had only become head of the university in 1895 and no doubt saw expansion as the route to institutional greatness. He would not recommend a retreat from the status—unusual for British universities—of having two physics professors, nor was he obliged to consider it, given the laboratory's financial resources. Cox, the senior professor, was a mathematician who did well enough on the Cambridge tripos to be a wrangler, and who became a fellow of Trinity College. In 1890, in mid-life, he was appointed to the McGill physics professorship, and immediately began building a laboratory with funds donated by a generous patron. It was felt at the time that being a wrangler qualified one for any task, from governing India to judging art, and, indeed, there was much to justify this view. In any case, Cox, who had done no experimental work in physics before this, toured the laboratories of Europe and America and designed what was acknowledged on its opening in 1893, shortly before Callendar's arrival, to be one of the finest and best equipped in the world.[6]

These facilities for research made McGill highly attractive to Rutherford, who otherwise might have remained longer in Cambridge. The explanation for McGill's allure lies very much in the remarkable generosity of Sir William Macdonald, a tobacco dealer who made his millions by selling the Confederate crop to the Union army during the American Civil War, yet a man who regarded smoking as a disgusting habit. More than once, Rutherford had quickly to air out the laboratory as he saw Macdonald coming up the walk. Macdonald endowed not only numerous professorships, but provided funds for the construction and equipment of several laboratories. In the early 1890's, he was responsible for the physics building, whose construction cost £29,000,[7] and for a much larger engineering building. Equipment for both structures was purchased for an additional £100,000 (£22,000 for physics), a sum which can be placed in perspective by comparing it to the £23,000 desired to construct and equip the engineering laboratory of Cambridge University. Yet, even these remarkable sums do not fully convey the quality of the furnishings. As Cox reported at the dedication ceremonies, Macdonald insisted: "Let us have everything of the best, with a definite aim for everything, but always the best." This put certain enviable pressures on Cox, who assembled a magnificent collection of apparatus from the best craftsmen in the field, though at a cost overrun of some four hundred percent. But Macdonald's largesse did not end here; his gifts to McGill eventually totaled several million dollars, including a further £30,000 to physics as an endowment expected to yield £1,500 annually, to be used for demonstrators' salaries, the cost of utilities, equipment repairs, and building maintenance. And he remained an enthusiastic godfather, proud of the accomplishments of his laboratory, and ever willing specially to purchase radium, induction coils, and a liquid-air plant, to provide a library for £1,000, and a special research fund of £400.[8] In these magnificent new surroundings, supported by the equivalent of a one-man National Science Foundation, Rutherford could dispense with the seamier side of Big Science, money-grubbing, and concentrate on his research. Thus, without effort on his part, though with the not difficult ability to recognize a good thing when it came his way, Rutherford *did* achieve one of the features of Big Science, namely adequate—or even lavish—support for his work.

Another characteristic of Big Science is the ability to convince your colleagues and the public that your specialty is of great importance. This has the obvious benefit of encouraging a flow of funds and graduate students, and support for them, as well as bestowing less apparent institutional leverage in academic infighting and in the distribution of prizes, medals, honorary lectureships, and memberships in prestigious societies.

At the laboratory dedication ceremonies in 1893, John Cox confessed that the conception of the Physics Building was almost an "incident" in the plans for the Engineering Building opened at the same time. He might equally have remarked that the guest list for these festivities showed the same bias. While the physics structure grew from an incident into "the finest physical laboratory in [North] America," according to George F. Barker, of the University of Pennsylvania, it apparently still played a minute role in the campus priorities. Of the 5,000 guests that day, including many representatives of engineering societies from the United States, Barker was the only foreign physicist of any note whose name was recorded in the official proceedings.[9]

The stated function of the laboratory further hints at the orientation. The primary purpose, Cox revealed, was to give scientific training to those intending to pursue engineering, medicine, and industrial chemistry. Also important was its place in the liberal education of students from the Faculty of Arts. Lastly, research would be conducted to extend the boundaries of knowledge.[10] Given the mores of the day, this ranking could not have been otherwise. Technology was transforming the globe, science was considered vaguely connected to engineering and as having intellectual merit worthy of inclusion in general education, and, in some quarters, research was not considered necessarily a waste of time. Credit must be given to Macdonald, Cox, and others at McGill for encouraging this minor function, and to Callendar and Rutherford for justifying their confidence. Rutherford, in particular, raised the respect toward research to that accorded a national resource.

He did this in two general ways: by actively proselytizing—being a missionary—and by happily, but without conceit, accepting the honors that came his way. He was clear in his own mind that physics was the most fundamental science; chemistry was "stinks," and all other branches of natural philosophy were merely stamp collecting. Within physics, radioactivity was of primary importance, because it was a basic phenomenon of Nature, to be compared with electricity, magnetism, heat, and gravitation, and because it promised to unlock that puzzle confronting all physicists—an understanding of the nature of matter. In fact, he did not have to work hard to convince people of the significance of radioactivity. Since the Curies' discovery in 1898 of the new elements polonium and radium, the subject enjoyed a good press. Rutherford's own discovery of the new element thorium emanation—more exciting still because it was both radioactive and a member of the novel family of rare gases—and his proposal, with Soddy, that in radioactive decay one element was transmuting spontaneously into another, were intrinsically fascinating to both scientists and laymen.[11]

A measure of this fascination may be gleaned from the newspapers and magazines of the early twentieth century. Scarcely a person in the civilized world could have been unfamiliar with that cornucopia of energy, radium, or with the name of its discoverer ("our lady of radium"). The element's spectacular properties, vanishing small quantities, and enormous price were eagerly discussed by lecturers, poets, novelists, bartenders, physicians, and society matrons. Early and not always well controlled testing led to speculation that it would be valuable in killing bacteria, curing blindness, turning the skin of Negroes white, determining the sex of unborn children, and curing cancers. The wonder element also had applications in the world of entertainment when it was found that self-luminous paint of long duration could be made from it. Fischer's, a night spot in San Francisco, boasted the performance of "fancy unison movements by eight pretty, but invisible, girls, tripping noiselessly about in an absolutely darkened theater, and yet glowingly illuminated in spots by reason of the chemical mixture upon their costumes."[12] In wide-open New York gambling chips and equipment were washed in a radium solution to provide luminous "radium roulette," after which the weary gambler might wash away his troubles, or toast his gains, with cocktails that glowed in the dark.[13] One American asked Madame Curie to allow him to baptize a race horse with her name, while another wrote a poem in her honor.[14] And the concentration of so much energy in such small quantities of matter provoked numerous "gee whiz" calculations, such as that the energy stored in but one gram of radium could raise 500 tons a mile high, and an ounce could drive a 50 horsepower vehicle at 30 miles an hour around the globe.[15]

The scientific community shared the public's wonder at radium and radioactivity. But they had additional reasons to regard the phenomenon with awe. Every new branch of physics, it seemed, was touched in some way by radioactivity. Beta rays and cathode rays alike were electrons, with the former exhibiting relativistic mass increases. Alpha particles were charged helium atoms, and emanation was another member of this new group in the periodic table. The gamma rays also found a match, in the still exciting X-rays. These radiations produced ions in gases, carried energy, caused chemical changes in substances they struck, generated luminescent effects, and burned human tissue, extending their interest to medicine, chemistry, mineralogy, and biology. How could a subject so all-pervasive and apparently important not be enchanting?

Radioactivity, furthermore, had the good fortune to impinge on some questions of perennial interest. The source of the sun's heat and the age of the earth were topics glamorous enough to capture popular imagination. Rutherford was quite cautious in suggesting that solar energy was derived from radioactive decay because he recognized the lack of real evidence, but the idea of dating geological samples by their lead:uranium or helium:uranium ratios seems to have been his, and the techniques were developed by his good friends, Bertram Boltwood at Yale, and R.J. Strutt in London, respectively.[16]

Rutherford took full advantage of the attractiveness of his subject and helped keep it before the public and professional eye. While he was especially effective among scientists, his effort to reach a wider audience furnished the relatively few lectures and articles that contained sober and accurate information on the subject. In early 1904, for example, *Harper's Monthly Magazine* carried an article of his on radioactive disintegration, and a year later another on the source of the earth's heat and its connection to geological dating.[17] He lectured widely, in England at summertime meetings of the British Association for the Advancement of Science,[18] in St. Louis at the 1904 International Congress of Arts and Science,[19] at many colleges and universities in the United States, before other professional societies,[20] and even conducted a summer course in 1906 at the University of California, at Berkeley—perhaps a precursor to the famous summer schools in physics of the 1930's.[21] Everywhere, he left his audiences figuratively radioactive. Michael Pupin, of Columbia University, wrote that Rutherford's frequent reports to the newly founded (1899) American Physical Society, "even without the many other good things which came along, amply justified the existence of the society."[22] Sometimes, Rutherford left them literally radioactive, as when he lectured at Dartmouth College and used a folded square of paper to pour some radium salt into a glass tube. Gorden Ferrie Hull, his host, retained the discarded paper, which became his laboratory's radium source for nearly 40 years.[23] So much did Rutherford seem to be away from Montreal, that Oliver Lodge, one of the elders of British science, felt constrained to write: "I trust you will not waste your time in lecturing but will go on with your experiments and leave lecturing to others."[24]

Institutions not only wished to hear Rutherford, they desired also to honor and to hire him. Honorary degrees were conferred upon him by the Universities of Pennsylvania and Wisconsin, job offers came from Yale, Columbia, Stanford, and the Smithsonian Institution, while inquiries of his availability came from University College, London, Kings College, London, and possibly Berkeley.[25] Columbia, in fact, set its sights extremely high, with simultaneous invitations to Rutherford and J.J. Thomson to join its faculty in 1902.[26]

Fellowship in the Royal Society of Canada came in 1900, and in the Royal Society of London in 1903.[27] Rutherford served as president of the Canadian society's mathematics, physics, and chemistry section in 1906, and was on the council of the American Physical Society from 1904 to 1907.[28] Prestigious speaking engagements came his way, particularly the Bakerian Lecture of the Royal Society of London in 1904, and the Silliman Lectures at Yale in 1905. And the medals and prizes began to flow in his direction. Sir William Huggins, as President of the Royal Society, presented the Rumford Medal in 1904, warmly praised Rutherford's achievement, yet was reluctant to believe its full meaning. "It perhaps still remains a task for the future," he said, "to verify or revise the details of these remarkable transformations of material substances, resulting apparently in the appearance of chemical elements not before present...."[29] Arthur G. Webster, president of the American Physical Society, had no such reservations. Public interest in radioactivity, he noted, was rivalled only by that in X-rays, but the scientific community did not share the public's fear that radium would "undo the chief conquests in physics of the past." Rather, he was confident that the new discoveries would be satisfactorily incorporated into established science, and rejoiced that Rutherford was a member of the APS and on its council.[30]

The point of all this is that whether one subscribed to the interpretations of the work in radioactivity or not, this research was universally regarded as being profoundly significant. Both scientists and laymen were fascinated by the subject, and Rutherford, through his active efforts and passive acceptance of many honors, became an acknowledged leader of an important field. He was, of course, not the only leader nor the only one honored—Pierre and Marie Curie received the Royal Society's Davy Medal in 1903, and in the same year shared the Nobel Prize in physics with Henri Becquerel—but more than anyone else he developed this science and the general behavior of scientists. In the process he became a "personality," someone to be introduced to and someone to invite when other distinguished people were about.[31]

I would suggest that the traits described—being highly visible and vigorous, serving as a leader of a field others are convinced is important, and, even better, glamorous, showing the impact of your specialty upon other subjects, and performing missionary service to professionals and to non-scientists—are characteristics of today's Big Science, and that Rutherford was almost unique in pursuing them so well. But there is more.

Alvin M. Weinberg, both a prominent practitioner and a critic of Big Science in his former post as director of the Oak Ridge National Laboratory, claimed that the method of Big Science is not always *planned* research, but rather to spend money instead of thought. Rather than reflect calmly on how best to solve a problem with existing apparatus, every possible new approach is funded in a shotgun attack that one hopes will hit the target. Big Science, consequently, tends to be economically wasteful science, thriving on publicity, and often emphasizing the spectacular.[32]

Rutherford would have agreed with parts of this analysis. "Go home and think, my boy," was his admonition to those who spent too much time at the work-bench.[33] But if the research of his laboratory covered a spectrum of topics, and if he was sometimes willing to try any "damn fool experiment" on the off-chance that it might work,[34] the shotgun approach was not his style. He was far more inclined to plan his laboratory's attack on the unknown, as shown, for example, in the annual lists of research tasks allotted to his troops, which are preserved in the Cambridge University Library. And if he was aided by publicity that emphasized the spectacular, its origin could not be attributed to him. Such publicity, moreover, was not always beneficial, for the rising medical demand for radium resulted in steep price increases and limited availability for the scientists.

In fact, Rutherford was a sober, conscientious leader of his field, and leadership, to be sure, is a vital feature in our discussion of Big Science. Rutherford was instrumental not only in setting the direction of radioactivity research, he strongly influenced the *style* of scientific activity.

The historian of science, Roy MacLeod, once noted that awards "codified schools of thought, and legitimized scientific paradigms."[35] Certainly, the prizes mentioned above, to Rutherford and others, did just that. In particular, the transformation theory of radioactivity, which succeeded admirably in explaining most of the observed phenomena, benefitted from its warm reception—and from the inability of its few opponents to criticize it except in vague terms. This theory, iconoclastic because it specifics subatomic chemical changes, then led the subject into new directions. From the time of Becquerel's discovery of radioactivity in 1896, the alpha, beta, and gamma radiations had been of primary interest, along with the physical properties of the several radioelements detected. After the transformation theory was presented, interest shifted from the emissions to the emitters, the radioelements, for now the need to determine the decay series' components and their sequence and chemical identities was recognized.

Rutherford also fashioned the field in other ways. He was concerned with terminology, and he coined the usage of "alpha" and "beta" for the two uranium radiations he examined;[36] he gave the name "emanation"—because he was not sure if it was a gas or a vapor—to the mysterious substance emitted from thorium which could be blown about by currents of air;[37] and he and Soddy made an ill-fated attempt to call radioelements "metabolons," to denote their instability.[38] Rutherford tried to bring order to his subject by further standardization of nomenclature and by comparisons of the radium sources used in different laboratories.[39] This led to his active involvement in the decision in 1910 to prepare an international radium standard, and to his writing several articles on nomenclature and standards during his years in Manchester.[40] Rutherford, moreover, showed the utility of electrometers, electroscopes, ionization chambers, and, after his move to England, of scintillation and electrical counting, such that C.T.R. Wilson's cloud chamber was perhaps the only major instrument to be developed beyond his influence.

Even more intellectual leadership was given by his writings. Though others such as Soddy also published books on radioactivity,[41] Rutherford's *Radio-Activity* of 1904, and its vastly enlarged and revised edition the following year, were recognized immediately as *the* bibles of the subject, and his published Silliman Lectures added still more up-to-date information to the bound literature of radioactivity.[42]

The published paper, of course, has for centuries been the primary vehicle for announcing scientific discoveries. Rutherford, while never the editor of a journal, was on the editorial boards of the two specialist periodicals for his subject, *Le Radium* (from its foundation in 1904 to its absorption by another journal in 1919) and the *Jahrbuch der Radioaktivität und Elektronik* (from its creation, also in 1904, to the start of World War I). However, he regarded English-language publications as of greater importance and directed most of his papers to the *Philosophical Magazine,* the *Proceedings of the Royal Society,* and to *Nature,* and he also communicated to them a steady stream of articles by his students and acquaintances. I would go so far as to say that he personally was one of the small band responsible for a noticeable improvement in the quality of the *Philosophical Magazine,* changing it from a somewhat lackluster monthly that reprinted articles from other journals and printed the proceedings of the Geological Society, to the foremost physics periodical of the day, heavily flavored with radioactivity. Similarly, he transformed the letters-to-the-editor section of *Nature* from one of genteel comments on scientific activity and reports of the first robin of spring, to announcements of the greatest fundamental importance and hard-hitting scientific controversy.[43]

The reason for Rutherford's concern with periodicals is obvious: He felt he was in a race to make discoveries, and the laurels went to the person who obtained priority.[44] Thus, *Nature,* with its weekly publication schedule, was exceedingly valuable, for he found he could often get letters in print in the very next issue. By contrast, the *Philosophical Magazine* had such a backlog of papers that a delay between reception and publication of three months was normal, and six months not unusual, though on occasion Rutherford was able to shorten that period considerably. As might be expected, his interest in *Science Abstracts* and *Chemical Abstracts,* both founded around the turn of the century, was minimal, since they simply recorded work already published.

He and his students maintained a flow of research reports, another characteristic of Big Science. Rutherford himself averaged about eight papers each year he was in Montreal, not counting the three books he wrote in this period. In addition, the many papers which listed his name as communicator indicated his judgment, as something of a public referee, that the work was of value. Not content with the pace and scope of the printed word, Rutherford also engaged in a massive correspondence[45] in which he exchanged prepublication information with his colleagues—perhaps a forerunner of today's duplicated preprint—and, rather surprisingly considering his busy schedule, was often the instigator of these communications.[46] If we wish to continue with the Invisible College analogy, these personal contacts, which sometimes replaced the slower, formal communications, led to the condition where anyone wishing to pursue radioactivity seriously found it advisable to tap into the pipeline. Entry was not exclusive, but the research front was reached with less effort by being connected in some fashion to one of the centers of radioactivity. Such acceptance, of course, made it more likely that one would be invited to any conference planned (though there were few during these early years), and also increased the probability of receiving a Nobel Prize or other award for meritorious research.[47]

The term Big Science conjures up visions of a large enterprise concentrating on a particular problem. When Rutherford first arrived in Montreal, he moonlighted for perhaps half a year, gathering data on vibrations caused by an electric street railway, for a pending lawsuit.[48] He also dabbled now and then with his first research topic, wireless telegraphy,[49] with N-rays,[50] and in later years occasionally toyed with other interests, such as X-rays. But his career concentrated remarkably on radioactivity. Such specialization is reminiscent of his teacher, for J.J. Thomson had increasingly and daringly devoted the resources of the Cavendish Laboratory to the discharge of electricity in gases, before his big breakthoughs could be foreseen.[51] Because of the early recognition of radioactivity's importance, Rutherford could concentrate his efforts upon it with far less fear of obtaining trivial results.

Furthermore, he attracted and enlisted the aid of people with other specialties, whose talents could also be trained on radioactivity. In particular, he recognized the need for chemical expertise and was fortunate in his associations with Frederick Soddy, Bertram Boltwood, and Otto Hahn at McGill, and Kasimir Fajans, A.S. Russell, and Georg von Hevesy in Manchester. Looking beyond chemistry, H.T. Barnes, a disciple of Callendar, collaborated with Rutherford on measurements of the heating effect of various radioactive products; S.J. Allen joined him for atmospheric radioactivity studies and continued in this area for the rest of his career; a few distinguished mathematical physicists were to be found in his circle in Manchester and Cambridge; and several others also carved out for themselves specialties within the specialty of radioactivity.[52] At Manchester, Rutherford took an additional step in encouraging team research by consistently pairing off newcomers to the laboratory with old-timers.

A surprisingly large fraction of Rutherford's work was collaborative. Comparison figures are not available for physics early in this century, but in chemistry about 80 percent of all published papers had a single author, and about 20 percent boasted double authorship (papers with three or more authors were exceedingly rare).[53] Assuming roughly comparable practices between the two sciences, it would seem that Rutherford's collaboration in about 35 percent of his McGill papers—even higher if we do not count published lectures—projects him some 50 years into the future, to the 1950's, when both this incidence of dual authorship and Big Science were to be found.

The practice of team research, with the professor or two research students together, has so expanded that today some papers bear several dozen names. This implies much about specialization; it also suggests the creation of a "school." By this I mean not a building in which classes are taught, but a cohesive group of people, with common methods, goals, and ways of viewing their subject. Rutherford had the necessary leadership traits to attract to him and his projects faculty colleagues, matriculating students, and postdoctoral researchers. They came from Canada, Germany (Otto Hahn, Max Levin, Gustave Rümelin), and Poland (Tadeusz Godlewski). Rutherford was even ahead of his age in having a woman (Harriet Brooks) in his laboratory. Here, as in many other examples, the influence of J.J. Thomson—who married a woman who had done research in the Cavendish Laboratory—must be acknowledged, but we must also recognize that discrimination remained such that, for example, Lise Meitner in 1907 was forced to work in a basement wood shop in Emil Fischer's Chemical Institute in Berlin, to keep her apart from the male students.[54]

Montreal became the Mecca for those interested in radioactivity, and the laboratory always had several research students busily at work. In these early days, Rutherford had little or no money directly at his disposal for supporting their living expenses, though he took full advantage of opportunities to recommend his gifted people for awards elsewhere, such as the John Harling Fellowship at Manchester[55] and the 1851 Exhibitions.[56] These financial honors were fledgling steps in the tradition that includes the Rockefeller fellowships of the 1920's and 1930's and the post-World War II American National Science Foundation support. They enabled students without private means to continue their scientific studies, and in many cases permitted them to do this abroad, thus fostering another tradition, that of internationalism in science. Whether due to his colonial origins or to the influence of such men as J.J. Thomson and Arthur Schuster, Rutherford developed and nurtured his international connections, publishing in foreign journals, attending meetings abroad, corresponding widely, serving on the editorial boards of the two journals mentioned above, and welcoming foreign students—not just those from the British Empire—to his laboratory. Such activity no doubt enhanced his position of leadership in radioactivity; it also benefitted him personally, as when the Curies sent him a sample of radium far more active than he was otherwise able to obtain, and with which he was finally able to deflect alpha particles magnetically.[57]

Thus, in having team research, numerous workers, a steady flow of publications, an international orientation, specialized research efforts, the means of disseminating information, and the mental attitude of being in a race against others, Rutherford set a tone of science that is easily recognized today.

Though he could not have been aware of it at the time, he was also involved in a few other trends. His work in radioactivity dealt with probability of decay, a statistical phenomenon. Over the years this would lead to the collection of enormous quantities of data and their processing and evaluation, and some of this development would take place in his own

Manchester and Cambridge laboratories. His use of alpha particle projec-
tiles from naturally decaying radio-elements is a forerunner of particle
beam accelerators. Another toe-hold on Big Science was the advent of the
big machine, something too large and complex to be built in the laboratory's machine shop. Electrostatic generators and banks of batteries could
be purchased in the nineteenth century, while the accelerating machines
and Peter Kapitza's apparatus for producing large magnetic fields are examples of engineered items from a later period. During Rutherford's years
at McGill, however, the device that comes to mind is the liquid-air machine. While it was apparently a fad in the many institutions that acquired one early in the century, for Rutherford it was a valuable research
tool. Thanks to Macdonald, a Hampson liquid-air plant was purchased
and set up in late 1902. With characteristic directness and speed, Rutherford and Soddy, within twenty-four hours, had condensed both radium
emanation and thorium emanation, showing their material nature.[58] Perhaps they were wise to work so rapidly, for they had competition for the
cryogenic product: Once, for example, when liquid air was desired for
research, Rutherford learned that the "prepared supply had been taken to
a church social for a demonstration."[59]

Research in those days was far from the "megabuck" stage of today,
yet it could be expensive in the contemporary economy. At a time when
the military and government would just as well have cared to finance
studies of witchcraft as of physics, and industrial research was just beginning, Rutherford surely was fortunate to have so generous a patron in
Macdonald. It must also be noted that Rutherford was wise enough not
to be greedy. He desired what he needed, and no more. In fact, when
Marie Curie was given a full gram of radium by public subscription in
America in the 1920's, and James Chadwick remarked to Rutherford that
it was a pity no one gave him such a huge amount of the precious element, he replied, "My boy, I'm glad no one has. How would I justify each
year the use of one gram of radium?"[60] Here, according to the Big Science
scorecard, we must fault Rutherford's unwillingness to write grant proposals and reports. Despite this minor "flaw," however, we must conclude
that Rutherford was a great scientific administrator. He trained, guided,
provided for, and inspired a legion of research students. Most likely, he
learned from his own seniors—A.W. Bickerton in New Zealand, J.J.
Thomson, and Cox—that it is productive to give able people minimal
control. Indeed, he encouraged them to work on their own ideas if they
had them.

One final aspect of leadership deserves comment. As the Immanual

Velikovskys, William Shockleys, and Linus Paulings (regarding vitamin C) have shown contemporary culture, it is difficult to get a hearing for the views of a maverick or an outsider. It is far more desirable to join the scientific "Establishment," or, better still, to become that Establishment yourself. Rutherford had a keen appreciation of the need to have his work accepted on its merits and not be ridiculed because it ran against tradition or because he was locked in public argument with colleagues.

When he and Soddy concluded that in radioactivity there is a subatomic "process of disintegration or transmutation steadily going on," he appealed to Sir William Crookes to deflect the initial hostility of any chemists who might object to this resurrection of alchemy.[61] Though he believed in atoms, he would much rather examine them experimentally than engage in such philosophical debates about their reality as raged at the 1904 Congress in St. Louis.[62] When he felt that the heat generated in radioactive decay overturned all of Lord Kelvin's calculations on the age of the earth, based on its rate of cooling from a once-molten mass, he softened the criticism by noting that the grand old man of British science had allowed that a new phenomenon might one day require such a revision.[63] And when Kelvin, Lodge, Soddy, Strutt, Henry Armstrong, A.S. Eve, and others, in 1906 conducted a heated controversy in *The Times* (of London) about the transmutation of one element into another, and whether radium was indeed an element, Rutherford, who then happened to be away from Montreal, submitted a belated, mild contribution that ruffled no feathers.[64] Only when he felt that someone was doing sloppy or dishonest work did he strongly criticize them in print, as happened with Henri Becquerel and Sir William Ramsay (a man with a reputation for making no small mistakes), but even then the public controversy did not become intensely personal.[65] This may perhaps be considered another violation of the characteristics of Big Scientists—a recent author, discussing those she calls "visible scientists," notes their willingness to argue controversial positions and use the media to a great extent[66]—but Rutherford found himself visible enough without it and better able to establish good relations with the older generation of scientific leaders. Yet, when he felt the need for it, he could be tactfully aggressive, as when, in 1904, Royal Society Secretary Joseph Larmor informed him that he was being considered for the Bakerian Lectureship, and Rutherford replied with a strong letter describing how he was wrapping up his subject, while at the same time soliciting Larmor's advice on the most appropriate type of lecture.[67]

While the quality of his research gained him entry to the inner circles, his good natured personality made him welcome there. The biggest obstacle he faced in maintaining this role was not time or effort, but distance. The Atlantic Ocean prevented him from participating in most activities of the Establishment, except on summer visits to England. It was not to acquire a better laboratory or finer students or to be nearer centers of radioactivity that Rutherford accepted the call to Manchester; it was primarily to be closer to the world's scientific center of gravity, to be with more people who could talk physics, and to carve out for himself a position among them.[68] McGill thus suffered two major losses in 1907, the destruction by fire of the engineering and medical buildings,[69] and Rutherford's departure, the latter an example of the increasing mobility of academics in their desire for advancement.

A.S. Eve once playfully depreciated his good friend's immense contributions to physics by charging that he rode the crest of a wave. Rutherford responded, "Well! I made the wave, didn't I?"[70]

I would like to suggest that Rutherford not only made and rode the wave of modern physics, but of Big Science as well.[71] In both cases there were other important figures, to be sure, but Rutherford's own career seems to hold the seeds of this transition, a change that effectively began in Montreal.

Notes

1. L. Badash, "The completeness of nineteenth-century science," *Isis*, 1972, *63*:48–58.

2. Quoted in the *Proceedings of the 28th All-University* [of California] *Faculty Conference*, 26–28 Mar. 1974, pp. 36–37.

3. Obituary of Hugh Longbourne Callendar, *Proc. Roy. Soc. London*, 1931, *A134*:xviii–xxvi.

4. Testimonial by J.J. Thomson, 28 May 1898, in the Rutherford collection, Cambridge University Library (hereafter RCC), Papers section, Add 7653/PA 296. Also see Rutherford letter to Mary Newton, Sept. 1899, printed in A.S. Eve, *Rutherford* (Cambridge: University Press, 1939), p. 68, and John Cox letter to George Ellery Hale, 6 Aug. 1903, Hale collection, California Institute of Technology Archives.

5. Rutherford letters to Mary Newton, 14 July 1898 and 30 July 1898, printed in Eve (note 4), pp. 52–53.

6. Obituary of John Cox, *Nature*, 16 June 1923, *111*:817.

7. The pound sterling was then equal to five dollars, U.S. or Canadian.

8. *Formal Opening of the Engineering and Physics Buildings. McGill University, Montreal. February 24th, 1893* (Montreal: Privately printed, 1893), pp. 11, 12, 23, 40–42. "Physics and engineering at the McGill University, Montreal," *Nature*, 4 Oct. 1894, *50*:558–564. A.S. Eve, "Some scientific centres. VIII.—The Macdonald Physics Building, McGill University, Montreal," *Nature*, 19 July 1906, *74*:272–275.

9. *Formal Opening* (note 8), pp. 6, 40, 46, 48.

10. *Formal Opening* (note 8), p. 40.

11. For the transformation theory, see L. Badash, "How the 'newer alchemy' was received," *Sci. American,* 1966, *215*:88–95.

12. *San Francisco Chronicle,* 29 May 1904. .

13. *New York Evening Journal,* 30 July 1904. *Electrical World and Engineering,* 13 Feb. 1904.

14. Eve Curie, *Madam Curie* (Garden City, N.Y.: Doubleday, Doran, 1938), p. 217. J.H. Ingham, "Radium," *Lippincott's Magazine,* May 1904, *73*:640.

15. *Potsdam* (New York) *Courier,* 9 Dec. 1903. Note that the energy in question is that released in the ejection of alpha particles, not the $E = mc^2$ transformation of mass into energy.

16. Rutherford, "Some cosmical aspects of radioactivity," *J. Roy. Astronomical Soc. Canada,* May–June 1907, 145–65. L. Badash, "Rutherford, Boltwood, and the Age of the Earth: The origin of radioactive dating techniques," *Proc. Am. Phil. Soc.,* 1968, *112*:157–169.

17. Rutherford, "Disintegration of the radioactive elements," *Harper's Monthly Magazine,* Jan. 1904, *108*:279–284; "Radium—the cause of the earth's heat," *ibid.,* Feb. 1905, *110*:390–396.

18. "Physics at the British Association," *Nature,* 22 Oct. 1903, *68*:609–611.

19. Rutherford, "Present problems in radioactivity," *Popular Sci. Monthly,* May 1905, *67*:5–34.

20. E.g., to the Royal Astronomical Society of Canada, on 3 Apr. 1907, and printed in their *Journal* (note 16).

21. Rutherford letter to Mary Rutherford, 25 June 1906, printed in Eve (note 4), p. 148. Leonard B. Loeb letter to the author, 30 Nov. 1962.

22. M. Pupin, *From Immigrant to Inventor* (New York: Scribner's, 1925), p. 353. Also see H.A. Bumstead letter to Rutherford, 4 Jan. 1903, printed in Norman Feather, *Lord Rutherford* (London and Glasgow: Blackie & Son, 1940), p. 102.

23. G.F. Hull, "The new spirit in American physics," *Am. J. Phys.,* Feb. 1943, *11*:23–30.

24. O. Lodge letter to Rutherford, 4 Jan. 1904, RCC.

25. Feather (note 22), pp. 109–110. The Berkeley possibility is inferred from Rutherford's letter to Jacques Loeb, 3 Feb. 1907, Loeb collection, Library of Congress, Washington, D.C.

26. Rutherford letter to J.J. Thomson, 26 Dec. 1902, Thomson collection, Cambridge University Library.

27. Eve (note 4), pp. 138, 437.

28. Eve (note 4), p. 138. Minutes of meetings of the American Physical Society, preserved in the Center for History of Physics, American Institute of Physics, New York City.

29. "Address delivered by the President, Sir William Higgins, K.C.B., O.M., F.R.S., at the Anniversary Meeting on November 30th, 1904," *Proc. Roy. Soc. London,* 22 Apr. 1905, *A76*:22–23.

30. A.G. Webster, "Some practical aspects of the relations between physics and mathematics," *Phys. Rev.,* Apr. 1904, *18*:303–304.

31. See, e.g., Rutherford letter to Mary Rutherford, 2 Nov. 1904, printed in Eve (note 4),

pp. 115–116, in which he tells of being invited to Principal Peterson's home to meet John Morley, the well known statesman and author, but has been quiet about it for fear of raising jealousies among his colleagues.

32. A.M. Weinberg, "Impact of large-scale science on the United States," *Science*, 21 July 1961, *134*:161–164.

33. Eve (note 4), p. 132.

34. James Chadwick interview by the author, 19 Feb. 1970.

35. R. MacLeod, "Of medals and men: a reward system in Victorian science, 1826–1914," *Notes and Records of the Royal Society*, 1971, *26*:99.

36. Rutherford, "Uranium radiation and the electrical conduction produced by it," *Phil. Mag.*, Jan. 1899, *47*:109–163.

37. Rutherford, "A radioactive substance emitted from thorium compounds," *Phil. Mag.*, Jan. 1900, *49*:1–14.

38. Rutherford and F. Soddy, "Radioactive change," *Phil. Mag.*, May 1903, *5*:576–591.

39. See, e.g., B. Boltwood letters to Rutherford, 4 Oct. 1905, 1 Feb. 1906, 1 Apr. 1906, 17 May 1906, RCC, and Rutherford letters to Boltwood, 28 Jan. 1906, 28 Feb. 1906, 3 Apr. 1906, Boltwood collection, Yale University Library (hereafter BCY); all correspondence between these two is printed in L. Badash (ed.), *Rutherford and Boltwood, Letters on Radioactivity* (New Haven: Yale University Press, 1969).

40. Rutherford, "Radium standards and nomenclature," *Nature*, 6 Oct. 1910, *84*:430–431; (with H. Geiger), "Transformation and nomenclature of the radioactive emanations," *Phil. Mag.*, Oct. 1911, *22*:621–629; "The British radium standard," *Nature*, 1913, *92*:402–403; "Radium constants on the international standard," *Phil. Mag.*, Sept. 1914, *28*:320–327.

41. F. Soddy, *Radio-Activity* (London: The Electrician, 1904).

42. Rutherford, *Radio-Activity* (Cambridge: University Press, 1904, revised 1905); *Radioactive Transformations* (New Haven: Yale University Press, and London: Henry Frowde, Oxford University Press, 1906 and 1911). H. Bumstead letter to Rutherford, 5 June 1904, printed in Eve (note 4), p. 111.

43. Personal communication from Roy MacLeod, 19 Nov. 1969, regarding *Nature*.

44. See, e.g., Rutherford letter to his mother, 5 Jan. 1902, printed in Eve (note 4), pp. 80–81.

45. L. Badash (ed.), *Rutherford Correspondence Catalog* (New York: American Institute of Physics, 1974).

46. See, e.g., Badash (note 39).

47. Diana Crane, *Invisible Colleges* (Chicago: University of Chicago Press, 1972).

48. Rutherford letters to Mary Newton, 4 Oct. 1898, 7 Nov. 1898, and May 1899, printed in Eve (note 4), pp. 64–66.

49. Eve (note 4), pp. 67, 83, 88–89.

50. W.C.D. Whetham letter to Rutherford, 13 Feb. 1904, printed in Eve (note 4), p. 102.

51. Derek J. Price, "Sir J.J. Thomson, O.M., F.R.S.," *Nuovo Cimento*, 1957, *4*:1609–1629.

52. For a bibliography, see *The Collected Papers of Lord Rutherford of Nelson* (New York: Interscience, 1962); this first volume covers the Montreal period.

53. Derek J. Price and Lawrence Badash, "Statistical studies of the history of chemical publication and manpower," an unpublished report to the American Chemical Society, 1961.

54. *Otto Hahn: A Scientific Autobiography* (New York: Scribner's, 1966), p. 51.

55. Rutherford letter to Arthur Schuster about Harriet Brooks, 25 Mar. 1907, Royal Society of London.

56. *Annual Calendar of McGill College and University, Montreal, 1903-4,* p. 147. The 1851 Exhibitions were placed at McGill's disposal every odd year since 1891. Rutherford's students R.K. McClung won it in 1901, and H.C. Cooke in 1903.

57. Rutherford, "Early days in radio-activity," *J. Franklin Inst.,* Sept. 1924, *198*:285.

58. John Cox, "The Hampson liquid air plant at McGill University, Montreal," *Canadian Electrical News,* Nov. 1902, *12*:191-192.

59. A. Norman Shaw, "Rutherford at McGill," *McGill News,* Winter 1937.

60. James Chadwick interview by the author, 11 Feb. 1970.

61. Rutherford letter to W. Crookes, 29 Apr. 1902, RCC.

62. Robert A. Millikan, *Autobiography* (New York: Prentice-Hall, 1950), pp. 22, 84-85.

63. Eve (note 4), p. 107.

64. *The Times* letters are reprinted in *The Chemical News,* 14, 21, and 28 Sept. 1906, *94:*125-127, 144-145, and 153-154. Rutherford, "The recent radium controversy," *Nature,* 25 Oct. 1906, *74*:634-635.

65. Rutherford letters to B. Boltwood, 10 Oct. 1905, 12 Nov. 1905, 23 Aug. 1908, 20 Sept. 1908, and 8 Nov. 1908, BCY.

66. Rae Goodell, *The Visible Scientists,* (Boston: Little, Brown, 1977).

67. Rutherford letter to J. Larmor, 19 Jan. 1904, Royal Society of London.

68. Rutherford letter to J.J. Thomson, 26 Mar. 1901, RCC. Rutherford letter to A. Schuster, 26 Sept. 1906, Royal Society of London.

69. "New disaster to McGill," *Montreal Medical Journal,* 1907, *36*:333-336.

70. Eve (note 4), p. 436.

71. For an analysis of this change, see Derek J. Price, *Little Science, Big Science* (New York: Columbia University Press, 1963).

Physics at McGill in Rutherford's Time

J.L. HEILBRON

When Rutherford left Cambridge for Montreal in the fall of 1898, he expected to be "practically boss man in the laboratory" of the McGill physics department.[1] Officially the boss was John Cox, a mathematician trained at Cambridge, the senior professor of physics and the director of the physical laboratories. But Cox, though he had designed the physics building and chosen its furnishings, left research to others; he preferred teaching and administration, and allowed his junior professor great freedom with the laboratory resources under his control.[2]

Rutherford had learned about these preferences when Cox visited the Cavendish Laboratory, the nursery of British physicists, to find a successor to his junior professor, Hugh L. Callendar, who had left in the spring of 1898 for a chair at University College, London. Callendar had, indeed, enjoyed a free hand in the laboratory: He directed all its best research students into his specialty, high-precision measurements of thermodynamic quantities. No doubt Cox wished Rutherford to have the privileges and opportunities that Callendar had enjoyed. But that could not be. Callendar had had no predecessor; Rutherford had Callendar's legacy. That consisted of a strong research line altogether different from Rutherford's, and a disciple, a demonstrator named Howard T. Barnes, eagerly pursuing it.

The physics building had the material resources to support research of both Rutherford's and Callendar's type. It was the most costly, and perhaps the largest, physics institute in the world when it opened in 1893.[3] The donor of the institute, its furnishings and professorships, was William Macdonald, who had spared no expense. "Let us have everything of the best," he had told Cox, who had asked for £ 5,000 for equipment and had received £ 6,000.[4] Macdonald gave money to hire three demonstrators, a mechanic, and an assistant, to pay the operating expenses of the building, and to buy more instruments. Cox made certain that Rutherford knew about the "magnificent supply of apparatus which alone cost £ 25,000" during negotiations about the professorship.[5] That sum was over four times the cost of Callendar's physics institute at the University of London, an exact contemporary of McGill's. Callendar was to lament the loss of the material resources of the "MPB" (as its users called the Macdonald Physics Building); Rutherford was to find the laboratory "everything that can be desired."[6]

It takes more than matériel to accomplish the purpose Rutherford brought to Canada: "to do a lot of original work and to form a research school."[7] One needs colleagues, associates, assistants, disciples, and of these McGill had short supply. There were not enough research students to go around when Rutherford arrived, and no sure supply was established during his stay. Rutherford by no means always won the competition for the few advanced students raised at McGill. Barnes and the Callendar tradition held its own against the new alchemy, as appears from the accompanying Table. The numbers for Rutherford's group only exceed those for Barnes' because of recruitment of independent associates trained abroad.

Callendar began to learn experimental physics in 1887, at the Cavendish, after having earned first-class honors in both classics and mathematics. J.J. Thomson, then in his third year as Cavendish Professor, was continuing the work of his predecessors, Maxwell and Rayleigh, on exact electrical standards. He proposed to Callendar that he try to make a dependable electrical instrument of the capricious platinum-resistance thermometer.[8] After years of work and refined observations Callendar succeeded, and even (as Thomson put it) "revolutionized thermometry."[9] In 1899 the Committee on Electrical Standards of the British Association for the Advancement of Science accepted Callendar's proposal to base

Research Papers Published from the MPB
1897/8–1906/7

	1898/9	1899/00	1900/1	1901/2	1902/3	1903/4	1904/5	1905/6	1906/7
A. Rutherford's Group	2	3	8	16	14	14	19	28	21
By Rutherford		2	6	5	4	7	7	6	8
Coauthored	1	1	1	8	6	1[a]	2[b]	2[c]	
By Associates	1		1	3	4	6	10	20	13
B. Barnes' Group	3	11	4	13	8	6	8	7	5
By Barnes	2	10	2	8	4	3	4	3	3
Coauthored	1	1	1	4	4	3[a]	4[a]	4	2
By Associates			1	1					
C. Others	1	1		1	2		1		2

sources: McGill Univ., *Ann. Rep.,* 1897–1907; McGill Univ. Archives, *A Guide to the Records of the Department of Physics* (Montreal, 1977); J.C. Poggendorff, *Biographisch-Literarisches Handwörterbuch zur Geschichte der exacten Wissenschaften;* Rutherford, *Collected Papers,* I (London, 1962); indexes to *Phil. Mag.,* RSC, *Trans.,* and RSL, *Proc.* Papers are referred to the academic year in which they were presented or submitted for publication.
a. Includes collaboration between Rutherford and Barnes, each credited with half.
b. Includes collaboration with Barnes and one paper with B.B. Boltwood (New Haven).
c. One paper each with Boltwood and Hahn.

conventional temperature scales on that of the newly docile platinum thermometer. It is still the accepted means of interpolation between the boiling point of liquid oxygen and the melting point of antimony.[10]

At McGill Callendar used his thermometer for exact measurement of the dependence of the electromotive force of standard cells on temperature, of the specific heat of water, and of the mechanical equivalent of heat. In all three researches, he had the help of Barnes, who later extended and refined them. Callendar also used his thermometry on engineering problems of steam turbines and internal-combustion engines. The determination of thermodynamic quantities has a practical side that he did not disdain to follow.

It appears that Callendar's conception of the physicist's role agreed with the expectations of most promoters of physics in Canada. For Macdonald, who had had to work for his money, the exemplar of the scientist was Benjamin Franklin, a man of thought and action, the inventor both of a new conception of electricity and of the lightning rod.[11] Franklin had understood the relative importance of theory and practice. "It is of real use [he had written] to know that china left in the air unsupported will fall and break; but *how* it comes to fall, and *why* it breaks, are matters of speculation. It is a pleasure indeed to know them, but we can preserve our china without it."[12] Study of the practical pleased Macdonald; besides the physics building, he gave one for chemistry and mining, another for engineering, and an entire college for agriculture.

Macdonald gave McGill a physics building not because he admired the subject, but because it seemed necessary to support the curriculum of the Faculty of Applied Science. He reached this conclusion under the guidance of H.T. Bovey, Dean of the Faculty, with whom he toured the leading engineering schools of the United States. The experience showed him that a first-class program in engineering required equivalent instruction in physics.[13] The MPB was created as a service to the Faculty of Applied Science; beginning in 1898, it helped the Faculty of Arts as well. In 1902–1903, a representative year during Rutherford's tenure, its clientele, some 324 students, was the largest of any teaching department in the university. Very few of these students worked towards degrees in physics. Fewer than ten of the 324 physicists of 1902–1903 hoped for honors in the subject; of the rest, about one-third were freshmen in the required curriculum in Arts, and two-thirds were students in the Faculty of Applied Science.[14] So few honors graduates in physics remained to work for M.A.s that the MPB had to recruit many of its demonstrators from among graduates in engineering, who would leave after a year or two for what Cox

called "commercial posts." Commitment or appeal to the practical doubt-
less inhibited the development of a research school in physics at McGill.

Government also stressed the practical, the applied, or, to use modern
cant, "the mission-oriented," on the rare occasions that it supported physical science.[15] The Royal Society of Canada urged all its proposals for government expenditures, whether a hydrographic survey or an exact triangu-
lation, on the ground of utility. Its own section on physical science split over
the proper occupations of its members. For some years before 1900 it could
not agree how to fill its vacancies. The first elections of the new century
brought a practical man and Rutherford; the next year balanced a professor and a government meteorologist; in the next, 1902, Barnes entered in
tandem with the Inspector of Public Schools in Ottawa.[16]

There was something in Callendar's work for followers of the *vita ac-
tiva* as well as for Canadian contemplatives. As for his personal accomplishments, all could but admire. Callendar was an athlete, a mathematician, physicist, classicist, and a Fellow of the Royal Society of London,
the first of Thomson's students to rise so high.[17] Withall he was modest,
unrivalled in "skill and flair for accurate work," a gifted and conscientious teacher, clear and inspiring, free from affectation, kindly and
generous; in short, a "versatility of talent that does all things easily."[18]
When Callendar left McGill his colleagues naturally doubted that anyone
so fine could be found to replace him.

The replacement, just as naturally, felt ambivalent about his predecessor. On the one hand, Rutherford was gratified that Callendar should
have been, and been esteemed to be, so excellent. "I think my appointment is a very much discussed matter at Cambridge as Callendar was
considered a very great man," he wrote his fiancée, Mary Newton. "Your
acute mind will at once gauge my importance if they place me in his shoes
when the beard of manhood is faint upon my cheeks."[19] On the other
hand, Rutherford objected to being measured against the great measurer,
whose old-fashioned physics, with its tedious exactness and proximity to
engineering, he did not admire.[20] At the end of his first year in Montreal,
Rutherford wrote Mary, still waiting for him in New Zealand: "I am getting rather tired of people telling me how great a man Callendar was, but
I always have the sense to agree. As a matter of fact, I don't quite class
myself in the same order as Callendar, who was more an engineering type
than a physicist, and who took more pride in making a piece of apparatus
than in discovering a new scientific truth."[21]

This expression of snobbery makes clear enough where Rutherford
then stood on the relative merits of pure and applied research. It also

points to a significant change in the character of Cavendish physics. Callendar's researches, which excited interest in the 1880's, would have been peripheral a decade later, when the chief subject of study was the gaseous ion.[22] Rutherford himself affords an example of the change. He had arrived in Cambridge in 1895 intending to continue work on his system for detecting radio waves. It was not pure research. "I have reason to hope that I may be able to signal miles, without connections, before I have finished. The reason I am so keen on the subject is because of its practical importance. If I could get an appreciable effect at 10 miles I would probably be able to make a considerable sum of money out of it."[23]

In the spring of 1896 Rutherford set these experiments aside to work with his professor on a new line of research. He was one of several advanced students mobilized by Thomson to study the behavior of ions produced in gases by X-rays.[24] He took up the subject as a respite from telegraphy, which declined to extend itself to ten miles, and as an opportunity to work with Thomson.[25] The collaboration laid the foundations for the theory of gaseous ionization. It also brought Rutherford heart and soul to the purer physics, a transition eased no doubt by an additional scholarship that brought his income up to adequate.[26] At Cambridge he became an expert in the theory of ions, or "jolly little beggars" as he later called them, and in the apparatus required to detect them. These instruments—electrometers, parallel-plate condensers, X-ray tubes, devices for creating air currents—remained his pet equipment for most of his career.[27]

Rutherford took up the study of uranium rays in 1897 as an expert in ionizing radiations; he used the same methods on them that he and Thomson had developed for the study of gaseous ions produced by X-rays. The work led directly to the discovery that uranium rays consisted of at least two components, one easily absorbed and heavily ionizing (which he called α), the other penetrating and weakly ionizing (baptized β).[28] Similar rays emitted by thorium were to be the subject of Rutherford's first successful research at McGill.

Two other points about Rutherford's experience at the Cavendish must be mentioned. Firstly, he learned (or had confirmed) that one need not strive for precision in pioneering work. In measuring the mechanical equivalent of heat, infinite pains are required; in chronicling the activities of the jolly little beggars, two-place accuracy normally sufficed. Sometimes, to be sure, Rutherford's semi-quantitative results misled, as in the conclusion, supported by a 20 percent error, that positive and negative ions in a gas drift at about the same velocity.[29] The policy of leaving the next figure to the next fellow allowed him to cover vast territory. It took Callendar and Barnes six years to perfect the constant-flow calorimeter and apply it to measurements on water. In the same time Rutherford and his collaborators established much of the basis of experimental radio-activity and invented the transformation theory.

Secondly, Rutherford brought with him a model for an effective re-search school. The ion group at Cambridge consisted primarily of gradu-ates of other universities admitted, like Rutherford, under a novel regulation adopted in 1895. For the first time an alien baccalaureate could earn a Cambridge degree—another A.B.—for research done at the Cavendish. This reform brought a windfall of eager talent. Thomson was able to work it into an effective research group by capitalizing on the possibilities of X-rays, which entered his laboratory along with the first of the new students.[30] The group developed data about the formation, veloc-ities, rates of recombination, and numbers of ions, and about the behavior of the ubiquitous mini-ion, or corpuscle, that their professor found in 1897. They devised ways to measure the charge of the corpuscle produced in gases by X-rays, or liberated from metals by ultraviolet light, or shot from hot cathodes. By 1900 these researches had established the existence of the electron and provided the foundation for a theory of atomic struc-ture.[31] Evidently a group of talented researchers directed in individual but related projects by a man of genius might accomplish something.

A small group already existed at McGill. In 1897 three demonstra-tors (Barnes, H.M. Tory, F.H. Pitcher) and three graduate students (R.O. King, R.W. Gill, R.W. Stovell) worked under Callendar's guidance at tasks related to constant-flow calorimetry.[32] This technique, which he de-vised, is easy to understand but difficult to perform. Water is made to flow through a long narrow tube containing a current-carrying wire; platinum thermometers measure the difference in temperature of the water entering and leaving the tube; appropriate electrical instruments determine the Joule heat supplied by the wire. To attain the accuracy sought—one part in 100,000—refined precautions are necessary. To calculate the Joule heat, for example, one must know the potential of the Clark cells supplying the current, and the resistances of the wires, to five figures. Callendar and Barnes began studying the behavior of Clark cells in 1896; King joined the investigation the following year. Resistances had to be measured against the standard ohm, of which the MPB had several specimens certi-fied by the Electrical Standards Committee.[33] An expensive instrument for testing and comparing resistances was procured from England and set up on a special free-standing pier in the laboratory. Gill, Barnes, and others used it. Stovell helped Barnes.[34] Tory, a McGill graduate in mathematics who had been recycled into physics at the Cavendish, looked into details of platinum thermometry.[35] And there were, or were to be, separate studies of the heat jacket surrounding the tube, of the radial distribution of heat within it, of the stream lines of water through it, and so on. Constant-flow calorimetry perfectly suited the purposes, staff, and resources of the MPB.[36]

The heart of the apparatus was Callendar's patented resistance box. To measure the difference in temperature of the entering and exiting water, the difference in resistance of two immersed thermometers had to be ascertained. A Wheatstone bridge provided a resistance in equilibrium with the thermometer in the entering water. This resistance, from which one calculates the required temperature difference, was made up from the coils and bridge wire in Callendar's box. To compensate for the change in the coils' resistance arising from the Joule heat produced by the small current passing through them, Callendar associated with each coil a compensator with the same temperature coefficient but different specific resistance. When the current passed, the compensating coil added its contribution to the other side of the bridge, cancelling any change in the resistance of the measuring coil. Callendar made and adjusted all the coils himself, at the "cost of a month or more continuous work."[37]

Callendar left Barnes the wonderful box and responsibility for continuing work on the specific heat of water. During Rutherford's first year at McGill, Barnes so perfected the apparatus that he could take all the readings himself, a requirement forced on him because he could not find an "experienced observer" able to devote sufficient time to the task. Others continued at the old jobs: King took up the Clark cell; Tory helped Barnes and went on with platinum thermometry; and a student in electrical engineering, J.W. Fraser, standardized resistances.[38]

Cox supported Barnes throughout, "placing every facility at my disposal that could aid me in the work."[39] Cox had a particular concern with the physics of gross bodies. He taught mechanics with as little mathematics as possible, developing the principles, as he said, "in their historical order, starting from real problems, as the subject started." He drew his history and philosophy from Mach's *Mechanics,* of which his own was but a "poor and incomplete abridgement."[40] Like Mach he emphasized the intuitive, the immediately given, the practical, "the [physics] of the objects about us."[41] Barnes' studies of these objects were Machist good works. So was his relentless measurement of the mechanical equivalent of heat, an artifact of the doctrine of energy conservation, "the central landmark of the science of the nineteenth century."[42]

Callendar thought that Rutherford might eclipse the light from Cox to Barnes. And he thought he had proof: To enable Barnes to proceed with his measurements ("worth all the previous work on the variation of the specific heat of water put together"), Callendar had left his box in McGill on the understanding that Cox would procure a duplicate and return his. It did not come. Callendar "naturally considered [Rutherford] partly to blame"; evidently the management of the MPB had not been willing to provide an expensive piece of apparatus for a mere demonstrator.[43] This comedy of Cox and Box was entirely in Callendar's head: The MPB had provided, and he eventually recovered his property. The point of interest is his impression of Rutherford, acquired during a conversation between them in 1898.[44]

In 1899 Barnes was named Joule Scholar of the Royal Society of London. The income enabled him to resign his demonstratorship for a year; the statutes allowed him to remain at McGill.[45] He completed his immaculate measurements and brought them to England. They were added, as the last word on the subject, to the Anglo-American report on recent heat determinations presented to the International Congress of Physics in Paris in 1900. Cox advertised Barnes' European successes as the outstanding research achievement of the MPB in the session 1898–1899. "[He] has specially distinguished himself" by presenting his work personally to the Royal Society, work "so important as to be taken for the basis" of reports to the international congress.[46] This was the same year in which Rutherford discovered the emanation and the active deposit, and "1000 new facts which have been undreamt of."[47]

Rutherford made most of these discoveries alone, following up the work of R.B. Owens, a colleague from the Faculty of Applied Science. Owens, an electrical engineer, had needed a research topic to occupy his time during tenure of a fellowship.[48] Rutherford suggested that Owens examine the radiation from thorium in the same way that he had studied uranium rays. Preliminary results, announced in May, 1899, mentioned the odd sensitivity of the activity of a piece of thorium oxide (thoria) to air drafts in its vicinity. It was Rutherford's masterful analysis of this sensitivity that brought the discovery of thorium emanation and of excited activity.[49] Subsequent work on the emanation led to the puzzles that inspired the collaboration with Soddy and the discovery of radioactive transformation. That was in the future. At the beginning of his second year in Canada, Rutherford still felt the weight of Callendar's legacy: "[He] left such a reputation behind him that I of necessity have to keep in the background."[50]

Since the advanced research men were occupied, Rutherford proselytized among the few undergraduates taking the honors course in physics.[51] He chose a fourth-year student, R.K. McClung, to help him measure the energy ε expended by X-rays in creating a pair of ions in a gas. Rutherford's purpose was to deduce the energy output from radioactive substances on the assumption that their rays also lose ε in making gaseous ions. To obtain ε he and McClung built a special bolometer—apparently without Barnes' advice—with which to determine H, the heat given off in the absorption of a certain quantity of X-rays. Next, using methods that had been devised at the Cavendish, they found n, the number of ion pairs created by the same quantity of rays. Evidently, $\varepsilon = H/n$. Their result, equivalent to an ionization potential of about 200eV for an air molecule, is not very good. Their inference, that electrons removed by ionization are bound close to the electric center of the atom, was badly misleading.[52]

They proceeded straightforwardly and inexactly to compute the total energy E radiated per second by a gram of thorium or uranium. They limited themselves to the contribution of the easily absorbed α-rays. They measured the number of ions produced by a thick layer of radiator, then by a thin one, in order to compensate for self-absorption in the source; and they calculated E from these data and the measured absorption coefficient of the rays. The result: $E \simeq 10^{-9}$ cal/g-sec. Rutherford did not have enough radium to determine its E directly. But he knew that Pierre Curie had mentioned using a specimen "at least" 100,000 times more active than uranium. Rutherford reasoned that, if the ratio holds for αs and for equal weights and areas, E of radium should be "at least" 10^{-9} cal/g-sec or 0.4 cal/g-hr.[53] It is at least 350 times that.

Ions made McClung's career. He continued with them and with Rutherford through the spring of 1900, and then worked alone at their rate of recombination as a function of pressure, which served for his M.A. thesis, awarded in 1901.[54] That year he went to the Cavendish on an 1851 Exhibition, the same scholarship that Rutherford had won. McClung made himself useful in England by reading proofs of Rutherford's papers. He returned to McGill as a demonstrator in 1904, and held the post until 1907. He ended as professor of physics at the University of Manitoba.

Rutherford had one other research student at this time, Harriet Brooks, raised up, like McClung, while still an undergraduate. She began, not with ions, but with an application of Rutherford's method of wireless reception to measuring the damping of oscillations in the Leyden discharge.[55] She then worked with him on a clever scheme to deduce the atomic weight of radium emanation by measuring its coefficient of diffusion in air. They estimated its atomic weight at between 40 and 100 times that of hydrogen. Using this approximation, which at best is off by a factor of 9/4, they inferred that the emanation could not be a vapor of radium, the atomic weight of which had been estimated at "very much greater than 174" by the Curies in 1900.[56] This inference may serve as an example of what Rutherford called his "devilish luck." It is, of course, correct; but it would not have followed had he come closer to the true atomic weight of the emanation (222).

Brooks received an M.A. for her research in 1901. She subsequently went to the Cavendish on a fellowship from Bryn Mawr, and returned to McGill to discover the recoil of atoms decaying by α emission.[57] In 1907 she resigned the John Harling Fellowship, given her to continue work with Rutherford at Manchester, in order to marry Callendar's former student Pitcher, a miscegenation that Rutherford did not approve.[58]

A new era for the MPB began in 1901, when Frederick Soddy accepted Rutherford's invitation to help in the continuing attack upon the emanations.[59] The experiments with Brooks indicated that radium emanation was a gas of moderate atomic weight. But what sort of gas? Owens and Rutherford had showed that the emanating power of a sample of thoria depended on its prior physical treatment. What might be the effect of chemical treatment? Rutherford needed a chemist. Chance threw a superb one in his path.

The first investigation by Rutherford and Soddy concerned the nature of thorium's emanating power and of its emanation. Completed by January, 1902, it revealed that the emanation was a gas similar to those of the argon family, and that the emanating power was a very complicated affair.[60] While this work progressed, Rutherford also studied the other end of the problem, the nature of the activity excited on surfaces touched by the emanation. When he exposed a negatively-charged electrode for some time, its induced activity fell immediately after separation from the emanation. When the exposure lasted only a few seconds, however, the activity at first increased. Three puzzles resulted: Whence comes the active material? How does it acquire a positively-charged carrier? What causes the initial rise in the electrode's activity? Rutherford inclined towards Thomson's view that the molecules of the emanation give out electrons, and that the positive ions thus produced come to the negative electrode to constitute the active layer.[61] The initial rise might be the mark of a substance that needs time to disclose itself. Perhaps it suffers a gradual molecular or chemical change or slowly induces activity in the particles of the electrode.[62]

These ideas, published before the discovery of the rise and fall of the activity of thorium *X*, foreshadow the disintegration theory. Rutherford seemed to imply that particles of the active deposit differ from those of the emanation only in the number of their constituent electrons. Since the deposit decays at a rate different from the emanation's, it had to be considered a distinct radioactive species: Apparently, one radioactive substance might derive genetically from another. Rutherford also allowed that molecular or chemical change, resulting in alteration of radioactivity, may occur in the active deposit. Note the implicit relation between the radiation and these presumed changes: first the change, then, without further alteration of radiative species, emission of radiation. Since a radioactive species was then defined by the radiation it emitted, as well as by chemical analysis, it would have been difficult even to state the relation later found to hold. One naturally assumed that radiating particles or atoms belonged to a single species, not (so to speak) to two at once. This assumption—first species change, then radiation—survived into the second paper by Rutherford and Soddy, the first published form of the disintegration theory, which was finished around April, 1902.[63]

The main clue to the invention of the disintegration theory was the discovery in January, 1902, that a specimen of ThX that had stood during the Christmas holiday had lost its activity.[64] Study of the rise and fall of the activity of the ThX and of the thorium from which it had been separated resulted in the theory that ThX arises from Th, and the emanation from ThX, by "sub-atomic chemical change" (presumably a rearrangement of electrons preceding α or β emission) of which radioactivity is a manifestation.[65] In their first formal announcement of the theory, Rutherford and Soddy did not try to specify the connection between the change and its manifestation. But it is clear that they had not yet associated the emission of α-rays from purified thorium (or uranium) with the *production* of ThX (or UX).[66] That possibility first appeared in print in the fourth of their papers, published in November, 1902.[67] They proposed it definitively in a paper finished the following February.[68]

The chief ground of this endorsement might very well have been Rutherford's success in deviating α-rays in a magnetic and electric field.[69] These effects, which he had sought for some time, made possible an assimilation of α- and β-rays, at least in respect of radioactive transformations: Apparently, both were material parts projected or left over during sub-atomic change.[70] A consequential shift in the meaning of "radioactive substance" resulted: One no longer understood such a substance to be made up of actually radiating particles, but rather of atoms that radiated only when spontaneously changing their chemical species.

Concurrently with the work with Soddy, Rutherford directed and participated in the research of three advanced students. It was the closest approach to group work in the Cavendish style that Rutherford was able to manage at McGill. All the students—Brooks, S.J. Allen, and A.G. Grier—had been trained at the MPB; both Allen and Grier earned M.Sc. degrees during the session 1900–1901. Rutherford's collaboration with Grier, which reached definitive results at precisely the same time that the first form of the disintegration theory was worked out, may have contributed something to it.

The main object of Rutherford and Grier was to determine the connection, "if any," between the deviable (β) and the non-deviable (α)-rays emitted by each of the principal radioactive substances. They succeeded in putting out of court the old theory, once endorsed by Rutherford, that αs are secondaries, analogous to X-rays, stimulated by βs in their passage through matter: Uranium and thorium could each be separated into two fractions, an "X" product that carried *all* the β activity and the residual "uranium" and "thorium" that emitted *only* αs.[71] Leaving aside the question of the nature of the α-rays, Rutherford and Grier asked about the relation between the X product and its source: "It seems probable [to us] that most of the deviable rays from uranium and thorium are given out by a secondary product produced by a disintegration of the uranium or thorium atom or molecule.... The non-deviable radiation may be either due to the other secondary product of the reaction [i.e., whatever is left after UX or ThX is removed], or may be due to an action of the product responsible for the deviable rays in the mass of the radioactive material."[72]

One is struck by the broad hint at the disintegration theory, which had not been published when Rutherford and Grier finished their paper, and by the fact that they thank Soddy only for providing preparations. Later Rutherford also credited Soddy with showing that the radiation from uranium X is almost entirely β, reserving for himself and Grier the honor of demonstrating that ThX emits both α and β.[73] These acknowledgments imply that, in Rutherford's thinking at least, the work with Grier contributed importantly to the construction of the disintegration theory. It certainly made acute the old question of the nature of α radiation. Rutherford took up this question at his earliest opportunity, at the beginning of the session 1902–1903.[74]

A second result of Rutherford and Grier brought the α-ray still closer to the center of interest. Having measured the ionization created by the αs and βs together, and then by the βs alone, they could compute—roughly, of course!—the ratio of the energies expended in ionization by each sort of ray. The calculation requires the values of the absorption coefficient of the β-rays in air and of both rays in their sources, none of which was known. Rutherford got around this ignorance with his customary ingenuity, adjusting or extrapolating data on absorption in aluminum. The result— that over 99 percent of the total ionizing energy radiated from U, Th or Ra is carried by the αs—could only underscore their importance.

The collaboration with Allen and with Brooks might seem remote from the creation of the disintegration theory. With Brooks Rutherford inventoried the radiations from most known radioactive substances; with Allen he measured the amount of radioactivity collected on a negatively-charged wire exposed to the atmosphere. In both cases, however, he had an opportunity to discuss the rate of decay of excited activity, which he insisted arose from radioactive particles deriving from the emanation; he did so in much the same terms as he was to use to describe the behavior of "thorium" and separated thorium X. For example, both papers mention the rise of the activity of a surface in contact with the emanation, and its decline after separation. They reassert and extend an important proposition from Rutherford's work on thorium emanation.[75] The proposition: If the emanation supplies "active particles" to the surface at a constant rate and contact is sufficiently prolonged, equilibrium will set in when the flow of fresh particles equals the "rate of decay of the excited radiation." If the excited radiation, or active deposit, decays as $I_0\exp(-\lambda t)$ after separation, then (under the assumption of constant and prolonged deposit) it had risen as $I_0[1-\exp(-\lambda t)]$. This manner of speaking was to be transferred to the rise- and fall-curves of thorium: The separated ThX plays the part of the separated active deposit, and the purified "thorium" that of the uncontaminated surface in contact with the emanation.

This transference deserves comment. In the case examined by Rutherford and Soddy, the activity of ThX *rose* for about a day after separation; only after the second day did it begin a regular, exponential decline. The "thorium" behaved contrarily: Its activity immediately after separation was about 45 percent of its value before; it then *fell* for one day and began to rise exponentially after two (see fig. 1). The capital point was that the half-life of the regular rise of "thorium" and of the regular decline of ThX came out about the same, namely four days. Further, the sums of the activities after the second day approximately equalled the intensity of the original thorium sample. Rutherford perceived in this behavior the working of the scheme he had developed to describe the decay of the active deposit.

Let the initial ionizing power of the thorium be Q_o, its residual intensity immediately after separation, I_o, and that of ThX, J_o. Then $Q_o = I_o + J_o$. If one ignores the first days' dips and rises, $J = J_o \exp(-\lambda t)$. Since, by experiment,

$$J_o \cdot \exp(-\lambda t) + I = Q_o = J_o + I_o,$$
$$I = J_o[1 - \exp(-\lambda t)] + I_o.$$

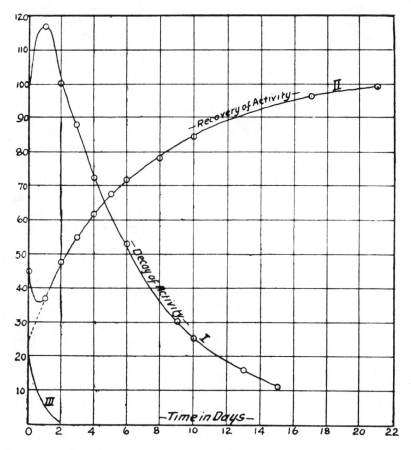

Fig. 1. The Rise and Fall of *Th* and *ThX*. From Rutherford and Soddy, *Phil. Mag.*, 1902, *4*: 380.

This is the behavior of a compound radioactive substance, of which one constituent radiates constantly (the hypothetical α emitter in "thorium"), and the other is generated constantly and decays exponentially (ThX).[76]

These considerations suggest what Rutherford at first understood by "sub-atomic chemical change." "Thorium" gives rise to ThX in the same way that, according to Thomson's theory endorsed by Rutherford, the emanation produces the "particles" of the deposit: by sending off electrons. Now ionization is also a loss of electrons and, according to the mistaken results of Rutherford and McClung, even deep-lying ones. How could the theoretician distinguish between ionization and ordinary chemical processes on the one hand, and radioactivity and "sub-atomic chemical change" on the other? In Thomson's model no clear distinction was possible:[77] Ionization and the emission of radiation did not differ qualitatively. Consequently, Rutherford did not at first recognize the profound conflict between the disintegration theory and accepted chemistry. At least that is the natural way to construe Soddy's complaint that he had "failed utterly" to make Rutherford realize the width of the gap between "our recent work and anything preceding."[78] Soddy, the Oxford chemist, disliked the electron theory of matter.[79] Rutherford, the Cambridge physicist, accepted it as the nature of things and had it constantly before him in the collaborations with Allen, Brooks, and Grier.

The detection of the materiality of the α particle brought Rutherford to accept transmutation even though he could not represent it persuasively by the electron theory. What choice had he? If an atom ejects a particle as heavy as a hydrogen molecule, is it not obliged by the principles of the periodic table of the elements to change its chemical species? So he reasoned: "The expulsion of heavy-charged particles of the same order of mass as the hydrogen atom leaves behind a new system lighter than before, and possessing chemical and physical properties quite different from those of the original element."[80] Soddy complimented Rutherford on writing so clearly: "Your unqualified pronouncement on sub-atomic change has much simplified the treatment. ...No metaphysics [electron theory?] left."[81]

The disintegration theory was put forth in April, 1902, and refined during the next several months primarily on the basis of the behavior of thorium. This was not a strong position from which to topple received ideas about the nature of matter. To strengthen it Rutherford and Soddy showed parallels between uranium or radium on the one hand, and thorium on the other;[82] and they devoted great ingenuity to demonstrating the truth of Rutherford's old claim that emanations are gases. They succeeded early in 1903 in condensing emanations with the help of a liquid-air plant newly contributed by Macdonald.[83] This exploit, which confirmed the materiality of emanations, seemed to many a stronger support of the disintegration theory than the odd behavior of the rise and fall of such phantoms as ThX.[84]

Meanwhile Barnes was busy perfecting calorimetry and building a career. In 1901 he rose to the assistant professorship and married on its strength. He assumed a large portion of the teaching chores of the department. He supplied laboratory exercises codified by the ancient demonstrators Tory and Pitcher.[85] He supervised advanced students, notably H.L. Cooke (A.B., 1900, M. A., 1903), who was perhaps unique at McGill in doing productive research under both Barnes and Rutherford. Cooke rose and fell rapidly: From 1903 to 1906 he held an 1851 Exhibition at the Cavendish; in 1906 he became Assistant Professor at Princeton, where he made a career in physics without doing much research.[86]

While Rutherford and Soddy practiced alchemy, Barnes continued to study hotness and coldness and the behavior of electrolytic cells. He had the help of two students besides Cooke, J. Guy W. Johnson (B.A., 1900, M.A. 1903), and A.S.S. Lucas (B.Sc., 1903). He also worked with E.G. Coker, a civil engineer, on water flow in pipes (an interest stimulated by continuous-flow calorimetry), and with Tory, now Associate Professor of Mathematics, on thermometry and electrochemistry.[87] And he worked with Rutherford. In the summer of 1903, in a demonstration that received more attention than it deserved, they successfully communicated wireless signals to a moving train.[88]

Their casual collaboration had an important sequel. Soddy returned to England in February, 1903,[89] leaving Rutherford with a lively impression of the occasional utility of experts in lines of work other than his own. He soon needed a specialist in heat measurement. In March, 1903 Pierre' Curie and his associate, A. Laborde, announced a new value of the heat output of radium, about 100 cal./hr, the uncertainty resulting from ignorance of the exact proportion of radium in the source.[90] In contrast to the roundabout method of Rutherford and McClung, Curie had measured the output directly—rather too directly, for he burned his fingers so badly that he could scarcely write.[91] The magnitude and constancy of the output created a "furore in the Press," as the overheated Soddy wrote Rutherford.[92] Soddy was concerned; Curie had challenged the disintegration theory. "This production of heat [he said] can also be explained by supposing that radium exploits an external source of energy of unknown type." To the uninitiated Curie's vague alternative to transmutation may have gained plausibility because his measurement of radium's heat was over 50 times the estimate Rutherford and Soddy had made by applying transmutation theory to measurements of the ionizing power of the emanation.[93] (They worked with emanation to avoid the problem of absorption of radiation in the source.) Guessing that emanation contributed about two-fifths of the heating of the "radium" in equilibrium with it, they reckoned the total output at 1.7 cal./hr. "Curie got more per day than we do per year," Soddy worried, miscalculating by a factor of ten. The paper containing this result was then (31 March) in final draft. Rutherford and Soddy decided to let it stand, to keep silent about Curie, and to add a qualification that reduced the menace of his big number. "Only the energy employed in producing ions has been considered, and this may be only a small fraction of the total energy of the rays."[94]

Leaving the size of the fraction aside, Rutherford saw that a partial answer to Curie, and a good test of the transformation theory, would be to obtain the outputs from radium and its descendents separately. The outputs should add up to that of natural radium. Moreover, if almost all the energy of decay was carried by α particles, as Rutherford and Grier had concluded, then the output of the various products measured directly as heat should be proportional to the ionizing power of their α-rays. Rutherford had determined this power with the help of Brooks and Grier. It remained to determine the heat. Who was more likely to do it right than Barnes?

Delicate apparatus was required. Rutherford had only 30 milligrams of radium bromide to hand; he needed to measure a few hundredthousandths of a gram calorie each second, a few hundred ergs. Barnes used special platinum-resistance thermometers and a differential air calorimeter. He fed the current from the thermometers into his version of Callendar's compensated resistance box. Rutherford's part was to supply the samples, radium freed from its emanation (and, consequently, of the short-lived products of the active deposit) and the emanation itself, allowed to stand until coming to equilibrium with its active deposit. The outcome corroborated the value obtained by Curie and Laborde, and confirmed the transformation theory.[95]

Someone had the misfortune to disagree with these immaculate measurements. It was Friedrich Paschen, a man usually cautious and accurate, but, in this particular, the supporter of a theory menaced by the experimental results.[96] He believed γ-rays to be particulate, to travel at or near the speed of light, and so to carry a sizeable fraction of the energy from "radium." Using a comparatively crude apparatus, an ice calorimeter, he tried to find the heat imparted by all the radiations of radium to a lead shield thick enough to stop most of the γs. According to him, the total heat of "radium" is over twice what Rutherford and Barnes had made it. Paschen's claim sent the McGill professors back to their calorimeter. They too arranged matters so as to trap much of the γ radiation, and they confirmed that it made a negligible contribution to the total radiated heat. Paschen, who had recognized the faults of his method, agreed.[97]

Barnes was to continue measurements of the heat output of radioactive substances after Rutherford left McGill.[98] The collaboration and collegiality had meant much to him. "As I look back over the time we have known each other here I feel how fortunate I have been in being placed with you," he wrote after the separation. "How much I should like to see you in your laboratory and have a good old talk with you about the many things we used to discuss together."[99] But Barnes was not the man to take another's direction. He was already well advanced on a line that was to have interesting scientific and important commercial consequences.

In the winter of 1895, the chief engineer of the Montreal harbor works asked Callendar to take the temperature of the St. Lawrence River. He hoped to learn how far the river stood from freezing and how its temperature related to the formation of "frazil" ice, a fine spicular ice that can clog navigation channels and intake pipes to power plants. Callendar was otherwise engaged and sent Barnes.[100]

Using a differential platinum thermometer, more accurate and more convenient than the usual mercury thermometer (which had to be removed from the water at each reading), Barnes found that the river temperature never departed from freezing by as much as $0.01\,^\circ$C. And that, as he said, was "a matter of great interest," since the air temperature sometimes reached $-33\,^\circ$C. He followed up the investigation the following winter, at rapids five miles upstream from town; frazil formed in great quantities on cold days near the rapids, when the ice-cold spray froze instantly on contact with the sub-zero air. At night, in backwaters, Barnes followed the growth of "anchor ice," which forms on the river bottom. This odd violation of gravity occurs only on cold, cloudless nights, and never under bridges or surface ice; often it is terminated by the first rays of the morning sun. With these facts Barnes supported an old hypothesis that radiation from the river bottom drops its temperature just enough to freeze the contiguous layer of ice-cold river water. The ice thus anchored grows, sometimes very quickly, owing to the adhesion of frazil created in the rapids and mixed with the water. By the spring of 1897, Barnes had a complete theory of the formation of river ice; frazil emerged as the chief menace, a mucilagenous slush that could freeze a river solid by attaching itself to firm ice on surface or bottom.[101]

Barnes returned to the study of ice formation after finishing his classic memoir on the specific heat of water. He began with the density of ice, for which discordant values had been published, latterly by E.F. Nichols, who had found that old ice and natural ice were denser by about two parts in 1000 than new ice and artificial ice. In a beautiful investigation, Barnes and Cooke reviewed the several methods of measuring the density, chose weighing in air and water, and found no differences of Nichols' kind. Barnes guessed that the discrepancies arose from stresses (and consequently changes in internal structure and density) set up in specimens by the process of making artificial ice. Cooke looked into the business and found it to be so.[102]

To confirm his theory of the formation of river ice, Barnes wished to make frazil in the laboratory. He needed a blast of air cold enough to simulate a wind whipping the spray of rapids at temperatures far below freezing. The liquid-air plant answered: By venting boiling liquid air into ice-cold water, Barnes got frazil to his complete satisfaction. The air machine corroborated his theory of ice formation as neatly as it had Rutherford's ideas about the emanation. Naturally, Barnes went beyond qualitative confirmation. He found that frazil forms when the water temperature falls to $-0.0060°$C. He concluded that a slight warming of the water near intake pipes or moving parts of power plants might prevent the agglomeration of unwanted frazil there.[103]

Effective measures of frazil control by heating were soon forthcoming.[104] Barnes himself did not play a part in designing these devices. Perhaps because of Rutherford's example, he had wavered about the propriety of exploiting his discoveries. On the one hand, he and Tory patented a pyrometer and pointed out its uses to industry;[105] on the other, he was reluctant to exploit his knowledge of ice: "I am interested altogether in the scientific side of ice and never expect to get the commercial end.... I have steadily refused commercial propositions as I hate being involved in such things and I believe it would act against the scientific value of my work."[106]

In 1912, when he wrote these lines, Barnes' value had recently been recognized by election to the Royal Society of London, on his second trial. He was proposed by Callendar, seconded by Rutherford, and supported by J.G. Adami, F.D. Adams, Bovey, Griffiths, E.W. MacBride, Sir Arthur Schuster, Sir Joseph Swan, F.T. Trouton, and W.C.D. Wetham.[107] The group represented Barnes' full range of interests as well as the solidarity of

Canadian Fellows. Adami, Adams, Bovey, and MacBride were acting or former McGill professors; Griffiths and Wetham were specialists in Barnes' specialties, heat measurements and electrolytes, respectively; and Swan and Trouton were concerned with practical applications of physical theory. Schuster, Rutherford's colleague at Manchester and a senior member of the Society, may have been added for weight.

Barnes was to apply his knowledge of ice with spectacular success. The sight of icebergs cracking themselves to pieces in sunlight suggested to him that ice jams might be broken by exploding small, hot charges in them. The heat of explosion could melt but a negligible amount of ice; but it might set up mechanical stresses that would propagate through the mass. Before Barnes could turn to such work he, too, had to suffer severe stress. In 1912 his wife died suddenly, leaving him with four young children; the directorship of the MPB, which he assumed on Cox' retirement in 1909, became too much; he had a breakdown from which he was not expected to recover.[108] He recovered to become a roving destroyer of ice menaces. In February, 1925, at his first trial, he removed a jam of 250,000 tons of ice from the St. Lawrence with three ninety-pound explosive charges.[109]

During Rutherford's last years in Canada, 1904–1907, the staff of the MPB occupied, or pacified, research territory it had earlier invaded. To speak plainly, Rutherford and Barnes wrote books. Rutherford began his *Radioactivity* in 1903; it came out the following year and reappeared reworked in 1905. Barnes published his *Ice Formation* in 1906. Each dedicated his book to his master, Rutherford to Thomson and Barnes to Callendar.

Honors, awards, and further opportunities for advertisement were thrust upon the willing McGill professors. In the spring of 1904 Rutherford gave the Bakerian lecture at the Royal Society; in the fall he explained radioactivity at the International Exposition at St. Louis; in the winter he was writing for *Harpers Magazine.* He gave the Silliman lectures at Yale (published as a book in 1906) and lesser performances in Boston, Columbus, Ithaca, Madison, and Berkeley. He received the Rumford medal of the Royal Society. Barnes was a delegate of the Royal Society of Canada to the St. Louis Exposition, where he acted as secretary to the Electrical Convention. He, too, was invited to lecture, for example to the American Academy of Mechanical Engineers.[110]

As for research, Barnes continued his old investigations and moved toward meteorology and geophysics. We already know the importance of this work for ice engineering. Rutherford's main study was the behavior of α particles. His demonstration of the deviability of their paths in electric and magnetic fields had made possible the determination of their charge, mass, and velocities of projection. Their manner of passage through matter also claimed his attention. He discovered that they ceased to ionize while still possessed of considerable energies and that—contrary to everyone's expectations—they could be scattered through appreciable angles by the molecules they encountered. In his last year at McGill, he tried to count the number of αs given off by radium, a project completed at Manchester with the help of Geiger. Everyone knows how the research on α scattering and α counting later led to the invention of the theory of single scattering and of the nuclear model of the atom.[111]

As Rutherford's reputation rose, advanced research workers, not trained in his laboratory, began to go to McGill. The first foreign worker was Fanny Cook Gates, head of the physics department at Goucher College, Baltimore, a peripatetic lady who had studied at Northwestern, Bryn Mawr, Göttingen, and Zürich.[112] She cleared up two points of minor interest during her stay in 1902–1903. She showed that the apparent destruction by heat of excited activity was in fact volatilization: The rule that radioactivity could not be affected by physical or chemical treatment survived without exception. And she showed that the odd ionizing radiations provoked from sulphate of quinine by altering its temperature differed altogether from the rays from radioactive substances.[113] She thereby rescued radioactivity from the weak grasp of Gustave Le Bon, who found rays everywhere and considered them all—αs, βs, γs, Xs, blacklight, quinine rays, N-rays—to be standard physico-chemical processes.[114]

The next foreign worker was Tadeusz Godlewski, who perceived that the alchemy of McGill would make gold back in Poland. He spent the year 1904–1905 chasing decay products in the actinium family, distributed his results in three papers, and received a chair at the University of Lemberg.[115] He was followed in 1905–1906 by Otto Hahn and Max Levin, who also did well after learning to manage "with hardly ever drinking anything" in Rutherford's teetotal environment.[116] Hahn had a new radio-element to his credit when he came to McGill; he soon found another, which Godlewski had overlooked among the products of actinium.[117] Levin too helped to clarify the actinium series, and both he and Hahn, mopping up after W.H. Bragg, measured the ranges of α particles from actinium and polonium.[118] Nothing very exciting, as Rutherford wrote Boltwood, but good exercise. "Things are going on fairly satisfactorily here—nothing particularly novel. Hahn and Levin are both indefatigable workers."[119] They were replaced in 1906–1907 by Levin's brother-in-law, Gustav Rümelin, who remeasured the rate of transformation of radium emanation. All three returned to promising academic careers in Germany. Levin abandoned his for the family business; Rümelin died in World War I; Hahn continued working indefatigably, discovered fission and won a Nobel Prize.[120]

Rutherford did not work closely with any of these foreign students. Only Hahn was admitted to co-authorship; and their joint paper, on the mass of the alpha particles from thorium, was in fact almost entirely Rutherford's work. Hahn's contribution was an active preparation of thorium.[121]

Several junior members of the MPB staff also published papers on radioactivity during these years. McClung, returned from Cambridge and once again a demonstrator, worked on what was becoming Rutherford's central problem, the absorption of α-rays.[122] H.F. Bronson came to McGill to learn radioactivity after receiving a Ph.D. from Yale in 1904. He helped to confirm the independence of radium's activity of temperature, which had again been challenged, and the decay sequence in the radium active deposit.[123] A.S. Eve, one-time Cambridge wrangler and secondary-school teacher, drifted to McGill in 1903, at the age of 42. Employed first as demonstrator in physics, then as lecturer in mathematics, he discovered a talent for tracking the rays of radioactive substances. He became Macdonald Professor on Cox' retirement in 1909, and Director of the MPB on Barnes' retirement in 1919.[124]

Eve's first, and perhaps his most important, research concerned the nature of γ-rays. The majority view, which likened γs to X-rays, then faced a serious objection: The soft X-rays usually employed ionize gases much more powerfully than do γ-rays from radium. At Rutherford's suggestion, Eve worked with very hard X-rays. He found that they ionized more like γs than like soft X-rays; if the bulb could be made hard enough, its penetrating radiations would presumably be identical with radium's.[125] The only evidence remaining against such an identification was Paschen's claim that γs could be deflected by a magnetic field. Eve showed that Paschen had confused the γs with secondary electrons created by them in passing through lead.[126]

Rutherford concluded that γ-rays are the short electromagnetic pulses that, on Maxwell's theory, should be emitted when fast charged particles (the β-rays) are projected from decaying atoms. Later he made the βs photoelectrons knocked out of atoms by γs originating in or near the nucleus.[127] Neither model has stood up.

The achievement of the workers at the MPB during Rutherford's time may draw attention because as an institution their research school was very fragile. It depended for its personnel on recruits from its own undergraduates, on demonstrators, and on occasional foreign students able to support themselves for a year in Montreal. The supply was uncertain. The only recruit in the session 1905–1906 was R.W. Boyle, B.Sc. in 1905. He went on to earn a Ph.D. in 1909, the first in physics at McGill.[128] The Ph.D. program was not stable until 1906; had it been available earlier, the MPB might have drawn more graduate students.

There is evidence that the quality of the demonstrators declined after 1905. The office, which paid very little, $500 or $750 a year, could attract only the dedicated or the desperate. In the session of 1905–1906, the full complement of demonstrators could not be filled. In 1907–1908 an employment agency was required.[129] The bright young men thus assembled did not compare favorably with their opposite numbers at Manchester or Cambridge. "The demonstrators are not very bright, not much 'ginger' in them." That was the opinion of Rutherford's student, J.A. Gray, just after taking up a lectureship at the MPB in 1912.[130]

As for foreign students, even Americans did not seek advanced training in physics at McGill. Gates and Bronson had finished their degrees before they came. Europeans could not be expected in any numbers after continental universities began to teach Rutherford's theories and methods. Godlewski, Hahn, and Levin came before or during this transfer. Rümelin made the journey not because the MPB was the only place to go, but because his brother-in-law recommended its friendly, if beerless, scientific life.[131]

Rutherford and Barnes were keen and energetic young men, with international reputations; they worked very hard; they encouraged beginners; they helped promising people to scholarships and appointments. The contagion of Rutherford's enthusiasm is well known: He could extract "almost incessant work willingly given."[132] In return he generously acknowledged help received: "I am really no more than a humble servant," Harriet Brooks once protested. "Please do not give me any more credit than I deserve. ... You are far too generous in that respect."[133] As for Barnes, he "devote[d] himself untiringly" to advancing the skills and broadening the training of his students.[134] The failure to establish a self-generating research group in physics at McGill was not the fault of the professors.

Manchester offered Rutherford not only proximity to European civilization, but also an established research school. The perceptive Godlewski correctly assessed the force of this attraction. He had noticed his boss' "great satisfaction to see the people working under your direction.... [At Manchester] you will have plainty [*sic*] of students of all the countries of the Continent, and have so a great school."[135]

As Rutherford had expected, he did have "a good number of researchers to look after"[136] at Manchester, about 20 a year on the average. About 80 percent of their work concerned radioactivity: As Director of the Laboratory Rutherford had no obligation to share his resources with physicists of the macrocosm. The size of the corps of organized researchers at Manchester impressed visitors from McGill.[137] Well it should: While Rutherford had as many workers as he could profitably employ—as many in one year as during his entire stay in Canada—Barnes had to put off projects important to him, "not having the advanced men to work in the laboratory."[138] In number there is strength, and weakness. It cannot be said that Rutherford's accomplishments were always in proportion to the size of his research staff.

Notes

It is a pleasure to thank L. Badash and T. Trenn for helpful comments, and L. Pyenson and B. Wheaton for critical readings of the penultimate draft. I am further indebted to Professor Pyenson for generously putting at my disposal information he gathered from the McGill University Archives.

1. Rutherford to Mary Newton, 3 Aug. 1898, in A.S. Eve, *Rutherford* (New York: Macmillan, 1939), p. 55.

2. *Nature*, 1923, *111*:817.

3. P. Forman, J.L. Heilbron, and S. Weart, *Physics circa 1900. Personnel, Funding and Productivity of the Academic Establishments* (Princeton Univ. Press, 1975), p. 92 (*Historical Studies in the Physical Sciences,* vol. 5).

4. J. Cox, "Physics and Engineering at the McGill University, Montreal," *Nature*, 1894, *50*:558–564.

5. Rutherford to Mary Newton, 30 July 1898, in Eve, *Rutherford,* p. 54; cf. *ibid.*, pp. 57, 64.

6. Forman et al., *Physics,* p. 92; Callendar to Rutherford, 19 Jan. 1900. This letter is in the Rutherford Correspondence (RC) at Cambridge University Library. Copies exist at the depositories of the Archive for History of Quantum Physics; see T.S. Kuhn et al., *Sources for History of Quantum Physics* (Philadelphia: American Philosophical Society, 1967).

7. Rutherford to Mary Newton, 30 July 1898, in Eve, *Rutherford,* p. 54.

8. J.G. Crowther, *The Cavendish Laboratory, 1874–1974* (New York: Science History Publications, 1974), pp. 95–98; R.T. Glazebrook, "The Rayleigh Period," in *A History of the Cavendish Laboratory, 1871–1910* (London: Longmans, Green, 1910), pp. 49–71.

9. J.J. Thomson, "Survey of the Last Twenty-Five Years," in *ibid.,* pp. 75–101, on p. 84; H.F. Newall, "1885–1894," in *ibid.,* pp. 102–158, on pp. 143–144.

10. H.A.M. Snelders, art. "Callendar," *Dictionary of Scientific Biography (DSB),* III (New York: Scribners, 1971), pp. 19–20.

11. Macdonald to his brother, 6 Jan. 1852, in J.F. Snell, "Sir William Macdonald and his Kin," *The Dalhousie Review,* 1943, *23*:317–330.

12. Franklin to Collinson, 29 July 1750, in *Benjamin Franklin's Experiments,* ed. I.B. Cohen (Harvard Univ. Press, 1941), p. 219.

13. W.M. H[icks], "Henry Taylor Bovey, 1850–1912," Royal Society of London (RSL), *Proceedings,* 1913, *88A*: x–xii. Cf. E.A. Corbett, *Henry Marshall Tory* (Toronto: Ryerson, 1954), p. 46, and Cyrus Macmillan, *McGill and its Story* (Oxford Univ. Press, 1921), pp. 236–238, 257.

14. McGill Univ., *Annual Report,* 1898/9, p. 40; 1899/1900, p. 32; 1903/4, p. 40; 1904/5, p. 46; *Calendar,* 1902/3.

15. Cf. L. Pyenson, "The Incomplete Transmission of a European Image: Physics at Greater Buenos Aires and Montreal, 1890–1920," American Philosophical Society, *Proceedings,* 1978, *122*:92–114.

16. Royal Society of Canada (RSC), *Proceedings,* 1899, *5*: viii, xxii–xxiii, xxxviii–xxxix; 1900, *6*: vi, xii–xiii; 1901, *7*: v, xli; 1902, *8*: xxxi; 1903, *9*: xxii–xxiii. Cf. C.H. McLeod, "A Trigonometrical Survey for Canada," RSC, Section III, *Transactions,* 1899, *5*: 3–7, on p. 5: "The commercial advantages of such a work as this [triangulation] will be at once recognized, even by those who do not see eye to eye with us in scientific affairs. [It will assist shipping.] It will also afford an illustration of how readily the purely practical may be made to serve the highest scientific ends." Prof. McLeod, director of the McGill observatory, is reduced to deriving the scientific from the practical.

17. J.J. Thomson, *Recollections and Reflections* (New York: Macmillan, 1937), p. 435.

18. *London Times,* 8 Jan. 1930, p. 6a, and 31 Jan. 1930, p. 8ab; *Nature,* 1930, *125*: 173–174; S.W.J. S[mith], "Hugh Langbourne Callendar, 1863–1930," in RSL, *Proc.,* 1932, *134A*: xviii–xxvi.

19. Letter of 11 Aug. 1898, in Eve, *Rutherford,* p. 56.

20. *Ibid.,* pp. 55, 57, 65, 68–69.

21. Rutherford to Mary Newton, Sept. 1899, *ibid.,* pp. 68–69.

22. Cf. Rutherford, "1895–1898," in *A History of the Cavendish,* pp. 158–194, who devotes two of 35 pages to "general physics."

23. Rutherford to Mary Newton, 15 Jan. 1896, in Eve, *Rutherford,* p. 23.

24. Rutherford, "1895–1898," pp. 176–177.

25. Rutherford to Mary Newton, 20 April 1896, in Eve, *Rutherford,* p. 34.

26. A total of £400, £100 less than Rutherford's beginning salary at McGill. Eve, *Rutherford,* p. 47.

27. *Ibid.,* pp. 43, 85.

28. J.L. Heilbron, "The Scattering of α and β Particles and Rutherford's Atom," *Archive for History of Exact Science,* 1968, *4*:247–307, on pp. 250–251; Rutherford, "Uranium Radiation and the Electrical Conduction produced by It," *Phil. Mag.,* 1899,

47:109–163; *Collected Papers (CP)*, I (London: George Allen and Unwin, 1962), pp. 169–215.

29. Eve, *Rutherford*, pp. 48–49; H.L. Bronson, "Some Reminiscences of Professor Ernest Rutherford during his Time at McGill University, Montreal," in Rutherford, *CP*, I, 163–164.

30. Rutherford, "1895–1898," pp. 159–160; Lord Rayleigh, *The Life of Sir J.J. Thomson* (Cambridge Univ. Press, 1942), pp. 74, 125; G.P. Thomson, *J.J. Thomson and the Cavendish Laboratory in His Day* (Garden City, New York: Doubleday, 1965), pp. 38–41.

31. J.L. Heilbron, art. "Thomson," *DSB*, XIII (1976), 362–372; "Lectures on the History of Atomic Physics, 1900–1922," in *History of Twentieth Century Physics*, ed. Charles Weiner (New York: Academic Press, 1977), pp. 40–108, on pp. 40–41, 53–56.

32. McGill Univ., *Ann. Rep.*, 1897, pp. 26–29.

33. Cf. *ibid.*, 1894, pp. 34–37.

34. Barnes, "On the Capacity of Water between the Freezing and Boiling-Points," RSL, *Phil. Trans.*, 1902, *199A:* 149–263, on p. 150; Callendar, "Continuous Electrical Calorimetry," *ibid.*, 55–148, on pp. 59, 65, 82, 86, 97.

35. Corbett, *Tory*, pp. 39, 44–45. Tory and Pitcher were the first demonstrators at the MPB; McGill Univ., *Ann. Rep.*, 1894, p. 34.

36. Callendar, "Continuous Electrical Calorimetry," pp. 57, 78–79, praising the "facilities," "solidity of construction," and "perfection of the heating arrangements" at the MPB.

37. Callendar to Rutherford, 19 Jan. 1900 (RC). Callendar describes the box in "Continuous Electrical Calorimetry," pp. 87–92.

38. McGill Univ., *Ann. Rep.*, 1898/9, pp. 40–41; Barnes, "On the Capacity," pp. 151–152, 172, 217.

39. *Ibid.*, p. 152.

40. Cox, *Mechanics* (2nd ed. Cambridge Univ. Press, 1909), pp. vii–xi.

41. *Ibid.*, p. 1; cf. J. Bradley, *Mach's Philosophy of Science* (Univ. of London Press, 1971), pp. 4–14.

42. Cox, *Mechanics*, p. 151.

43. Callendar to Rutherford, 19 Jan. and 26 Feb. 1900 (RC).

44. Rutherford's notes of this conversation are not among his papers at Cambridge.

45. The award, first given in 1890, was made every two years. RSL, *The Record* (4th ed., London: Royal Society, 1940), p. 125.

46. McGill Univ., *Ann. Rep.*, 1899/1900, p. 32; J.S. Ames, "L'équivalent mécanique de la chaleur," in Congrès International de Physique, *Rapports* (4 vols., Paris: Gauthier Villars, 1900/01), I, 178–213, on pp. 195, 213; E.H. Griffiths, "La chaleur spécifique de l'eau," *ibid.*, I, 214–227, on pp. 216, 220–225.

47. Rutherford to Mary Newton, 2 Dec. 1899, in Eve, *Rutherford*, p. 69. "A Radioactive Substance emitted from Thorium Compounds," *Phil. Mag.*, 1900, *49*:1–14 (*CP*, I, 220–231), was completed in September, 1899, and published in January; "Radioactivity Produced in Substances by the Action of Thorium Compounds," *Phil. Mag.*, 1900, *49*:161–192 (*CP*, I, 232–259), completed in Nov., published in Feb.

48. McGill Univ., *Ann. Rep.*, 1898/9, pp. 40–41; Eve, *Rutherford*, p. 61.

49. *CP,* I, 220–259.

50. Rutherford to Mary Newton, Sept. 1899, in Eve, *Rutherford,* p. 68.

51. See L. Pyenson, "Incomplete Transmission."

52. Rutherford and McClung, "Energy of Röntgen and Becquerel Rays, and the Energy required to produce an Ion in Gases," RSL, *Phil. Trans.,* 1901, *196A*:25–59 (*CP,* I, 260–295), on pp. 283, 287.

53. *Ibid., CP,* I, 288–293; M. and P. Curie, "Les nouvelles substances radioactives et les rayons qu'elles émettent," Cong. Int. Phys., *Rapports,* III, 79–114, on p. 92.

54. McGill Univ., *Thesis Directory.* I, *1881–1959* (Montreal: McGill Univ., 1976), p. 1. This directory is not complete.

55. McGill Univ., *Ann. Rep.,* 1898/9, p. 40; Brooks, "Damping of Electrical Oscillations," RSC, Sec. III, *Trans.,* 1899, *5*:13–15.

56. Rutherford and Brooks, "The New Gas from Radium," *ibid.,* 1901, *7*:21–25, read 23 May, 1901 (*CP,* I, 301–305); Rutherford, "Emanations from Radioactive Substances," *Nature,* 1901, *64*:157–158 (*CP,* I, 306–308); P. and M. Curie, "Les nouvelles substances," p. 92. By July, 1902, Marie Curie had fixed the atomic weight of radium at about 225; "Sur le poids atomique du radium," Académie des Sciences, Paris, *Comptes rendus,* 1902, *135*:161–163.

57. Brooks, "A Volatile Product from Radium," *Nature,* 1904, *70*:270; T.J. Trenn, "Rutherford and Recoil Atoms: the Metamorphosis and Success of a Once Stillborn Theory," *Historical Studies in the Physical Sciences,* 1975, *6*:513–547, on pp. 530–531.

58. Rutherford to Schuster, 25 Mar. 1907 (RSL Archives): "Miss Brooks is a very good friend to my wife and myself...very able woman....J.J. Thomson informed me that she was the best woman researcher, next to Mrs. Sidgwick, he had at the Cavendish. She has already a good knowledge of experimental work in ionization of gases and radioactivity....She has as strong a claim as any probable candidate for the position." I am indebted to L. Badash for knowledge of this letter. Pitcher also committed the sin of entering industry.

59. Muriel Howorth, *Pioneer Research on the Atom* (London: New World Publications, 1958), pp. 83–90; Norman Feather, *Lord Rutherford* (Glasgow: Blackie, 1940), pp. 78–79.

60. Cf. T.J. Trenn, "Rutherford and Soddy: from a Search for Radioactive Constituents to the Disintegration Theory of Radioactivity," *Rete,* 1971, *1*:51–70; Marjorie C. Malley, *From Hyperphosphorescence to Nuclear Decay: A History of the Early Years of Radioactivity* (Unpubl. Ph.D. Thesis, Berkeley, University of California, 1976), pp. 56–73. Trenn's careful study, *The Self-Splitting Atom. The History of the Rutherford-Soddy Collaboration* (London: Taylor and Francis, 1977), came to hand too late to be used; it does not, however, require any important change in the discussion in the text. Cf. *Science,* 1978, *200*:1143–4.

61. Rutherford, "Übertragung erregter Radioaktivität," *Phys. Zs.,* 1902, *3*:210–214, read 29 Dec. 1901 (*CP,* I, 351–359), on pp. 357–358. Cf. Trenn, "Rutherford and Recoil Atoms," p. 517.

62. Rutherford, "Versuche über erregte Radioaktivität," *Phys. Zs.,* 1902, *3*:254–257, dated 14 Jan. 1902 (*CP,* I, 370–375), on p. 372.

63. "The Radioactivity of Thorium Compounds, II," Chemical Society of London, *Trans.*, 1902, *81*:837–860 (*CP*, I, 435–456), on pp. 452, 454.

64. E.g., Eve, *Rutherford*, pp. 77–80, 84–85, and Alfred Romer, "The Transmutation Theory of Radioactivity," *Isis*, 1958, *49*:3–12.

65. Rutherford and Soddy, "Radioactivity of Thorium Compounds, II," in *CP*, I, 455.

66. *Ibid.*, p. 454.

67. Rutherford and Soddy, "The Cause and Nature of Radioactivity, Part II," *Phil. Mag.*, 1902, *4*:569–585 (*CP*, I, 495–508), on p. 508; Rutherford, "The Magnetic and Electric Deviation of the Easily Absorbed Rays from Radium," *Phil. Mag.*, 1903, *5*:177–187, dated 10 Nov. 1902 (*CP*, I, 549–557), on p. 557; cf. Feather, *Lord Rutherford*, pp. 86–87. Rutherford and Soddy's first two papers, presented to the Chemical Society of London in January and May, 1902, were written in the course of the work; they concern, first, the emanating power of thoria and, second, the rise and decay of ThX. The next two papers, published in the *Philosophical Magazine* for September and November, 1902, are reworkings of the first pair, published in reverse order.

68. Rutherford and Soddy, "The Radioactivity of Uranium," *Phil. Mag.*, 1903, *5*:441–445, dated 20 Feb. 1903 (*CP*, I, 561–564), on p. 564.

69. Trenn, this volume, pp. 89–109; Heilbron, "Scattering," pp. 252–254.

70. Rutherford, "Magnetic and Electric Deviation," in *CP*, I, 549–557; Trenn, "Rutherford and the Alpha-Beta-Gamma Classification of Radioactive Rays," *Isis*, 1976, *67*:61–75.

71. Rutherford, "Magnetic and Electric Deviation," *CP*, I, 557.

72. Rutherford and Grier, "Deviable Rays of Radioactive Substances," *Phil. Mag.*, 1902, *4*:315–330, communicated to the American Physical Society, 21 April 1902, but dated 7 May (*CP*, I, 457–471), on pp. 470–471; cf. *ibid.*, pp. 452, 454.

73. *CP*, I, pp. 464, 471, 557. Rutherford and Grier's paper also appeared in *Phys. Zs.*, 1902, *3*:385–390, dated 21 April; it includes the sentence quoted in the text.

74. Cf. Trenn, "Rutherford and Recoil Atoms," pp. 519–520.

75. Rutherford, "Radioactivity Produced in Substances," *CP*, I, 248; Rutherford and Brooks, "Comparison of the Radiations from Radioactive Substances," *Phil. Mag.*, 1902, *4*:1–23, dated 6 March, published July, 1902 (*CP*, I, 415–434), on p. 431; Rutherford and Allen, "Excited Radioactivity and Ionization of the Atmosphere," *Phil. Mag.*, 1902, *4*:704–723, dated 9 June, published Dec., 1902 (*CP*, I, 509–527), on pp. 514–515.

76. Rutherford and Soddy, "Radioactivity of Thorium Compounds, II," in *CP*, I, pp. 437–438. The initial dips and rises come from short-lived products of the active deposit.

77. Heilbron, "Lectures," pp. 55–56.

78. Soddy to Rutherford, 7 Aug. 1903 (RC); cf. Soddy to Noyes, 22 Feb. 1936, in Howorth, *Pioneer Research*, p. 87, and *ibid.*, pp. 83–84.

79. *Ibid.*, pp. 80–81.

80. Rutherford and Soddy, "Radioactive Change," *Phil. Mag.*, 1903, *5*:576–591, dated 16 Oct. 1902, published May, 1903 (*CP*, I, 596–608), on pp. 598–599, 604.

81. Soddy to Rutherford, 31 Mar. 1903 (RC). Rutherford still cleaved to the electron theory, hence Soddy's taunt of 7 Aug. 1903.

82. Rutherford and Soddy, "Radioactivity of Uranium," *CP*, I, 561-564; "A Comparative Study of the Radioactivity of Radium and Thorium," *Phil. Mag.*, 1903, *5*:445-457, dated 20 Feb. 1903 (*CP*, I, 565-575).

83. Soddy to Rutherford, 31 July and 3 Aug. 1902 (RC); Rutherford and Soddy, "Condensation of the radioactive Emanations," *Phil. Mag.*, 1903, *5*:561-576, dated 9 Mar. 1903 (*CP*, I, 580-595).

84. Soddy to Rutherford, 7 Mar. 1903 (RC): "The condensation is what has struck them all [the men in Ramsay's laboratory] I think much more than the earlier work...."

85. H.M. Tory and F.H. Pitcher, *A Manual of Laboratory Physics* (New York: Wiley, 1901), p. v.

86. *American Men of Science*, ed. J.M. Cattell and D.R. Brimhall (3rd ed. Garrison, New York: Science Press, 1921), p. 143; McGill Univ., *Ann. Rep.*, 1900/1, p. 30.

87. *Ibid.*, 1901/2, p. 28; 1902/3, p. 41.

88. McGill Univ., *Ann. Rep.*, 1902/3, p. 35; Eve, *Rutherford*, p. 83. Rutherford recognized Barnes' merit from the beginning; *ibid.*, p. 70, quoting a letter of 31 Mar. 1899.

89. Soddy to Rutherford, 7 Mar. 1903 (RC).

90. P. Curie and A. Laborde, "Sur la chaleur dégagée spontanément par les sels du radium," Acad. Sci., Paris, *C.R.*, 1903, *136*:673-675, read 16 Mar.

91. Curie to James Dewar, 26 June 1903 (Dewar Papers, Royal Institution, London): "J'ai les doigts tellement abimés par les rayons du radium que j'ai peine à écrire."

92. Letter of 31 March 1903 (RC).

93. Rutherford and Soddy, "Radioactive Change," in *CP*, I, 607, published April, 1903. C.D.T. Runge and Julius Precht, "Über die Wärmeabgabe des Radiums," Akademie der Wissenschaften, Berlin, *Sitzungsberichte*, 1903, *2*:783-786, read 23 July, make the output 105 cals./hr; it is about 140.

94. Soddy to Rutherford, 31 March 1903 (RC), *CP*, I, 607.

95. Rutherford and Barnes, "Heating Effect of the Radium Emanation," *Nature*, 1903, *68*:622, dated 16 Oct. (*CP*, I, 611-612); "Heating Effect of the Radium Emanation," *Phil. Mag.*, 1904, *7*:202-219, dated 22 Dec. 1903 (*CP*, I, 625-639), on pp. 627, 629. Cf. Soddy to Rutherford, 27 Oct. 1903 (RC): "I got your letter of the 19th today, and congratulate you on having got out the heating effects so soon, which are so satisfactory."

96. F. Paschen, "Über die γ-Strahlen des Radiums," *Phys. Zs.*, 1904, *5*:563-568, dated 19 Aug., published 18 Sept.; B.R. Wheaton, *On the Nature of X- and Gamma Rays: Attitudes Toward Localization of Energy in the "New Radiations," 1896-1922* (Unpubl. Ph.D. Thesis, Princeton Univ., 1978), Chapt. 3.

97. Rutherford and Barnes, "The Heating Effect of the γ-Rays from Radium," *Nature*, 1904, *71*:151-152, dated 1 Dec. 1903 (*CP*, I, 723-724), and *Phil. Mag.*, 1905, *9*:621-628, dated 22 Feb. 1905 (*CP*, I, 792-798); F. Paschen, "Über die Wärmeentwickelung des Radiums in einer Bleihülle," *Phys. Zs.*, 1905, *6*:97, dated 30 Jan. 1905.

98. Barnes to Rutherford, 28 Jan. 1908 (RC). Callendar also joined in; Callendar to Rutherford, 16 June 1910 (RC).

99. Barnes to Rutherford, 19 Dec. and 28 Jan. 1908 (RC), respectively.

100. Barnes, "On some Measurements of the Temperature of the River Water...," RSC, Sec. III, *Trans.*, 1896, *2*:37–44; *Ice Formation* (New York: Wiley, 1906), pp. 103–106.

101. Barnes, "On some Measurements," pp. 40–44; "On some Measurements of the Temperature of the Lachine Rapids...," RSC, Sec, III, *Trans.*, 1897, *3*:17–30, on pp. 28–30; *Ice Formation*, pp. 106–113.

102. E.L. Nichols, "On the Density of Ice," *Phys. Rev.*, 1899, *8*:21–37; Barnes and Cooke, "On the Density of Ice," RSC, Sec. III, *Trans.*, 1902, *8*:143–155; Cooke, "The Variation in the Density of Ice," *ibid.*, 127–134. Barnes, "Notes on Frazil and Anchor Ice, with Considerations as to the Freezing Point of Water," RSC, Sec. III, *Trans.*, 1899, *5*:17–22, had at first accepted Nichols' results. Cf. Barnes, *Ice Formation*, pp. 30–44.

103. Barnes, "On the Artificial Production of Frazil Ice, together with Measurements of the Temperature Conditions in the Water," RSC, Sec. III, *Trans.*, 1904, *10*:29–32.

104. Barnes, *Ice Engineering* (Montreal: Renouf, 1928), pp. 144–148.

105. J.S. Foster, "Howard Turner Barnes," RSL, *Obituary Notices of Fellows*, 1952/3, *8*:25–35, on p. 35. Perhaps Barnes' enthusiasm for the British Science Guild, of whose Canadian branch he was secretary (McGill Univ., Archives, Acc. 454/592), is pertinent here. The Guild aimed to promote both science and its applications. See A.J. Meadows, *Science and Controversy. A Biography of Sir Norman Lockyer* (MIT Press, 1972), pp. 273–279.

106. Barnes to Rutherford, 13 Aug. and 25 Nov. 1912 (RC).

107. Information kindly supplied by N.H. Robinson, Librarian of the Royal Society. Who blackballed Barnes on his first trial, in 1908? Someone whom he had "revered as a master" and whose opposition, by then of long standing, had left a wound that Rutherford's "friendship all these years...helped to heal over." Barnes to Rutherford, 20 Mar. 1908 (RC).

108. Foster, "Barnes," p. 31.

109. Barnes, *Ice Engineering*, pp. 154–158.

110. L. Badash in *DSB*, XII (1975), 25–36; McGill Univ., *Ann. Rep.*, 1903/4, p. 40; *ibid.*, 1904/5, p. 46.

111. Heilbron, "Scattering," pp. 258–264, 280–300.

112. Women had a separate college at McGill and the right to work in the university's laboratories (Macmillan, *McGill*, pp. 253–254). From Rutherford's letter to the *London Times* of 8 Dec. 1920 ("On Women at Cambridge University"), one judges that he welcomed them, in small numbers.

113. Gates, "Effect of Heat on Excited Radioactivity," *Phys. Rev.*, 1903, *16*:300–305, dated Jan. 1903; "On the Nature of Certain Radiations from the Sulphate of Quinine," *ibid.*, 1904, *18*:135–145, dated June 1903. Cf. *American Men of Science* (3rd ed.), p. 250; Rutherford, *Radioactivity* (2nd ed. Cambridge Univ. Press, 1904), pp. 315, 530.

114. M.J. Nye, "Gustave Le Bon's Black Light: A Study of Physics and Philosophy in

France at the Turn of the Century," *Hist. Stud. Phys. Sci.*, 1974, *4*:163–195, esp. pp. 177–181.

115. McGill Univ., *Ann. Rep.*, 1904/5, p. 46; Godlewski, "Actinium and its Successive Products," *Phil. Mag.*, 1905, *10*:35–45; "Some Radioactive Products of Uranium," *ibid.*, 45–60; "On the Absorption of the β and γ Rays of Actinium," *ibid.*, 375–379.

116. Hahn, *My Life*, tr. E. Kaiser and E. Wilkins (New York: Herder and Herder, 1970), p. 73; cf. Hahn, *A Scientific Autobiography* (New York: Scribners, 1966), pp. 35–36.

117. Hahn, "On Radioactinium," *Phil. Mag.*, 1907, *13*:165–180; *Scientific Autobiography*, pp. 21, 24–28.

118. Hahn, "The Ionization Ranges of the α Rays of Actinium," *Phil. Mag.*, 1906, *12*:244–254; Levin, "On the Origin of the β Rays Emitted by Thorium and Actinium," *Phil. Mag.*, 1906, *12*: 177–188; "On the Absorption of the α Rays from Polonium," *American Journal of Science*, 1906, *22*:8–12; Rutherford, *Die Radioaktivität*, tr. E. Aschkinass (Berlin: Springer, 1907), pp. 379, 381. On Bragg ranges see Heilbron, "Scattering," pp. 255–256.

119. Letter of March 1906, in *Rutherford and Boltwood. Letters on Radioactivity*, ed. L. Badash (Yale Univ. Press, 1969), p. 126.

120. Rümelin, "The Rate of Transformation of the Radium Emanation," *Phil. Mag.*, 1907, *14*:550–553; Hahn, *Scientific Autobiography*, pp. 31–32; Eve, *Rutherford*, p. 147.

121. Rutherford and Hahn, "Mass of the α Particles from Thorium," *Phil. Mag.*, 1906, *12*:371–378; Hahn, *Scientific Autobiography*, p. 28.

122. McClung, "The Absorption of α Rays," *Phil. Mag.*, 1906, *11*:131–142.

123. *Rutherford and Boltwood*, pp. 68–69, 84, 136, 140, 157; Bronson, "The Effect of High Temperatures on the Rate of Decay of the Active Deposit from Radium," *Phil. Mag.*, 1906, *11*:143–153; "On the Periods of Transformation of Radium A, B, and C," *ibid.*, 1906, *12*:73–82.

124. Wheaton, *Nature of X and Gamma Rays*, Chapt. 3.

125. Eve, "A Comparison of the Ionization Produced in Gases by Penetrating Röntgen and Radium Rays," *Phil. Mag.*, 1904, *8*:610–618, dated July 1904. Cf. Rutherford, *Radioactivity* (1st ed.), pp. 141–146, and McClumg, "Dependence of the Ionization produced by Röntgen Rays, upon the Type of the Rays," *Nature*, 1904, *69*:462–463.

126. Eve, "On the Secondary Radiation Caused by the β and γ Rays of Radium," *Phil. Mag.*, 1904, *8*:669–685, dated 27 Aug. 1904.

127. Rutherford, "Nature of the γ Rays from Radium," *Nature*, 1904, *69*:436–437, dated 18 Feb. 1904 (*CP*, I, 440); *Radioactivity* (2nd ed.), pp. 182–187; Heilbron, *H.G.J. Moseley. The Life and Letters of an English Physicist*, 1887–1915 (Univ. of California Press, 1974), pp. 52–54.

128. A.N. Shaw, "Recollections of Robert William Boyle, 1883–1955. A Distinguished Canadian Physicist," *Physics in Canada*, 1955, *10:4*:21–28.

129. McGill Univ., *Ann. Rep.* 1906/7, p. 49; Barnes to Rutherford, 28 Jan. 1908 (RC). Salaries are recorded in McGill Univ. Archives, Acc. 454/1226.

130. Gray to Rutherford, 11 Oct. 1912 (RC); Eve, *Rutherford*, p. 214.

131. Levin to Rutherford, 18 Nov. 1906 (RC): "It was very kind of you to write me about

what is going on in the Physics-Building, because all who have been with you will, if they hear from Montreal, feel as if they got news from home." Cf. Hahn to Rutherford, 21 Aug. 1906: "I was badly homesick for Montreal, but it is going better. We Germans cannot be as natural and pleasant against [i.e., towards] people we don't know, as English people are. Levin feels the same, it is our natural fault, we are too much soldiers and have too many degrees in social life."

132. A.N. Shaw, "Lord Rutherford," RSC, *Proc. and Trans.*, 1938, *32*:93-100, on pp. 95, 100.

133. Brooks to Rutherford, 18 Mar. 1902 and 8 Dec. 1901 (RC), resp.; cf. Eve, "The Macdonald Physics Building, McGill University, Montreal," *Nature*, 1906, *74*:272-275: "He is generosity itself...[in] giving a full measure of credit to those who do research under his guidance."

134. A.N. Shaw, "Howard Turner Barnes (1873-1950)," RSC, *Proc. and Trans.*, 1951, *45*:77-81.

135. Godlewski to Rutherford, 23 April 1907 and 11 Dec. 1905 (RC).

136. Rutherford to Hahn, 24 Sept. 1907 (RC).

137. Boyle to Rutherford, 15 Jan. 1908 (RC).

138. Barnes to Rutherford, 28 Jan. 1908 (RC).

Some Episodes of the α Particle Story, 1903–1977

NORMAN FEATHER

I remember as if it were yesterday, my last meeting with Rutherford. He knew that he was not well, and he summoned me to his house and asked me to take his next lecture for him. We sat talking for a while over a cup of tea in his study: there was a cake on the tea-tray, but neither of us, for different reasons, had the appetite for it. Then he handed me his lecture notes, and walked with me down the paved path to the door in the garden wall. He paused, then shook me awkwardly by the hand. This was an unusual gesture; hand-shaking was not his way, with intimates. The garden door closed behind me, I put the lecture notes in my bicycle basket and returned to my office in the Department. An hour later he telephoned me to ask after an experiment in progress in the laboratory. I had nothing of importance to report. So my association with the great man ended—on a note of inconsequence. It was his last contact with the Cavendish: Five days later he was dead. The odd lecture that I had been asked to give stretched out for a further seven years, and if during those years I had any success in keeping alive the tradition of the master, possibly the reason is to be found, in some measure, in the circumstance in which his mantle as lecturer fell on my shoulders.

You must forgive me this personal preamble. Its serious purpose is to establish the background from which I approach this paper. If you accept that background, you will not be surprised when I confess that any memorial that I give cannot be other than Rutherford-centered. The time will come—in fact it has come already—when the Rutherford lecturer will have had no direct contact with the man in whose memory he is speaking: Then he will be at liberty to choose his topic without constraint. That is not the case with me. In private duty bound—as a well-worn Cambridge formula runs—I must choose a Rutherfordian theme. Twelve years ago, Philip Dee, my classmate in the Cavendish of 1926, lecturing in Canada, was similarly motivated. His theme was built around Rutherford's speculations concerning the role of the α particle as a constituent particle of atomic nuclei in general.[1] That is one aspect of the α particle story. Today I wish to recall another.

Possibly, it was through some misunderstanding of the nature of his

74

achievement that Rutherford was awarded the Nobel Prize for chemistry rather than for physics in 1908, but the title which he chose for his prize lecture, "The chemical nature of the α particles from radioactive substances," while deftly accepting the compliment that was intended, turned the interest firmly back into the more familiar world of physics. Already in 1908 ten years had passed since Rutherford had himself brought the α particle into that world (little realizing, at the time, what in fact he had done); already during those years he had come to appropriate it as singularly his own creature, and for the rest of his life it remained for him his most reliable, most intimate, contact with the new world that he was creating. It was, of course, as any philosopher of science will insist, a conceptual world, but Rutherford's concepts followed the route from his fingers to his brain—they lodged in his bones. He knew in his bones that his α particles would not betray him.

"In private duty bound," I have said. On a much lower plane than his, my own interests have found continuity linked by a similar thread. My first substantial research (with Robert Nimmo, in the Cavendish) concerned the long-range α particles of the active deposits of radium and thorium. Now, fifty years later, I and my younger colleagues are still intrigued—and tantalized—by the problem of the long-range α particles of fission. However, those topics belong to later episodes in my story. Let me waste no more time on preliminaries. Let me start at the beginning.

The beginning was at McGill, in the Macdonald Physics Laboratories, in the winter of 1902–1903. It was there that the α radiation of 1898 finally assumed the character of a stream of "charged bodies projected with great velocity."[2] It was there that the α particle was born. In my view the relevant experiment, carried out with a tin-can electroscope and a miniscule array of metal plates at one-millimeter spacing, the intervening gaps half closed by a superimposed grid, is one of the most amazing experiments in the whole history of science.[3] It must surely be an inspiration—if a somewhat chastening experience—for the young physicist of today to examine Rutherford's original apparatus in the McGill museum.

Historians of science, presenting the success story, have passed over without notice an interesting fact recently brought to our attention by Dr. Trenn.[4] During the autumn of 1902, Rutherford had steadily been developing the view that the α radiation must be particulate in nature. The phenomenon of the deposition of "excited radioactivity" on solid surfaces exposed to emanation appeared to involve the recoil of positively charged atoms arising from the emission of α radiation from atoms of the emanation. This could be understood if the radioactive emission process itself were to involve the expulsion of a particle of atomic mass—an α particle—provided that the particle was negatively charged. It was with real surprise, therefore, that Rutherford found a positive charge when his deflection experiments established beyond peradventure that the α radiation was indeed particulate, as he was coming to believe.

To what extent his partial failure of his expectations troubled Rutherford we shall never know. With hindsight, however, we can appreciate the sureness of his instinct in disregarding it completely at the time—no mention is made of it in "Radioactive Change" of May, 1903. In that remarkable paper,[5] α radioactivity consists in the emission of positively charged α particles from individual atoms—just simply that and nothing more. If there was a skeleton in the cupboard, Rutherford kept the cupboard door securely closed for ten years or more, until the complexity of the recoil process could be understood in terms of the nuclear atom model as developed by Bohr.

My next episode, like the first, is centered in McGill. In 1903 it had been necessary to employ an array of 20 channels, with an electroscope as detector, to derive significant information concerning the magnetic deflection of α particles. Three years later source strengths had been increased sufficiently for a single slit to be substituted, and for photographic detection to be possible. Even so, the apparatus was on a small scale: Rutherford's "photographic plates" were in general little more than one centimeter square. It was with such equipment that, in 1906, he investigated the loss of velocity of α particles traversing thin sheets of mica.[6] Deflections were minute, and in one series of exposures, Rutherford sought to record the two groups of particles—those slowed down by the mica, and those coming directly from the source, simultaneously—by covering only half of the slit by the mica sheet. He noticed that the traces on the photographic plate—they were, of course, shadow images of the slit—were different in appearance: Those produced by the particles that had passed through the mica were slightly more diffuse than the others. He, therefore, made exposures with the magnetic field switched off, so that the two traces appeared one above the other in the undeflected position. The difference was now undeniable. Rutherford was not entirely surprised by this result: he had previously obtained rather fuzzy traces when exposures had been made with a certain amount of air in the apparatus,[7] and he had interpreted the effect as due to "scattering" of the α particles in the air. But the circumstances of his new observation immediately brought home to him the full implication of his observation. Using the most intense magnetic field at his disposal, he had at last been able to deflect an α

particle through two or three degrees over a path of a few centimeters in vacuum. Here a deflection of the same magnitude was occurring naturally along a path of three thousandths of a centimeter in mica. For him it was a matter of simple arithmetic: "[this] would require over that distance an average transverse electric field of about 100 million volts per cm," and he concluded, "Such a result brings out clearly the fact that the atoms of matter must be the seat of very intense electrical forces."[6] This was not a skeleton to be locked in a cupboard; it was a live issue to be kept in the forefront of the mind for future exploration. I must not pursue the matter farther; in 1906 Rutherford had taken the first step on the road to the discovery of the nucleus—but you know the rest of that story.

I had the privilege of going through Rutherford's collection of papers after his death. Among them I found some slips of photographic plate belonging to the series that I have just been describing. I have had these in my possession ever since. I think they should now return home to McGill. With the agreement of Rutherford's grandchildren, I propose to leave them where they rightly belong.

At this stage I must refer to an early Manchester episode—Rutherford moved there in 1907—though I have recounted it in detail in other places. When he left McGill, Rutherford had a reasonably accurate value for e/m for the α particle—effectively the same value whatever the source of the particles investigated.[8] He had only to measure the charge in order to know the mass. He could envisage three possibilities: that the α particle "is (1) a *molecule* of hydrogen carrying the ionic charge of hydrogen; (2) a helium atom carrying *twice* the ionic charge of hydrogen; or (3) *one-half* of the helium atom carrying a single ionic charge."[8]

In the next year, in collaboration with Geiger, he determined the α particle charge.[9] It was 9.3×10^{-10} esu. At that time direct determinations of the ionic charge were quoted as giving values in the range 3.0×10^{-10} to 3.4×10^{-10} esu. Could it be, as the crude results appeared to suggest, that the α particle was triply-charged? Rutherford would have none of it. He knew in his bones—he had known it, as he might say, with increasing conviction for the past five years—that α particles were charged helium atoms. They must be doubly-charged. Thus the fundamental unit of charge must be 4.65×10^{-10} esu, or thereabouts, whatever the earlier experimenters had said.

In 1909 the British Association came to Canada for its annual meeting. J.J. Thomson was the Association's President and Rutherford was President of Section A. His presidential address, delivered in Winnipeg, was devoted largely to a discussion of "the various methods that have been devised to determine the values of certain fundamental atomic magnitudes," as he said in his introduction.[10] Naturally, the value of the fundamental unit of charge was high on his list for attention. It was a masterly survey. The printed account reveals only the modesty of the speaker: "I trust that my judgment is not prejudiced by the fact that I have taken some share in these investigations ...," [he said] and again: "It is difficult to fix on one determination as deserving of more confidence than another; but I may be pardoned if I place some reliance on the radioactive method previously discussed...." If only the lecture had been recorded on video-tape, we might today be able to hear the tell-tale inflection in that sonorous voice, and catch the glint in the president's eye.

So Rutherford returned to Manchester, and to the discovery of the nucleus. Within four years the α particle was not merely a doubly-charged atom of helium, it was the bare nucleus of that atom—a single minute entity, positively charged, unencumbered by attendant electrons so long as it was moving rapidly enough through matter. How small, then, was the α particle—how small, indeed, were the nuclei of atoms other than helium—and had it, possibly, a shape different from the spherical? Rutherford's scattering law, which the experiments of Geiger and Marsden had so extensively verified in relation to α particle scattering in thin foils of gold, had been based on the coulombian force-law and the point-change approximation. Rutherford was no follower of Boscovich, as Faraday, in his time, was inclined to be: He expected to find evidence for the failure of his point-charge model in collisions of closer approach, if only these could be studied. In Manchester, as World War I was drawing to its close, he found that evidence in experiments on the scattering of α particles in hydrogen.[11] Obviously, his observations would have to be extended before any significant conclusions could be drawn, but he saw no reason why such observations should not eventually find explanation in purely electrostatic terms, if the α particle and the hydrogen nucleus were assigned finite size, and the distribution of charge on one, or both, of them was other than spherically symmetrical.

Soon after the war, Rutherford succeeded to the Cavendish Chair. Almost continuously over the next eight years there were experiments in progress in the laboratory on α particle scattering. He was not personally involved in all of them, but the overall strategy was obviously his alone. To begin with he set Chadwick and Bieler to extend his Manchester experiments with hydrogen.[12] Then Bieler was left on his own to investigate scattering in aluminum and magnesium.[13] Rutherford and Chadwick took over this investigation in due course and extended it to cover the scattering in gold and uranium.[14] Finally, in 1927, continuing their collaboration, they investigated the scattering of α particles in helium.[15] I wish, at this stage, to refer only to the first and the last of these studies.

Having accumulated much more detailed information concerning the scattering of α particles in hydrogen than Rutherford had obtained two years previously, Chadwick and Bieler concluded that their observations could not be explained on the basis of purely electrostatic forces as Rutherford had hoped, even though finite size were attributed to the charge distributions. Forces of shorter range and of a different origin had to be invoked. The model they suggested, assuming the hydrogen nucleus to be small and spherical, involved an α particle which had the form of "an oblate spheroid of semi-axes about 8×10^{-13} cm and 4×10^{-13} cm respectively, moving in the direction of its minor axis."[12] Electrostatic forces would determine the distribution of charge over the spheroid; its elasticity represented the short-range forces effective in the closest collisions.

It is a little surprising, in retrospect, that, with this result achieved, Rutherford did not immediately switch the investigation to the scattering in helium. Six years later, when that study was at last undertaken, he stated what must have been self-evident from the beginning: "In this case both particles concerned in the collision have the same structure. There is therefore no need to assume a structure for one nucleus in order to deduce that of the other."[15] Broadly, the experimental results were consonant with those obtained in hydrogen: a marked departure from the predictions of the classical law based on an inverse-square-law repulsive field, increasing rapidly as the energy of the α particle was increased beyond 5 MeV. Rutherford and Chadwick concluded: "It does not seem possible to explain the collisions with hydrogen or helium nuclei without some additional assumption about the non-spherical "shape" of the α particle."[15] This conclusion, as I have said, was reached in 1927.

During the next two years, the whole language of the subject was changing. The ideas of de Broglie and Schrödinger had been found to be fundamentally relevant to the physicist's world; theorists began treating the phenomena of particle scattering on the basis of the new mechanics; and Gamow, and Condon and Gurney, independently gave the first inherently reasonable account of the process of α disintegration on the same basis. About the same time, Heisenberg formulated the uncertainty principle, and this fundamental result, all other considerations apart, immediately raised the question how far the classical impact-parameter approach to the scattering problem could be justified. It had been the basis of Rutherford's calculations of α particle scattering by the heaviest elements in

1911, and the experiments of Geiger and Marsden in the following year had verified the predicted angular distribution over a range which involved a factor of 10^5 in the intensity observed.[16] In 1920 Chadwick had identified the nuclear charge number of the medium-light element copper with the atomic number of that element, with near one percent accuracy, on the basis of an absolute determination of the probability of α particle scattering—again using the classically-derived scattering law.[17] There was no conflict whatsoever between theory and experiment, thus it appeared quite paradoxical to suggest that in some fundamental way the classical theory was misconceived. Yet this is precisely what the adherents of the new mechanics were compelled to assert. The concept of the classically determinate path of the particle during the scattering process was altogether foreign to the new approach.

In point of fact, by 1929, the paradox had been resolved, at least at the level of experiment. Wentzel[18] and Mott[19] had already shown that, uniquely for scattering in an inverse-square-law field, the final result—the expression for the differential cross-section for scattering—is precisely the same whether classical mechanics or wave mechanics is used in the calculation.

My object in introducing this episode of the α particle story is to pose a question. How did Rutherford himself react, after a quarter of a century of knowing the α particle, his own peculiar creature, as an honest-to-goodness bit of primordial matter, structured no doubt, but secure in its individuality—how did he react to this fundamental revolution in the theorist's way of describing its behaviour?

I am not sure that I can give a comprehensive answer. There could be no doubt that with the aid of the α particle he had discovered the "real" nucleus. The theoretical ground from which that discovery sprang was now believed to have been insecure, his success the result of an accident of circumstance. Was it a pure accident, however? Was it conceivable that the structure of the universe is such that fundamentally the only long-range interaction capable of persisting is of an inverse-square-law character as seen within our framework of space and time—and that this constraint is mirrored in another, so that any reasonable being who is daily in contact with that universe at the macroscopic level inevitably fashions his theories of the micro-world to give prominence to this fact? There is no evidence to show that Rutherford ever asked himself such questions.

On February 7, 1929 he took the chair at a discussion meeting at the Royal Society in London, the day's topic being "The Structure of Atomic Nuclei."[20] In his opening address he welcomed Gamow as one of the invited participants and referred very briefly to his application of the wave mechanics to the problem of α disintegration. His only comment, in anticipation of Gamow's contribution, was "It will be seen that this theory makes the radius of the uranium nucleus very small, about 7×10^{-13} cm. . . . It sounds incredible but may not be impossible." The reflex of disbelief, followed by the gesture of tolerance, is strongly reminiscent of the last sentence in the paper of February, 1914 in which Rutherford reviewed the then current situation regarding the structure of the atom as a whole.[21] You may remember that he wrote: "While there may be much difference of opinion as to the validity and of the underlying physical meaning of the assumptions made by Bohr, there can be no doubt that the theories of Bohr are of great interest and importance to all physicists. . . ." Fifteen years had not changed Rutherford's attitude to the theorist. "I have, however, such a strong belief in the ingenuity of our theoretical friends," he said in another context in his 1929 opening address, "that I am confident that they will surmount this difficulty in some way. . . ."[20]

I have, perhaps, dwelt too long on this particular episode. In conclusion, I think it may be said that Rutherford soon came to accept the wave-mechanical description of the process of α disintegration as providing an acceptable vehicle for his own thoughts on the matter; for the phenomena of α particle scattering the situation was probably otherwise. For some years after 1929, he continued to be involved in experiments on rare modes of α disintegration, but 1927 saw his last paper on α particle scattering. Indeed, between 1927 and his death ten years later, only one experimental paper on α particle scattering was published from the Cavendish.

This paper was published by Chadwick in 1930.[22] It reported a reinvestigation of the scattering in helium, with particular attention to the more distant collisions—those of α particles of the lowest attainable energy. Earlier that year Mott had discussed the special case in which projectile and target nuclei in a scattering experiment are identical particles and had examined theoretically the interference effects which a wave treatment must predict, and for which there is no counterpart in a classical mechanical treatment of the problem.[23] In this connection we may say loosely that a collision between two nuclei of the same mass and charge is necessarily a collision between 'completely identical' particles only if the nuclei are devoid of any axis of rotational symmetry—otherwise, for example, if the nuclei possess intrinsic spin, there are various possible aspects at collision in some of which the particles appear 'more identical' than in others. Chadwick's experiments fully confirmed the predictions which Mott's calculations made about 'completely identical' particles according to our loose classification. There could be no other conclusion than that

the α particle was spinless and that its force field was spherically symmetrical in the undisturbed state. The model of the spheroidal α particle
had been consigned, once for all, to the limbo of ancient conceits.

I have said that Rutherford continued his life-long involvement in
problems of α disintegration for some years beyond 1929 in experiments
on certain disintegration modes of relatively small yield. If I make this the
next episode of my story, I must go back in time to discover its origins. In
fact, it is a long-drawn-out episode with a tortuous history, covering a
span of seventeen years. It shows Rutherford for once bemused—and for a
while misled through his own enthusiasm—by the "ingenuity" of one of
his "theoretical friends." However, he soon recovered his characteristic
scepticism and won through in the end. It is the episode of the long-range
α particles; it began in 1916 and was not finally concluded until 1933.

In February, 1916 Rutherford sent forward for publication in the
Philosophical Magazine a short paper in joint authorship with A.B. Wood.[24]
It described an unfinished investigation which "neither of the authors is
likely to have time to continue...in the near future." The opening sen-
tences of that paper were worded positively: "In the course of an examination of a strong source of the active deposit of thorium by the
scintillation method, one of us observed the presence of a small number of
bright scintillations...[which] were undoubtedly due to α particles...of
greater velocity than any previously observed." A later sentence in the
same paragraph made it abundantly clear that the "one of us" mentioned
was indeed Rutherford himself—though it does not explain why he had
been examining a thorium preparation at the time. He was not using such
sources for any other purpose just then—in fact, it was nearly three years,
according to the evidence of his published papers, since he had used one.
Be that as it may, in 1916 Rutherford and Wood were convinced that
they had discovered a new mode of α disintegration arising in the active
deposit of thorium, of unusually high energy and very small yield—about
1 in 10,000 in relation to the previously known modes. For Rutherford,
who ever had an eye for the unconsidered trifle in any experiment, it was
an intriguing result.

World War I dragged on, and, as I have already said, towards its end
Rutherford began again to spend some time in his old laboratory pur-
suits, assisted only by William Kay, the steward. I have dealt with the
experiments on the scattering in hydrogen; in other experiments Rutherford examined the effects which could be observed in helium, carbon
dioxide, nitrogen, and oxygen. In all these experiments α particle sources
of radium active deposit were employed. The results were presented in

four papers dated from Manchester in April, 1919 and published under a
single title in June of that year. The first two dealt with the hydrogen
results;[11] the third and fourth were sub-titled, respectively, 'Nitrogen and
Oxygen Atoms'[25] and 'An Anomalous Effect in Nitrogen.'[26] The fourth
paper has become a classic; the third, on the other hand, has been forgotten. I wish to direct your attention to it now.

Again, I quote Rutherford's opening sentence: "Bohr has worked out
a general theory of the absorption of electrified *atoms* in passing through
matter, and has verified his conclusions by consideration of the absorption
of α particles." For Rutherford that was an unusual opening: Never before in any paper of the Manchester period had he made it clear at the
outset that basic to what he was going to say was the acceptance of a
particular theoretical result. And in this case, when he did so, he showed
himself in the outcome—and in retrospect—to have been bemused. Bohr's
theory[27] had worked very well in relation to the observations in hydrogen:
The hydrogen nuclei projected in the forwards direction in collision with
α particles had four times the residual range of the α particles projecting
them, as the theory predicted. Rutherford looked for similar success in
applying the theory to collisions in other light elements, such as nitrogen
and oxygen. But the situation was very different in the two cases. The title
of Bohr's papers referred to the absorption of "*swiftly moving electrified
particles*"—meaning electrons and bare nuclei, such as protons and α particles—not of "electrified *atoms*," as Rutherford misconstrued it.[25] The
theory had nothing to say about the range of an energetic recoil atom—a
nucleus carrying with it at least some of its extranuclear electrons. Rutherford, however, used the theory to calculate the forwards ranges of
singly-charged recoil atoms of the light elements, and on this basis predicted ranges for such atoms of nitrogen and oxygen as some 33 percent
and twelve percent greater, respectively, than the residual range of the
responsible α particle—and he set himself to look for the effect which he
had predicted. Sure enough, with his radium active deposit source, the α
particles of which have an air-range of seven cm, he found a few bright
scintillations which were not suppressed until nine cm air-equivalent absorption had been inserted. With complete objectivity Rutherford recorded other observations which might have given pause to an
uncommitted observer, but his experiments in oxygen and nitrogen had
been the 'cleanest' of the series, and he did not allow himself to be dis-
suaded from his adopted stance. However, his earlier confidence regarding the interpretation of the observations with thorium active deposit was
now undermined. He wrote "In [those] experiments, the α-rays...were

absorbed in mica.... This... raises the question whether these long range α particles are not in reality due to collisions of α particles with the oxygen atoms in the mica."[25]

It was not long, however, before he had to revise his views again. He had devised a crude method of examining the magnetic deflection of particles of small yield, and by June, 1920, he had proved to his satisfaction that the particles of nine cm range could not be singly-charged atoms of oxygen or nitrogen, after all; rather they were doubly-charged particles of more nearly the α particle's mass. It is clear, in retrospect, that Rutherford did not fully appreciate the difficulties of interpretation inherent in his experimental approach, since he was not content with that qualitative conclusion—which would have been unassailable—but proceeded to commit himself to the view that the long-range particles were of mass number three, rather than four, and that they were produced in the gas in disintegration collisions of greater intrinsic probability than those which gave rise to the disintegration protons which he had identified the previous year.[28]

Thus, when in the autumn he returned to the problem of the long-range particles from thorium active deposit, the question he was asking was not whether these had been recoil atoms of oxygen arising in the mica absorbers, but whether, either from the source itself, or in a secondary process in the absorbers, there were produced particles of ³He of long range and small yield.

At last he was able to do a really clean experiment. He had acquired a fresh supply of radiothorium which enabled him to use sources 400 times as strong as before. He could dispense with absorbers and carry out magnetic experiments in vacuum. Again, he had A.B. Wood as collaborator. Between them, they showed conclusively that the long-range particles came from the source, and that, if they were doubly charged, then they were of mass number four, not three.[29] Indeed, they were real α particles, as Rutherford had asserted when first he observed their scintillations four years previously. Here, I might add in parenthesis that on the basis of the experimental evidence—the measured range and the magnitude of the magnetic deflection—it could have been maintained, with almost equal conviction, that the particles were ³H. Happily, this possibility, if it was ever recognized, was not allowed to confuse the issue yet again.

What, therefore, was now the position regarding the less abundant long-range particles observed with sources of radium active deposit? Were they, despite all the observations previously made, real α particles originating in the source material, also? Before long, Rutherford was beginning to think that they must be. In the course of a lecture to the Chemical

Society in the spring of 1922, he said: "While a large amount of experiment will be required to fix definitely the nature of the radiation, the general evidence indicates that it consists of particles of mass four, which are projected from the source...."[30]

Some two years later, in collaboration with Chadwick, Rutherford found time to engage in the "large amount of experiment" to which he had referred, and when it was all published in the *Philosophical Magazine* of September 1924,[31] no one could seriously doubt the final conclusion—rare modes of α disintegration had been set in evidence in the active deposits of radium and thorium, presumably involving very short-lived bodies, having regard to the long ranges of the α particles. As we have seen, it took Rutherford eight years to win through to this conclusion. When he had done so, from one point of view, his problem had only just been identified—that is the problem of understanding the facts as he had finally established them. You will remember that I said that the episode of the long-range α particles lasted for seventeen years: I have covered only the first eight of them!

Obviously, I must be brief concerning the remaining nine, from 1924 to 1933. During that period there were three separate investigations mounted in Cambridge, two yielding a spectrum of ranges,[32] and the last a magnetic spectrum, by semi-circular focusing, using the purpose-built 'mushroom' magnet designed by Cockcroft.[33] When, in collaboration with Lewis and Bowden, Rutherford published the results of that last investigation in 1933, they had identified twelve separate long-range α particle groups, of combined intensity no more than 30 per million normal disintegrations, with radium active deposit. More importantly, they knew how to interpret this spectrum: It was essentially the spectrum of the energy levels of the radium C′ nucleus as populated in the β disintegration of radium C. The α particles of long range were emitted from these excited nuclei in competition with the generally more probable process of γ-ray emission. It had been a long haul, but the account was closed at last.

So I come to my last episode which concerns the long-range α particles of fission. It is, in fact, the longest enduring of the episodes I have identified—it began under cover of secrecy during the last war, and it is still in progress.

Let me digress for a moment on the fission phenomenon itself. As you all know, Rutherford did not live to read of the experiments of Hahn and Strassmann and Meitner and Frisch which early in 1939 set all the world of physics agog. But he was familiar with the liquid-drop model nucleus of von Weizsäcker and Bohr (strictly, he was present at the birth, at the Royal

Society discussion meeting of 1929 to which I have already referred—and the original progenitor was, in fact, Gamow, as reference to the published account[20] will confirm). He found it a comfortable classical model and would have been well pleased had he known that it provided such a satisfactory basis for the initial understanding of the fission process. Here was a new phenomenon of great interest and, for its consideration, a ready-made classical model congenial to his habit of mind; he would have been in his element. He would not have needed to be reminded, as Bohr and Wheeler reminded their readers,[34] that when an unstable jet of liquid breaks up into individual drops, a much smaller drop is frequently left behind in the space between neighbouring drops of normal size. The "splash" photographs of Worthington[35] would have been clear in his mind's eye.

In 1939 Bohr and Wheeler put forward this fact of classical physics as providing one possible model-explanation of the emission of secondary neutrons in fission. In that connection it did not survive for long. The other mechanism which they suggested for consideration proved to be more consonant with experiment: that the secondary neutrons are evaporated from the accelerated fission fragments as the nuclear temperature rises through the collapse of the initial deformation. However, the hydrodynamical analogy was not thereby rendered wholly irrelevant. It came into its own once the long-range α particles were discovered.

These particles were first observed by Alvarez in 1943, when he was working for the Manhattan Project.[36] Over the next ten years, their main characteristics were established: One α particle in some 400 fission events, or thereabouts; a broad spectrum of energies peaked at about 16 MeV; an angular distribution heavily peaked just to the light fragment side of the plane at right-angles to the fission axis. The conclusion was inescapable: These particles must originate in the space between the separating fragments, possibly at the very moment of scission, their initial velocities being quite small, and their final energies and directions being determined by the joint action of the coulomb fields of the fragment nuclei in the early stages of their separation. If the liquid-drop model were admissible for the primary process, these, indeed, were the droplets which, within the full scope of the analogy, the model demanded. In fact we now know as a result of detailed experiments that the fission droplets range in complexity from single protons to oxygen nuclei of mass number 20. However, I am concerned today with the α particle story, and in any case α particles comprise about 90 percent of the long-range particles of fission.

There were great expectations, once the general picture of long-range α particle emission had been accepted, that close study of the effect would provide a key to understanding the scission process itself. That expectation has yet to be realized; a thoroughgoing dynamical theory of fission has not yet been written. At the macroscopic level, although Rayleigh faithfully recorded the presence of the secondary droplets in his illustrations of the breakdown and collision of water jets, his successful theory of jet instability took no account of them.[37] In the fission situation the α particles are released predominantly in those events in which the filament of nuclear matter joining the nascent fragments becomes more than normally elongated before rupture occurs. That is about all we can say. Halpern has expressed our present ignorance more colloquially: "Ternary fission is just binary fission that happened to get over-enthusiastic at the moment of scission."[38] Some day, perhaps, we shall be able to describe in less anthropomorphic terms how that sudden burst of enthusiasm develops.

I thus conclude my episodic account of more than 70 years of α particle physics. Much, of course, has been omitted: Other episodes might have been chosen of comparable interest, and a better balance have been achieved by including more from the postwar era. In the upshot this paper has become even more Rutherford-centered than I expected it to be. I offer no excuses; I make no claim that the development of the subject over the last 40 years would have been different had Rutherford lived. I only know that as long as he lived he would have continued to take a fatherly interest in his α particles—in the long-range α particles of fission, and in all those α emitters among the transuranic elements whose discovery and systematisation resulted in the addition of the names of McMillan and Seaborg to the list of Nobel Laureates in Chemistry along with his own. In the spring of 1903, at the very beginning of the period covered by my survey, Rutherford and Soddy wrote: "If elements heavier than uranium exist it is probable that they will be radioactive. The extreme delicacy of radioactivity as a means of chemical analysis would enable such elements to be recognized even if present in infinitesimal quantity."[5]

Truly, there were certain things that Rutherford and Soddy had known in their bones from the beginning.

Notes

1. Dee, P.I. 1967 *Proc. R. Soc. Lond.* A298, 103–122.

2. Rutherford, E. 1903 *Phil. Mag.* 5, 95–117.

3. Rutherford, E. 1903 *Phil. Mag.* 5, 177–187.

4. Trenn, T.J. 1971 Ph.D. thesis (Wisconsin). 1975 *Historical Studies in the Physical Sciences* 6, 513–547.

5. Rutherford, E. and Soddy, F. 1903 *Phil. Mag.* 5, 576–591.

6. Rutherford, E. 1906 *Phil. Mag.* 12, 134–146.

7. Rutherford, E. 1906 *Phil. Mag.* 11, 166–176.

8. Rutherford, E. 1906 *Phil. Mag.* 12, 348–371.

9. Rutherford, E. and Geiger, H. 1908 *Proc. R. Soc. Lond.* A81, 162–173.

10. Rutherford, E. 1909 *Report Brit. Assn. Winnipeg,* 373–385.

11. Rutherford, Sir E. 1919 *Phil. Mag.* 37, 537–561, 562–571.

12. Chadwick, J. and Bieler, E.S. 1921 *Phil. Mag.* 42, 923–940.

13. Bieler, E.S. 1924 *Proc. R. Soc. Lond.* A105, 434–450.

14. Rutherford, Sir E. and Chadwick, J. 1925 *Phil. Mag.* 50, 889–913.

15. Rutherford, Sir E. and Chadwick, J. 1927 *Phil. Mag.* 4, 605–620.

16. Geiger, H. and Marsden, E. 1912 *Sitz. Akad. Wiss, Wien* IIa, 121, 2361–2390.

17. Chadwick, J. 1920 *Phil. Mag.* 40, 734–746.

18. Wentzel, G. 1926 *Z. f. Phys.* 40, 590–593.

19. Mott, N.F. 1928 *Proc. R. Soc. Lond.* A118, 542–549.

20. Rutherford, Sir E. (Discussion opened by) 1929 *Proc. R. Soc. Lond.* 123A, 373–390.

21. Rutherford, Sir E. 1914 *Phil. Mag.* 27, 488–498.

22. Chadwick, J. 1930 *Proc. R. Soc. Lond.* A128, 114–122.

23. Mott, N.F. 1930 *Proc. R. Soc. Lond.* A126, 259–267.

24. Rutherford, Sir E. and Wood, A.B. 1916 *Phil. Mag.* 31, 379–386.

25. Rutherford, Sir E. 1919 *Phil. Mag.* 37, 571–580.

26. Rutherford, Sir E. 1919 *Phil. Mag.* 37, 581–587.

27. Bohr, N. 1913 *Phil. Mag.* 25, 10–31. 1915 *Phil. Mag.* 30, 581–612.

28. Rutherford, Sir E. 1920 *Proc. R. Soc. Lond.* A97, 374–400.

29. Rutherford, Sir E. 1921 *Phil. Mag.* 41, 570–574. Wood, A.B. 1921 *Phil. Mag.* 41, 575–584.

30. Rutherford, Sir E. 1922 *Nature,* Lond. 584–586, 614–617.

31. Rutherford, Sir E. and Chadwick, J. 1924 *Phil. Mag.* 48, 509–526.

32. Nimmo, R.R. and Feather, N. 1929 *Proc. R. Soc. Lond.* A122, 668–687. Rutherford (Lord), Ward, F.A.B. and Lewis, W.B. 1931 *Proc. R. Soc. Lond.* A131, 684–703.

33. Rutherford (Lord), Lewis, W.B. and Bowden, B.V. 1933 *Proc. R. Soc. Lond.* A142, 347–361.

34. Bohr, N. and Wheeler, J.A. 1939 *Phys. Rev.* 56, 426–450.

35. Worthington, A.M. and Cole, R.S. 1897 *Phil. Trans. R. Soc. Lond.* A189, 137–148. 1900 *Phil. Trans. R. Soc. Lond.* A194, 175–199.

36. See Farwell, G., Segre, E. and Wiegand, C. 1947 *Phys. Rev.* 71, 327–330.

37. Rayleigh (Lord) 1879 *Proc. R. Soc. Lond.* 29, 71–97. 1882 *Proc. R. Soc. Lond.* 34, 130–145.

38. Halpern, I. 1971 *Ann. Rev. Nucl. Sci.* 21, 245–294.

Rutherford in the
McGill Physical Laboratory

THADDEUS J. TRENN

Early in his career, Rutherford was fortunate to have had both plenty of time and excellent facilities to carry out his scientific research. This is not to say that under different conditions he would have been unsuccessful. Rutherford was undoubtedly a very gifted experimental physicist, and he would very likely have made important contributions to science had he not come to Montreal. But these factors coupled with his innate research abilities certainly yielded a constellation of unique promise for modern, experimental physical science.

Rutherford fulfilled that promise to a remarkable degree. His nine years at McGill were among the most prolific and creative of his 40-year career, although he continued to have excellent laboratory facilities both for his twelve years at Manchester and his eighteen years at Cambridge. One only need compare the size of the three volumes of the *Collected Papers of Lord Rutherford*[1] to corroborate this point, for the McGill volume covering nine years is nearly as large as the Manchester and Cambridge volumes which, taken together, span a period three times as long.

Rutherford's focus upon the new and emergent science of radioactivity frequently required alternative applications of available standard equipment and even highly specialized home-made devices. Rutherford redesigned the bolometer to measure the heating effect of X-rays and hence to determine the energy of Röntgen and Becquerel rays.[2] He used a differential air calorimeter to measure the heating effect of the radium emanation and thus the energy involved in atomic disintegration, especially the degree to which this is transferred to the alpha particles in the form of kinetic energy.[3] The electroscope and the electrometer were both frequently utilized, and the latter became something of a workhorse. This electrical method of detection responded directly to changes in the state of ionization and hence indirectly to the ionizing radiation, the object of his investigation. Besides such alternative utilization of standard equipment, Rutherford produced various home-made devices which demonstrated his knack for simple, yet effective design in reaching the core of a specific problem. To measure the duration of the radioactivity of the emanation, which he correctly presumed to be gaseous, he constructed a long tube with a radioactive source at one end and a collecting vessel at the other.[4] A slow current of air then wafted the emanation downwind into the vessel, and its radiation produced ions within this container. Once the ionization current had reached a maximum, Rutherford stopped the air flow and measured the rate of loss of ionic current, which was taken to be proportional to the rate of decay of the emanation. Similarly, Rutherford established a correlation between the emanation and the so-called active deposit—later shown to be the radioactive daughter products of emanation—by gently wafting the emanation down a long wooden vessel fitted with four electrodes spaced at intervals along its length. After several hours he measured the ionic current at each of the four terminals, which gave a measure of the combined effect of both emanation and active deposit.[5] After quickly blowing out the electrically neutral emanation, Rutherford repeated the four measurements, thereby isolating the effect of the active deposit. The difference was due to the emanation alone, and this value was found to be proportional to that due to the active deposit at each of the four terminals. Rutherford also constructed a similar device, a long brass cylinder with three electrodes spaced at intervals, to compare the emanating power of various radioactive substances.[6] There is a great variety of such equipment still extant among the specimens preserved at the McGill museum through the efforts of Dr. F.R. Terroux. Perhaps the most innovative of such devices is the great variety of baffle systems of collimating slits which Rutherford developed to investigate the characteristics of radioactive radiations. We will dwell upon these at some length.

Rutherford's research program steadily moved toward radioactivity and related topics. His approximately 70 papers from the Montreal period can be roughly divided into several sub-categories which, although overlapping both in time and in topic, give an overview of his main interests. The emanation and the accompanying problem of the transmission of excited activity forms one such division up to 1903. The various problems surrounding the nature and production of the emanation led to a series of nine papers jointly with Frederick Soddy from 1901 to 1903 dealing with the cause and nature of radioactivity. Their classic "Radioactive Change" laid the foundation for a proper theoretical understanding of radioactivity and subsequently of all related processes.[7] This disintegration theory in turn opened up two new areas of interest. On the one hand, it gave impetus to clarifying the genetic connections between radioactive substances, a topic which Rutherford pursued in depth from 1904 following his Bakerian Lecture on "The Succession of Changes in Radioactive

Bodies."[8] On the other hand, it exposed a variety of questions concerning the properties of the radioactive radiations expelled during radioactive change. Rutherford concentrated here on the alpha radiation, demonstrating in 1902 that it can be electromagnetically deviated, and that hence it consists of charged particles. Professor Norman Feather has expressed the view that he considers this particular experiment of Rutherford to be one of the most amazing in the entire history of science.[9]

The experiments performed by Rutherford in the autumn of 1902, which changed the accepted status of alpha rays from radiations to particles, constituted an important step in the gradual unfolding of scientific knowledge about the nature of alpha rays from 1898 through 1908. Briefly summarized, alpha rays were identified in 1898 by Rutherford as the easily absorbed component of uranium radiation; and for the next four years were construed as a type of secondary X-ray produced by the beta rays whether directly, if these were construed as primary X-rays, or indirectly once the beta rays were found to be corpuscular cathode rays. But by the spring of 1902, a constellation of experimental evidence made this analogy of radiations untenable. Specifically, new chemical evidence demonstrated that alpha rays persisted even after the chemical separation of the source of beta rays.[10] Furthermore, Rutherford's research on the transmission of excited activity had yielded anomalous results which could best be explained by his tentative theory of recoil atoms. But for this he required a massive charged *particle* as part of the residue from atomic disintegration. Conservation of electric charge, as understood at the time, dictated that this massive particle ought to have a negative charge. Rutherford was accordingly induced to investigate, still in 1902, whether the alpha rays could not be heavy particles carrying a negative charge.[11] After the summer vacation, Rutherford performed the necessary experiments and thereby confirmed that alpha rays are massive charged particles; but he also found that the charge is positive instead of negative. His report to J.J. Thomson in a letter written in December, 1902 completed this phase of the investigation. During the next six years, Rutherford continued to unravel the mystery of the alpha particle, obtaining direct evidence by 1905 that it is positively charged; confirming in 1906 and 1907 that the alpha particles from various sources can vary in velocity but not in mass; demonstrating with Geiger in 1908 that alpha particles carry an anomalous dual electric charge; and finally proving with Royds late in 1908 that the residual helium observed spectroscopically after prolonged exposure to alpha rays is not occluded helium released by the impact, but is simply the accumulated, spent alpha particles themselves.[12]

Let us now return to 1902—to the McGill Physical Laboratory of Rutherford's day—and reexamine his research at the critical juncture when he experimentally established that alpha rays were corpuscular in character. To make this review, we will use his published paper, his laboratory notebooks, his correspondence, and an examination of some of his surviving equipment.

The ten-page paper describing his experiments on the field deflection of alpha rays was entitled "The Magnetic and Electric Deviation of the easily absorbed Rays from Radium" and was published in the February, 1903 number of the *Philosophical Magazine*.[13] It marked the successful completion of what had been expected since 1900, but which had hitherto yielded negative results. In January, 1900 Curie had suggested that the easily absorbed component might consist of uncharged particles. In December of that year, Strutt had urged that it would be well worth while to try to deflect the soft rays with a very powerful magnetic field. About one year later, in February, 1902, Crookes resurrected this dormant proposal of Strutt, suggesting that, despite the hitherto negative deflection results also obtained by Curie and Becquerel, these easily absorbed rays might well be particles.[14] Rutherford tried this experiment in the spring of 1902 but also obtained negative results: "No action of a magnetic field on the alpha radiation of uranium was observed."[15] This result misled Rutherford to reclassify the alpha rays. In May, 1902 he wrote: "We will call the non-deviable rays of *all* radioactive substances alpha rays."[16] But the breakdown of the analogy of radiations and the alleged "direct evidence that a negatively charged particle is projected,"[17] which could save his recoil theory, made Rutherford fully aware of the consequences. He, therefore, decided to repeat this experiment in greater detail at the next opportunity. Several more months intervened, since from late June to early September Rutherford was on a family vacation some distance from Montreal. When he returned to McGill, Rutherford spent about two weeks preparing the necessary equipment for these experiments. He constructed a few small deviation chambers consisting of a series of narrow parallel slits through which the rays must pass.[18] Some were designed to be placed between the pole pieces of a strong magnetic field, and others were wired to deflect the rays electrostatically. The deviation chambers were so arranged that the alpha rays would normally pass upward into an ionization chamber. When the field was turned on, some of these rays would be deflected from the vertical sufficiently so as to lose energy by bouncing off the plates and thus cause a reduction in the ionization effect. To determine the direction of deflection, Rutherford prepared one such deviation chamber with small caps on one side of each plate so as to trap the rays more when the magnetic field was on in one direction than in the other. The magnetic deflection would have been sufficient to establish the particulate nature of the alpha rays, and the sign of its charge could have been determined by magnetic deflection alone using the special deviation chamber with the capped plates. The electrostatic deflection was also necessary in order to permit a calculation of the velocity and e/m ratio for the alpha rays.

Using the largest electromagnet available in the physical laboratory, Rutherford recorded a deviation of only 30 percent of the alpha rays on October 6. The maximum field which this could produce was 2,200 C.G.S. (gauss) which was insufficient for total deviation.[19] Rutherford accordingly borrowed the field magnet from a 30 kilowatt Edison dynamo from Owens, the Macdonald Professor of Engineering. This type of dynamo employed a vertical bipolar yoke construction for the field magnets. The two parallel magnet limbs including windings left an air gap 12 cm wide, 45.7 cm high and about 45 cm in depth.[20] By placing a small deviation chamber within this slot, an intense, uniform magnetic field up to 8,400 C.G.S. (gauss) units could be obtained over the entire collimating grid. Rutherford continued to utilize this electromagnetic for the remaining experiments.

Besides this difficulty with the strength of the magnetic field, Rutherford found that the intensity of the radiation reaching the ionization chamber was hardly sufficient for meaningful measurements. This was due to two causes: The radioactive source was relatively weak, and the slits of the original deviation chamber were far too narrow. When "the rays were sent through sufficiently narrow slits to detect a small deviation of the rays, the rate of discharge of the issuing rays became too small to measure, even with a sensitive electrometer."[21] By defining the path of the rays, Rutherford had reduced the transmission of his source—although it was 20 times more active than what he had used in the spring—below the minimum operating conditions of his standard electrical method. He therefore switched from the electrometer to the electroscope. Rutherford wrote to J.J. Thomson that "I was working far below the range of my Dolezalek electrometer and used an electroscope instead."[22] While the electrometer combined sensitivity with flexibility and was able to measure currents over the range 10^{-8} to 10^{-14} amperes, a modified form of the gold-leaf electroscope can be used to detect currents from 10^{-15} to 10^{-17} amperes.[23] The normal mode of operation was to charge the gold-leaf system and observe its rate of fall. The rate of loss of charge was an indication of the rate of production of ions within the chamber, and thus a measure of the intensity of the rays issued through the slits. To make observations with ease and accuracy, a tele-microscope with a large field of view and giving a magnification of about 10 was used. The eyepiece was fitted with a scale of about 80 divisions, which were about one-tenth of a millimeter apart.[24]

In the preliminary measurements of October 6, a very narrow system of parallel plates was used spaced only about 0.013 cm apart. Typical transmission data recorded with this deviation chamber was proportional to one scale division in 43 seconds.[25] For the magnetic deflection experiments recorded in his published paper, Rutherford used deviation chambers with wider slits such as 0.042 and 0.1 cm. Even the narrowest of these could increase the intensity of the issuing rays so that the gold-leaf in one case fell one division in about 25 seconds,[26] which represents an increase in transmission and ionization of over 40 percent. Rutherford took the final data on magnetic deflection of the alpha rays during late October and early November under the following conditions: He used Owen's electromagnet to give sufficient field intensity, wider slits to yield sufficient transmission, and an electroscope to provide adequate sensitivity.

The electrostatic deflection proved to be even more difficult because of sparking between the slits when very high voltages were applied. Rutherford recorded the electrostatic deviation of 7 percent of the rays in experiments carried out between September 30 and October 9.[27] He was unable to improve upon this result until after he had submitted his paper about mid-November for publication. On December 11 and 12 he recorded data taken with a special apparatus, probably a single slit condenser, permitting an applied voltage of between 1100 and 1450 volts.[28] "The electric deviation is very difficult to get at," Rutherford wrote Thomson at the end of December, "as one reaches the limit of measurement in all directions. I have *completely* deviated the alpha rays by a magnetic field and about 45 percent by the electric field....It was the most difficult piece of work I have tackled for some time, as my radium (activity 19,000) was hardly active enough for the purpose."[29]

The experimental data and derivative calculations can be arranged under three major headings: 1. magnetic deviation; 2. electrostatic deviation; and 3. calculation of parameters. Let us now highlight some of the details surrounding these three points, as this will shed considerable light upon how Rutherford worked in the McGill Physical Laboratory.

The magnetic deviation data plotted on the graph accompanying his published paper were taken during the first week of November.[30] The magnetic deflection device had 25 plates—2 outside ones and 23 internal "active plates," each about 0.074 cm thick forming 22 collimating slits of average width 0.042 cm—the total length being slightly less than three centimeters. The height of the entire device was 5.23 cm; the height of each plate was 3.70 cm; and the radioactive source was positioned about 1.4 cm below the lower edge.[31] Operating Owen's electromagnet at full capacity with nearly 12 amperes flowing through the coils, produced a field of nearly 8,400 C.G.S. (gauss) units sufficient to deflect nearly 90 percent of the alpha rays using pole pieces about 2 cm in length.[32]

The data he took to make this determination consisted of counting the number of scale divisions passed in unit time both with and without the magnetic field, and then repeating these readings after inserting a thin sheet of mica 0.01 cm thick in the path of the rays, sufficient to stop all but the beta and gamma rays. This latter set of readings was the background effect, and its average value was subtracted from the first and second readings. The ratio of these differences was supposed to yield the percentage of the alpha rays not deviated compared to the total of the alpha rays. This proportion ranged between 10 percent and 15 percent for the several data runs Rutherford recorded. He therefore concluded that between 85 percent and 90 percent of the alpha rays had been deviated in these experiments.[33] These results were taken with maximum current flowing through the coils of the electromagnetic and producing a field of nearly 8,400 CGS (gauss) units. But Rutherford also took similar data over the full range of field strengths and plotted this in his published graph.

There are several remarkable points concerning this data which deserve further consideration. First, the background effect from the beta and gamma radiation is nearly half as large as the effect to be measured. This is because the beta and gamma radiation were not attenuated and confined in the manner of the alpha radiation which had to pass through the narrow slits before it produced an effect. It is one indication of what Rutherford meant when he said that he reached the limits of measurement in all directions. Second, it will be noted that the linear curve, if continued downwards, would not intersect the origin as it should have done. Rutherford extrapolated this curve upwards and thereby determined a value of $H = 9,600$ for 100 percent deviation, a value he used in his calculations. It turns out that two of the points are incorrectly plotted. If properly calculated, the points shown at 67 percent and 78 percent deviation respectively are off by about 12 percent and should be shifted leftwards to 5,800 CGS and 6,530 gauss respectively.[34] The five data points then form an elongated s-form curve. But if a *linear* relation is assumed, a best fit from the origin, upon extrapolation to 100 percent, still meets nearly the same value for H as that obtained by Rutherford. His data were fortunately sufficiently flexible to provide the right result in spite of this experimental error.

Finally, although this magnetic deflection data appeared in the published paper, they were superceded by a new set of data taken with another deviation chamber just a few days later, and this time he was able to deviate 100 percent of the rays. The full implications of why he decided to repeat the magnetic deviation experiment using the apparatus designed for the electrostatic deviation experiment will soon become apparent, for it exemplifies one of Rutherford's most characteristic and creative moments in the McGill Physical Laboratory.

At this stage of experimentation, Rutherford had demonstrated that alpha rays were charged particles, since they could be deviated in a magnetic field. To determine the sign of the charge, Rutherford constructed a special deviation chamber having an exposed slit width of about 0.1 cm where each slit was capped on the upper edge[35]. With the field current flowing in one direction, the rays would tend to be trapped in the corner, while with the field current reversed, the rays could easily escape through the remaining opening. The spacing in the collimating grid was accordingly constructed to be about twice that of the other deviation chambers. The data obtained indicated that the direction of deviation of the alpha rays was opposite in sense to that of cathode rays. Although this evidence that the alpha particles carried a positive charge was only indirect, it was sufficient to defeat Rutherford's original expectation that the alpha rays, if they should prove to be particles, would carry a negative charge. This new evidence did not accord well with his concurrent work on the recoil atom and the transmission of excited activity, but Rutherford made no issue of the point in his publication.

While the alpha rays at this point were taken to consist of positively charged particles, the electrostatic deviation was also required before he could calculate the velocity and e/m ratio. The four sets of data that Rutherford took between September 30th and October 9th also well illustrate what he meant when he wrote Thomson that one reaches the limit of measurement in all directions. The electrostatic deflection device had 25 plates—2 outside and 23 internal plates, each about 0.080 cm thick forming 22 collimating slits of average width 0.055 cm—the total length being about 3 cm. The height of the entire device was 5.40 cm, and the height of each plate was 4.50 cm.[36] The active material was placed 0.85 cm below the

bottom edge of the plates. Alternate plates were electrically connected together and charged by means of a battery of small accumulators to a potential difference of about 600 volts. The use of such a set of series-connected
electrolytic cells of about 2 volts each, which could be recharged by a
dynamo, was standard laboratory procedure. One major constraint in this
series of experiments was the width of the slits, which could not be increased
without losing definition regarding the deviation, yet were too close to
permit raising the voltage so as to obtain a significant deflection. Rutherford operated the electrostatic deflection device with a voltage ranging
between 580 and 630 volts, which was hardly sufficient; but beyond this
range sparking occurred across the narrow gap between the slits. Since his
radioactive source was relatively weak, the intensity of the issuing rays was
very low. Rutherford accordingly depended upon measurements which
yielded an extremely slow rate of fall of the gold-leaf, typically taking about
one minute to fall only one scale division. The low intensity of the rays
combined with the voltage restriction provided precious little evidence for
the electrostatic deviation. For in some cases, with the field turned on and
then off, the rate of fall of the gold-leaf through one scale division was
reduced only from 74 seconds to 70 seconds. This ratio is about 95 percent
to which Rutherford applied a small correction for background radiation.
The resulting 93 percent meant that about 7 percent of the rays had been
deviated. Yet the four sets of data were consistent over the range 91.4
percent to 93.5 percent, and taken together these yielded 93 percent for an
average value. Thus, in spite of the weak intensity and the minute differences in the data obtained, Rutherford concluded that he had indeed succeeded in deviating 7 percent of the rays electrostatically.[37]

But what of the direction of deviation which would indicate the sign
of the charge? Rutherford concluded that the "amount of deviation in
this experiment was too small to determine the direction of deviation by
the electric field."[38] Yet it was actually unnecessary, since the direction
could be adequately determined by the magnetic field alone. Was this
simply good fortune? In this context it might be mentioned that Rutherford was seldom caught out in the design and use of laboratory equipment. But during these electrostatic deflection experiments, his colleague
Soddy once saw him dancing like a dervish with one of these devices
clutched in his hand. Rutherford had forgotten to disconnect the chamber from the high voltage battery, and as he flung it in shock to the
ground, its beautiful canalization system lay strewn in ruins on the floor.[39]

For the magnetic deviation it had been possible to extrapolate the
field strength required for 100 percent deflection, but the very limited

electrostatic deviation did not permit such an extension of the data. Although his method of calculating the velocity and charge-to-mass ratio
(following that of J.J. Thomson on the electron), did not depend upon
100 percent electrostatic deflection, Rutherford did attempt to improve
upon his results. He did not succeed in this effort until early December,
since it was more urgent to calculate the parameters and send the paper
off for publication. Also it was necessary first to design and construct another type of electrostatic device. Rutherford added a note as his paper
was in press: "In later experiments, which are not yet completed, I have
been able to deviate about 45 percent of the alpha rays in a strong electric
field."[40] On the 11 and 12 of December, Rutherford used what he designated a "special apparatus," presumably a single condenser, with much
longer slits set 0.01 cm apart, and he was able to apply an electric field of
1,450 volts without incurring sparking.[41]

These experimental results may have been influenced in part by the
alpha particles glancing off the surface of the parallel plates and being
reflected into the testing vessel. Rutherford was well aware that the
"theory of the experimental arrangement where the parallel plates act
both as a slit and a means of applying the electric field, is more complicated than the ordinary case where a narrow pencil of alpha rays is made
to pass between the two parallel plates of the condenser without imping-
ing on the sides."[42] But in this particular experiment, he was trying to
deflect the alpha particles into the plates, and therefore such reflection
could hardly have been avoided.

But his admitted difficulties with the electrostatic deviation of alpha
rays did not hinder Rutherford from successfully completing his program
of experiments. On the contrary, about November 10 he turned what
seemed to be an impasse into an advantage, simplifying the matter in one
deft stroke by redoing the magnetic deflection experiment with the electrostatic device.

In order to appreciate the full significance of this maneuver, we must
now turn our attention to his method of calculation of the various parameters. One of these concerned the radius of curvature of the alpha rays
under 100 percent magnetic deflection to determine the $H\rho$ value for the
particles in a magnetic field.[43] The other involved the velocity and e/m
ratio of the alpha particles. These parameters are all related, as was
pointed out earlier by J.J. Thomson, according to the equation[44]

$$H\rho = \frac{v}{e/m} \quad \text{(I)}$$

Now the equations for determining these parameters in uniform electric and magnetic fields are as follows:[45]

$$v = \frac{d_m (1_e)^2 X}{d_e (1_m)^2 H} \quad \text{(II)}$$

$$e/m = \frac{2 d_m v}{(1_m)^2 H} \quad \text{(III)}$$

where d_m, d_e, are the distances of magnetic and electric deviation respectively in passing through uniform magnetic and electric fields of length 1_m and 1_e respectively. But the larger pole pieces used for the special experiment were 4.5 cm long and thus exactly of the same length as the plates producing the electric field! Since the same device was used both for magnetic and electric deviation, the values for d were also identical. Furthermore, Rutherford assumed that the same percentage of deviation could be so construed that the electric and magnetic fields were crossed and in balance with one another,[46] and he succinctly stated the implications of this in his laboratory notebook: "Now when electrostatic and magnetic field act on same apparatus over same length of plates

$$v = \frac{X}{H}$$

when magnetic and electric field give same deviation. Now 30 percent of magnetic [deviable] rays are deviated for a field of 1900. Therefore, 7 percent is deviated for a field of $\frac{7 \times 1900}{30} = 430$ units."[47]

Rutherford had thus simplified the calculation of the velocity from equation II. His special experiment had obviated the necessity of dealing with any factors other than the values for the two fields. It was only the ratio of the fields for the "same deviation" that was important. He had already found that 7 percent were deviated for an electric field of 600 volts. To convert this to electromagnetic C.G.S. units, it was only necessary to multiply by 10^6 and divide by the width of the gap in meters.[48] Hence the potential gradient is

$$X = \frac{600 \times 10^8}{0.055} = 1.09 \times 10^{12} \text{ C.G.S. (gauss) units.}$$

He then extrapolated backwards to estimate the value of the field sufficient to deflect 7 percent of the rays magnetically. This is surely an ingenious interpretation of the crossed field experiment!

It is of interest that he determined the value of the field strength at 30 percent not from the data—he had one reading at 29 percent with field strength 2086—but interpolated this result from the linear graph.[49] This is but one indication of his greater reliance upon data distributed over a given range and averaged out, rather than upon any specific bit of datum. With the field strength of 1900 at 30 percent, he should have obtained a value closer to 440 at 7 percent, although the result was not very sensitive to such small variations. From equation II Rutherford accordingly estimated the velocity of the alpha particles to be

$$V = \frac{1.09 \times 10^{12}}{430} = 2.5 \times 10^9 \text{ cm/sec.}$$

For the calculation of the e/m ratio, Rutherford made direct use of equation I, which is simply a modification of equation III.[50] To calculate $H\rho$, Rutherford introduced the relationship, that if a particle passes through a uniform magnetic field for a distance '1,' it is deviated from its original direction by a small distance 'd' according to the equation[51]

$$2\rho d = (1)^2. \qquad \text{(IV)}$$

He obtained the value for the magnetic field at 100 percent deviation, $H = 9{,}600$, by extrapolation from the graph. The value of '1' was technically 1.9 cm, the dimension of rough pole pieces used in late October and early November for the magnetic deflection. Operating the electromagnetic at full current, Rutherford examined the field strength at various points in the vicinity using the standard search-coil technique. The field strength tapered off beyond the edge in such a way that Rutherford estimated the total field to be equivalent to a uniform field of 8,400 gauss acting over a distance of 3.3 cm;[52] and this was the value he then used for '1.' For the value d he initially took simply the width between the slits of the magnetic deviation chamber, which on the average were 0.042 cm apart. This gave an excessively large value for ρ of well over a meter and hence a value of $H\rho$ over 10^6 units.[53] Rutherford discarded this value, since it seemed to him not to be of the correct order of magnitude. His intuition was right! The source of error appeared to him to lie in the value he had taken for d. He therefore tried to take the geometry within the slit into consideration, so as to effectively magnify the value adopted for d. The total length of the path of the rays from the source to the issuing end of the slits was about 5 cm but only 3.3 cm of this path was construed as passing through the uniform magnetic field, and the difference between these two values is 1.65 cm. Rutherford then took the ratio $3.3/1.65 = 2$

as his factor of magnification, and thereby obtained three times the slit width for his new value of d, *viz.*, $d = 0.126$ cm. This reduced the calculated radius of curvature for the alpha rays to about 40 cm and the value of $H\rho$ to 413,000 units, but through a miscalculation he obtained 378,000 instead[54].

Rutherford seems to have been unsatisfied with his assumption about the uniform magnetic field, and to replace the rough pole pieces he had special pole pieces constructed which were 4.50 cm high and thus guaranteed a uniform field over the entire grid of collimating slits.[55] He could have redone the experiment with the magnetic deflection device. Yet for a variety of reasons, Rutherford selected the *electrostatic* deviation chamber instead; and he made these decisive measurements on November 10 and 11. Since the slit width was 0.055 cm instead of 0.042, the first benefit was an experimental one, for the intensity of the issuing radiation was more than doubled from about 2.40 scale divisions per minute to about 5.90.[56] A second immediate advantage was that the larger pole pieces increased the field intensity sufficiently to permit the deflection of the entire stream of alpha particles passing through the collimating grid. He now had experimentally achieved 100 percent magnetic deflection. From the data obtained Rutherford was able to plot a curve,[57] and he noted that with "another apparatus, with a mean air space of 0.055 cm., the rays were *completely* deviated by a uniform magnetic field of strength 8400 units extending over the length of the plates, a distance of 4.5 cm."[58] In fact, this field was the maximum this electromagnet could produce, and with the larger pole pieces proved to be more than sufficient for complete magnetic deflection of the alpha rays. From the data at hand, Rutherford graphically estimated that a field of 6,500 units would have been sufficient, and he adopted this value for H in his calculations.[59]

Rutherford then recalculated the value for $H\rho$ using this data and the characteristics of the electrostatic deviation device. The value taken for '1' no longer depended upon an examination of the field characteristics but was simply 4.5 cm. The total depth of the chamber was 5.40 cm, which left only 0.9 cm of the total path of the rays outside the uniform portion of the magnetic field.[60] Taking the ratio 4.5/0.9 as the factor of magnification in this case, Rutherford obtained six times the slit width of 0.055 cm as his value for d, *viz.*, $d = 0.33$ cm. The corresponding value of ρ is about 30 cm, although Rutherford obtained twice this value through an arithmetical error.[61] The value for $H\rho$ in this case should therefore have been a low 198,000 instead of the 396,000 that he calculated.

It might be mentioned briefly that this factor of magnification, as worked out by Rutherford, has a most remarkable property, for if the pole pieces were just 1 cm larger so as to cover the entire depth of the deviation chamber, the denominator would be zero yielding infinite magnification! This fact, of course, casts doubt upon the validity of his values for d in each case.[62]

Rutherford now had two independent estimates of the value for $H\rho$ both of which were roughly consistent with one another. He averaged his 378,000 and 396,000 together and rounded this off to obtain his published value of 390,000 which he claimed "gives the higher limit of the value of $H\rho$."[63] From this value and that for the velocity of the alpha particles obtained from equation II, Rutherford calculated the e/m ratio from equation I as follows:[64]

$$Hev = \frac{mv^2}{\rho} \quad \text{(V)}$$

$$\frac{e}{m} = \frac{v}{H\rho} = \frac{2.5 \times 10^9}{387,000} = 6 \times 10^3 \text{ electromagnetic units,}$$

which again is incorrect, for this product is much closer to 6.5×10^3 But of far greater significance is the fact that his calculated value for $H\rho$ had depended upon a series of computational errors. Had he not made these arithmetical slips and obtained the values 413,000 and 198,000 instead, the average value would have been 306,000; a rather low order-of-magnitude approximation for the value of $H\rho$.[65] The value for e/m that Rutherford should have obtained on the basis of his data and method of calculation by means of equation I would thus have been

$$\frac{e}{m} = \frac{2.5 \times 10^9}{306,000} = 8.2 \times 10^3 \text{ electromagnetic units,}$$

which is an excessively high value compared with the true value of about 4.8×10^3.[66]

Rutherford's special experiment, whereby he repeated the magnetic deflection with the larger pole pieces and the deviation chamber designed for electrostatic deflection, was a creative venture that had both its benefits and its drawbacks. He could have reached the same goal without it and with results at least as good. But Rutherford was working with unknown quantitites, and he therefore resorted to the simplicity and security which this experiment seemed to offer. In the calculation of the velocity from equation II, Rutherford was able to avoid introducing the dimensions d and '1' from the two different deflection chambers and from the two different sets of pole pieces. This was surely a simplification. Yet had he attempted to make the same calculation without the special experiment and with these differing values for d and '1,' he would have obtained

$$v = \frac{0.126 \times 20.2 \times X}{0.33 \times 10.9 \times H} = 0.7 \times \frac{X}{H} \text{ cm. per second.}$$

And for the same values of X and H as before, this would yield
$$v = 0.7 \times 2.5 \times 10^9 = 1.75 \times 10^9 \text{ cm./sec.}$$

This value is actually much better, and also closer to that obtained almost simultaneously by Des Coudres, *viz.*, $v = 1.65 \times 10^9$; and it falls well within the subsequently known range of velocities of the alpha particles from radium which were measured between 1.6×10^9 and 2.06×10^9.[67] Thus, with his special experiment, Rutherford had gained simplicity of calculation and presumably a more reliable result. But it turns out, by chance, that the combined data from the two separate devices would have actually given a better value.

Again, the special experiment seemed to provide Rutherford with a control for his estimate of the value of $H\rho$ for the magnetic field and hence to add significantly to its reliability. Yet here he was certainly blessed by good fortune, for as we have seen it was only through computational errors that a correlation emerged in the first place, which in turn yielded an average value of the correct order of magnitude. Paradoxically it was actually the $H\rho$ value obtained from the special experiment that was deviant. Had Rutherford chosen to rely upon only the original magnetic deflection data, his value for $H\rho$ would have been 413,000, without arithmetical errors and taking $d = 0.126$ and '1' $= 3.3$ cm.[68] This would have yielded

$$\frac{e}{m} = \frac{2 \times 0.126 \times 2.5 \times 10^9}{10.9 \times 9,600} = 6.02 \times 10^3 \text{ electromagnetic units,}$$

which is a very good value nearly identical with the value he obtained by means of his various computational errors.

So there were at least two ways available by which to reach nearly the same results. The one was characterized by simplicity and redundancy to reduce the degree of risk, and this is the route taken by Rutherford. The other would have been more straightforward, and with less data would have yielded results at least as good. In retrospect, then, it might appear that the special experiment was not really so valuable. It had simplified the calculation, but the straightforward method would have yielded better results.

Here we may insert a general word of caution regarding evaluating the goodness of scientific results by applying subsequent or *post facto* standards. If there is no accepted standard available at the time such research is conducted, what could be more secure than simplicity and redundancy? This was certainly Rutherford's hallmark in laboratory work throughout his career, and the merits of this procedure can be gleaned from the specific case at hand.

The values for the velocity and the e/m ratio work out well in the straightforward method. But what if we calculate the e/m ratio using the magnetic deflection data obtained with the electrostatic deviation chamber? This would yield

$$\frac{e}{m} = \frac{2 \times 0.33 \times 2.5 \times 10^9}{20.2 \times 6{,}500} = 12.6 \times 10^3 \text{ electromagnetic units,}$$

which is far too excessive! Presumably this extreme value derives from the factor of magnification used in the determination of d for this device, since the velocity is the same; '1' is determined by the size of the special pole pieces; and H is extrapolated from experimental data. But if so, it points up the degree of chance involved in calculating the velocity in the straightforward manner. Although a good value would have been obtained for the velocity, compared with subsequent standards, the straightforward use of equation II would have included this same suspect value for d. It is eliminated from the calculation only through the special experimental procedure used by Rutherford. Thus, although his results may have not been the "best" that could have been obtained from the data at hand, Rutherford had gained a measure of reliability for his results without the benefit of standards of comparison.

There seems, therefore, little question that his use of the special experiment to simplify the calculation of the velocity was a brilliant stroke of ingenuity. It is equally clear and impressive that in spite of occasional mistakes, whether in computation or in data analyses, Rutherford invariably seemed to have his experimental program well under control. His innate caution had led him to use the results of his special experiment also to provide a second estimate for the value of $H\rho$, in order to gain control through redundancy. But he seems to have known all along what this value ought to be, since he discarded the original result obtained before he introduced his factor of magnification. This suggestion is reinforced by his incorporation of the redundant value for $H\rho$, since he was not even aware that his calculation had been off by at least a factor of two. The close correlation of his two values was of far more interest to him, and if the result was "right," it did not make all that much difference to him if an inadvertant miscalculation were required to achieve it. Had he noticed his mistake, Rutherford would no doubt either have relied upon the single case of the magnetic deviation chamber for the determination of the $H\rho$ value, or have introduced some other factor of correction until he obtained the desired correlation. Whatever the means that may have been required, it is unlikely that Rutherford would have accepted a value for $H\rho$ as reliable which differed significantly from 400,000. But this should not be surprising, since it is well known of Rutherford that he possessed an uncanny gift for sensing what the correct order of magnitude ought to be, and this for a great variety of physical problems throughout his experimental career.

The example we have chosen well illustrates his approach to laboratory work and experimental science, and it is by no means an extreme case. It might be added, however, that Rutherford was motivated to move rapidly in this fundamental question concerning his alpha particles and to have his results published as quickly as possible. These were intended only as preliminary results. Rutherford realized that his data were only approximate anyway and thus not conducive to any rigorous determination. Rather than allowing himself to be confined by such data or by accepted rules of procedure, Rutherford with his uncanny intuition rose above this level of laboratory practice. The results he obtained were judged by him to be right, because—as Professor Feather would say—he felt it in his bones.[69]

We have seen Rutherford struggle with the problem of the alpha rays. This was only one of many such experimental programs that Rutherford dealt with at McGill, but it was also admittedly one of the most difficult. The upshot of his results was that alpha rays were not wave-like radiations but corpuscular alpha particles. He had been induced to do the experiments, because of the breakdown of the analogy of radiations and his own expectations regarding the transmission of excited activity and the recoil atom. Alpha particles were indeed charged electrically, but the sign of the charge was positive rather than negative, and much further research was now necessary. It was 1905 before Rutherford obtained *direct* evidence of the positive charge on the alpha particle, and it was 1908 before he realized that it was doubly charged. But by 1902 Rutherford could sense the significance of these newly-born alpha particles. He had previously considered them to be a secondary effect due to beta rays, but after these deflection experiments he realized their primary character, not least of all, because alpha rays were much more energetic than beta rays. The alpha rays had suddenly become the primary phenomenon. These were no longer considered to be caused by the beta rays, and they were found to carry 99 percent of the total energy of radiation.[70]

For Rutherford the experimental breakthrough came on November

10 and 11 when he was able to perform the special experiment simplifying his calculation of the velocity which, in conjunction with his value of $H\rho$, also permitted him to make a reliable estimate of the e/m ratio. Perhaps this is why he dated his paper November 10, 1902. Technically, it would have been possible for him to have completed the paper by the eleventh, since by then he had all the required data and needed only to plot it graphically as well as make a few calculations. But the tenth, being a Monday, perhaps symbolizes work completed during the course of that week. That Rutherford felt impelled to send it off for publication at the earliest possible opportunity indicates how significant this experimental program had been for him. Also, he had conducted this program with great dispatch and efficiency. In a very short time, he had constructed several deviation chambers and taken all the data he required. None of this proved to be superfluous, and what little there was appeared either directly or indirectly in the published paper.

As we have seen, the straightforward procedure would have by chance yielded better results, but at the time there was no criterion available by which to make this judgment. Rutherford with his intuition seems to have known in advance what the correct order of magnitude for these parameters ought to have been. He preferred to take a short cut to reach these results, building a bridge when required both by design and by error in order to get there. He constructed apparatus specifically to solve particular problems, and he adapted equipment to a variety of uses. Rutherford made mistakes but always seems to have known where he was going. How he got there became of secondary importance.

Finally, the existence of alternative procedures and the implementation of a choice between them is perhaps not uncommon, and is of great interest, demonstrating as it does the range of freedom available in experimental research. The case of the birth of the alpha particle is in this respect a particularly fortunate one, for it clearly indicates the high degree of ingenuity and creativity of which Rutherford was capable within the constraining framework of experimental techniques and data while working in the McGill Physical Laboratory.

Notes

1. *The Collected Papers of Lord Rutherford of Nelson,* ed. Sir James Chadwick, 3 vols. (London: Allen & Unwin; New York: Wiley, 1962-1965). (These volumes will hereafter be cited as *CPR.*)

2. E. Rutherford and R.K. McClung, "Energy of Röntgen and Becquerel Rays, and the

Energy required to produce an Ion in Gases," *Philosophical Transactions of the Royal Society, London,* 1901, *196-A:*25–59 (*CPR* I, 260–295).

3. E. Rutherford and H.T. Barnes, "Heating Effect of the Radium Emanation," *Philosophical Magazine,* 1904, *7:*202–219 (*CPR* I, 625–639).

4. E. Rutherford, "A Radioactive Substance emitted from Thorium Compounds," *Philosophical Magazine,* 1900, *49:* 1–14 (*CPR* I, 220–231).

5. E. Rutherford, "Radioactivity Produced in Substances by the Action of Thorium Compounds," *Philosophical Magazine,* 1900, *49:* 161–192 (*CPR* I, 232–259).

6. E. Rutherford and F. Soddy, "The Radioactivity of Thorium Compounds: An Investigation of the Radioactive Emanation," *Transactions of the Chemical Society,* 1902, *81:*321–350 (*CPR* I, 376–402). The device is shown CPR I, pp. 383, 480 (plate), and 497.

7. T.J. Trenn, *The Self-Splitting Atom: A History of the Rutherford-Soddy Collaboration* (London: Taylor & Francis, 1977).

8. E. Rutherford, "The Succession of Changes in Radioactive Bodies," *Philosophical Transactions of the Royal Society, London,* 1904, *204-A:*169–219 (*CPR* I, 671–722).

9. Norman Feather, "Rutherford Memorial Lecture, 1977: Some episodes of the α-particle story, 1903–1977," *Proceedings of the Royal Society,* London, 1977, *357-A:*117–129; esp. p. 118. Lecture delivered at McGill University, Montreal, Canada on 28 September 1977.

10. John L. Heilbron, "The Scattering of α and β Particles and Rutherford's Atom," *Arch. Hist. Exact Sci.,* 1968, *4:* pp. 249–258; T.J. Trenn, "Rutherford on the Alpha-Beta-Gamma Classification of Radioactive Rays," *Isis,* 1976, *67:* 61–75.

11. T.J. Trenn, "Rutherford and Recoil Atoms: The Metamorphosis and Success of a Once Stillborn Theory," *Historical Studies in the Physical Sciences,* 1975, *6:*513–547.

12. T.J. Trenn, "Rutherfords Alpha-Teilchen," *Annals of Science,* 1974, *31:*49–72.

13. E. Rutherford, "The Magnetic and Electric Deviation of the easily absorbed Rays from Radium," *Philosophical Magazine,* 1903, *5:*177–187 (*CPR* I, 549–557).

14. Trenn, *op. cit.* (10), Classification, pp. 69–70.

15. E. Rutherford and H.T. Brooks, "Comparison of the Radiations from Radioactive Substances," *Philosophical Magazine,* 1902, *4:*1–23 (*CPR* I, 415–434): quote on p. 417.

16. E. Rutherford and A.G. Grier, "Deviable Rays of Radioactive Substances," *Philosophical Magazine,* 1902, *4:*315–330 (*CPR* I, 457–471): quote on p. 466.

17. E. Rutherford, "Excited Radioactivity and the Method of its Transmission," *Philosphical Magazine,* 1903, *5:*95–117 (*CPR* I, 529–548); quote on p. 545.

18. A photograph of this apparatus appears in *CPR* I, p. 480 (plate).

19. Rutherford Laboratory Notebooks, Cambridge University Library, Add. MSS 7653/ CLM-13, p. 43 and CLM-10, p. 41.

20. S.P. Thompson, *Dynamo-Electric Machinery* (London, 1904), pp. 24–27, 115–116, and 130; J. and E. Hopkinson, "Dynamo-Electric Machinery," *Philosophical Transactions of the Royal Society, London,* 1886, *177,* part i: p. 336 and Plate 18, fig. 4.

21. Rutherford, *op. cit.* (13) Deviation, p. 178 (*CPR* I, p. 550).

22. Letter from Rutherford to J.J. Thomson, 26 December 1902, Cambridge University Library, Add. MSS 7654/R67.

23. E. Rutherford, *Radio-Activity* (Cambridge, 1904), pp. 71–73, and 84.

24. W. Makower and H. Geiger, *Practical Measurements in Radio-Activity* (London, 1912), pp. 21–23.

25. Rutherford Laboratory Notebooks, C.U.L. Add. MSS 7653/CLM-13, p. 41.

26. *Ibid.,* p. 57.

27. *Ibid.,* pp. 46–47.

28. Notebook CLM-12, pp. 101–105.

29. Letter, *op. cit.* (22); cf. Rutherford, *op. cit.* (13) Deviation, p. 184 (*CPR* I, p. 555). For information about the level of activity see letter from Rutherford to F.O. Giesel, 3 March 1904, C.U.L. Add. Mss 7653/G79 published in part in *Dictionary of Scientific Biography,* vol. 5 (New York, 1972), p. 394.

30. Notebook, CLM-13, pp. 49 & 55.

31. *Ibid.,* p. 52. This is probably item R 14B of the Rutherford Collection at McGill.

32. *Ibid.,* pp. 49 & 55.

33. *Ibid.,* p. 53.

34. *Ibid.,* pp. 49 & 55.

35. This is probably item R 14D of the Rutherford Collection at McGill.

36. Notebook, CLM-13, p. 56. This is probably item R 14E of the Rutherford Collection at McGill.

37. Rutherford, *op. cit.* (13), p. 184 (*CPR* I, p. 555); Notebook CLM-13, pp. 46–7. The experimental arrangement from September 30th, 1902 yielded one scale division in about 40 seconds, whereas that of October 8th and 9th yielded one division in about 70 seconds. This difference is due in great part to the preparation and position of the radioactive material.

38. Rutherford, *op. cit.* (13), p. 184 (*CPR* I, p. 555).

39. M. Howorth, *Pioneer Research on the Atom* (London, 1958), p. 65.

40. Rutherford, *op. cit.* (13), p. 184 (*CPR* I, p. 555); cf. note 28 above.

41. Rutherford, *op. cit.* (23), p. 121.

42. E. Rutherford, "The Mass and Velocity of the α Particles Expelled from Radium and Actinium," *Philosophical Magazine,* 1906, *12*:348–371 (*CPR* I, 880–900); quote, p. 884.

43. It was standard practice to use the quantity $H\rho$, where H is the value of the magnetic field and ρ is the radius of curvature of the deflected particle, instead of the momentum $H\rho e$ where e is the elementary charge in electromagnetic units, since $H\rho$ is what is "directly determined by experiment." E. Rutherford, J. Chadwick, and C.D. Ellis, *Radiations from Radioactive Substances* (Cambridge, 1930), p. 343.

44. Rutherford, *op. cit.* (23), p. 122; cf. J.J. Thomson, *Conduction of Electricity through Gases,* (Cambridge, 1903), pp. 82, 92.

45. Rutherford, *op. cit.* (23), p. 122.

46. Thomson, *op. cit.* (44), pp. 92–3.

47. Rutherford, Notebook CLM-13, p. 58.

48. *Ibid.* The potential gradient is measured in volts per meter, where one volt is 10^8 electromagnetic units.

49. Notebook, CLM-13, pp. 56–7.

50. *Ibid.,* p. 58.

51. Rutherford, *op. cit.* (44), p. 122; Thomson, *op. cit.* (44), p. 92.

52. Rutherford, Notebook CLM-13, pp. 51, 59.

53. *Ibid.,* p. 59.

54. *Ibid.* According to his modified method of calculation, he should have obtained $\rho = (3.3)^2/2 \times 3 \times 0.042 = 43$ cm. instead of the 39 cm. that he did presumably from taking 0.047 for the slit width by mistake.

55. Rutherford, *op. cit.* (13), pp. 180–182 (*CPR* I, pp. 552, 554); cf. Notebook CLM-13, p. 57.

56. Notebook CLM-13, pp. 53, 57.

57. *Ibid.,* p. 56.

58. Rutherford, *op. cit.* (13), p. 182 (*CPR* I, p. 554). This "apparatus" was the electrostatic deflection device.

59. Notebook CLM-13, pp. 56–59. This value does not appear in the published paper.

60. Notebook CLM-13, pp. 56, 59.

61. *Ibid.,* p. 59. He should have obtained $\rho = (4.5)^2/2 \times 6 \times 0.55 = 31$ cm. instead of the 61 cm that he did.

62. Presumably Rutherford was trying to take the grazing case into consideration where the alpha particle just touches both edges of one side of the slit and nearly the center of the opposite side. He developed this theory during the next few years; Rutherford, op. cit. (42), CPR I, pp. 884–888; cf. CUL. Add. MSS 7653/NB 22, p. 67 dated 1918.

63. Rutherford, op. cit. (13), p. 184 (CPR I, p. 555); cf. Notebook CLM-13, p. 59.

64. Notebook CLM-13, p. 58.

65. E. Rutherford, "Retardation of the α Particle from Radium in passing through Matter," *Philosophical Magazine,* 1906, *12:*134–146 (*CPR* I, 859–869); especially p. 864.

66. Rutherford *et alii op. cit.* (43), p. 47.

67. Th. des Coudres, "Zur elektrostatischen Ablenkbarkeit der Rutherford-strahlen," *Physikalische Zeitschrift,* 1903, *4:*483–485; E. Rutherford, "Some Properties of the α Rays from Radium," *Philosophical Magazine,* 1905, *10:*163–176 (*CPR* I, 803–815). A velocity less than 1.5×10^9 cm. per second was below the range of detection, *CPR* I, p. 813.

68. The value d = 0.126 is derived from d = 3×0.042, cf. note 54 above.

69. Feather, *op. cit.* (9), *passim.*

70. E. Rutherford, "Charge carried by the α Rays from Radium," *Nature,* 1905, *71:*413–4 (*CPR* I, 789–791).

71. Rutherford, *op. cit.* (23), pp. 150–154.

The Reality Beneath:
The World View of Rutherford

STANLEY L. JAKI

In going through the literature on Rutherford one meets with regular frequency statements such as that Rutherford was the greatest experimental physicist since Faraday and that we owe him much of our modern views on matter.[1] These and similar statements carry a special force when theoretical and historical studies are supplemented by some very unpleasant experiences, such as being caught in agitated debates about breeding reactors or other offsprings of the discovery of the atom and of its nucleus. This is not to suggest that Rutherford carried out his probings of the core of the material reality with an eye on practical results. Talk about getting energy out of the atom on a practical scale was for him equivalent to talking moonshine,[2] an appraisal which was his only memorable blunder, quite an achievement on the part of a voluble man of science.

For this blunder no historian of science has raked him over the coals. The incident is merely recalled here as a delightful example of the dangers of making prophecies about the future course of scientific technology.[3] A historian of science with a certain philosophical preference may, however, be tempted to take for a monumental blunder the entire tone of Rutherford's research stretching over four decades—the tone of unabashed epistemological realism. His famous boast, "I know now what atoms look like,"[4] and his legislating, "There is no room for this particle as designed *by me,*"[5] were the voice of one for whom atoms, electrons, protons, and neutrons were as real as were the stones forming the walls of his laboratory. He, of course, knew that others derived the opposite conviction and with a reference to his work and findings. Probably, there have been but a few among the many readers of Eddington's *The Nature of the Physical World* who have disagreed with his caricature of Samuel Johnson's kicking a large stone to refute Berkeley's idealism. Eddington, the idealist, could hardly be wrong if he could claim for himself the authority of Rutherford and say: "What Rutherford has left us of the large stone is scarcely worth kicking."[6]

To be sure, physicists no longer probe reality by kicking stones, nor even by dropping stones from a tower. But an Eddington, who tried to derive the reality of the material world from the structure of his thinking, could hardly have taken comfort had he seen those huge stones or rather concrete walls which shield radiation from giant accelerators. The radiation, as is well known, comes from the acceleration of extremely hard bits of matter by which physicists "kick" other, equally hard particles. The results are veritable fireworks, the spectacular proliferation of elementary particles. Hard they ought to be, if analogy has any meaning. For the harder a stone is, and the harder it is hit by another stone, the greater is the number of sparks produced.

Of course, the hardness of those elementary particles is not hardness in the ordinary sense, nor is it elementary in the sense of being fundamental or ultimate. About fundamental particles we certainly know that none of them is fundamental.[7] The splitting of atoms was followed by the splitting of the nucleus, and now we live in an age which Rutherford would have certainly relished and would call, as he called the twenties, the heroic age of physics.[8] There is, indeed, something heroic in the experimental and theoretical efforts that try to find the parts of which nucleons, the constituents of nuclei, are made up. The heroism relates less to the fact that the smaller the particle under investigation is, the greater the energy must be in order to "kick" it and make it resonate or split, than to that urge which keeps physicists fascinated with the ever-new frontiers which material reality has in store for them.

When Rutherford started his work, those frontiers seemed to be fairly closed. The only exciting prospect for anyone interested in the basics of material stuff was the closing of gaps in the periodic table. True, the newly discovered phenomenon of radioactivity had added a new perspective to the more than two-decade-long search for missing elements, but it was largely an educated guess that there was a layer of matter beneath the elements. Mendeleev was not the only one who took each and every element for a fundamental species of matter, irreducible to one another. Otherwise the famous debate between Mendeleev and Crookes would not have taken place in 1886, a debate in which Crookes defended the view that all elements had constituent particles common to all of them.[9] But the most tangible detail that Crookes could offer about that stuff beneath any and all elements was a name, protyle, *proté hulé* or first matter, a name he coined, unless he remembered reading it in Aristotle.

Rutherford himself did not think of a layer of matter deeper than the level of elements when he wrote to his future wife Mary Newton in October, 1896: "I have some very big ideas which I hope to try and these, if successful, would be the making of me. Don't be surprised if you see a cable some morning that yours truly has discovered half a dozen new elements, for such is the direction my work is taking. The possibility is considerable, but the probability rather remote."[10] Once more he made a wrong prophecy but not in the sense in which forty years later he discounted the likelihood of atomic and nuclear energy. He not only discovered new elements but also found that their radioactive character was not due to an external factor, as the Curies and others thought,[11] but to that intrinsic property which linked them into a series, the so-called natural decay series. This was in sum the main achievement of his years at McGill, an achievement which looks very natural today, but which at the time appeared farfetched and upsetting to not a few at McGill and elsewhere. At McGill he was urged by some to go slow with his publications lest the reputation of the university be endangered.[12]

He went on publishing, for what on earth could have stopped that "lucky fellow, Rutherford, always on the crest of the wave," who retorted: "Well, I made the wave didn't I?"[13] The wave, nothing less than an irresistible tidal wave, is embodied in the three volumes of his collected papers, the first and thickest of which contains his papers written while he was at McGill. These papers have three chief characteristics: First, each is a reliable step in a straight advance. He never had to write a retraction, he never had to revise drastically, let alone to renounce, any major phase of his experimental findings and his interpretation of them.[14] Second, his main discoveries concerning material reality were invariably revolutionary: The laws of radioactivity, the structure of the atom, artificial radioactivity, to say nothing of his prediction of the existence of the neutron and other particles, were so many revolutions in our understanding of matter. About the neutron he stated in 1920 (a dozen years before its actual detection): "It should be able to move freely through matter...and it may be impossible to contain it in a sealed vessel."[15]

This phrase is a perfect summary of the third characteristic of his papers—a plain, matter-of-fact style which lost nothing of its realism even when dealing with the most unreal-looking, paradoxical features of some particles of matter. Rutherford could on occasion wax rhetorical, and he did not mind doing so in his more or less popular lectures. But in his scientific papers, he could not have sounded less revolutionary, not, of course, in the sense in which revolutionaries become excited and lose touch with reality. It was precisely because of his matter-of-fact style that Rutherford turned out to be a true revolutionary, although his revolution could only appear in his time as an already outmoded counter-revolution. The revolution, or rather counter-revolution, far transcended the question of style. By the time Rutherford came to the scene, the days when editors of scientific journals welcomed phrases, however matter-of-fact, about the material reality that lies beneath the realm of sensory experience were gone. But Rutherford wrote and spoke about that reality with an intense commitment, as if he were, as a perceptive biographer of his remarked, defending the honor of the woman he loved. On being told by Eddington that electrons possibly were only mental concepts and had no real existence, Rutherford exclaimed: "Not exist? Not exist? Why I can see them as plainly as I can see that spoon in front of me!"[16] The conviction exuding from similar utterances made him a revolutionary at a time when taking the realm of atoms for hard reality was equivalent to *lèse majesté*, to defying an imposing consensus.

Originally, the majesty was mainly embodied in the person of Ernst Mach, whose influence reached worldwide proportions precisely during the years Rutherford spent at McGill.[17] Later, the majesty was assumed by the scientist-philosophers, or at times just plain philosophers, of the Vienna Circle and the Copenhagen school of quantum mechanics.[18] Let Mach be considered first as there is a curious coincidence between Rutherford's life and the course of Mach's influence. The starting point of that influence is Mach's first book, *History and Root of the Principle of the Conservation of Energy*, a book completed in its original German in 1871, the year of Rutherford's birth. In turn, 1937, the year of Rutherford's death, marks the end of the formal existence of the Vienna Circle, first called Verein Ernst Mach. But the clashing contrasts between the deeds and words of Mach and Rutherford seem far more telling than these coincidences.

Possibly the most striking of these contrasts is the almost complete silence of Mach about radioactivity during the opening years of this century when the talk of the best laboratories was radioactivity, and when Mach was the talk of scientists, especially in their non-scientific hours. A year after Rutherford's splendid ten years at McGill were over, and dozens of his revolutionary papers on radioactivity had for years been in print, there appeared in 1908 the second improved edition of Mach's *Grundriss der Physik,* his textbook of university physics. Its 600 pages contain only seventeen lines on radioactivity and no mention whatever of Rutherford.[19] Two years later in Manchester, Rutherford was formulating his revolutionary theory of the atom, and he did so in a most realistic sense. On being informed by Geiger that some alpha particles not only were greatly deflected while passing through a thin gold foil, but that some of them simply bounced back, he could, like anyone else, only gasp. As he himself recalled his reaction years afterwards: "This is almost as incredible as if you fired a 15-inch shell at a piece of tissue paper and it came back and hit you."[20] Incredible as it may appear, Rutherford not only believed his eyes when seeing the evidence on a scintillating screen, but also believed that there ought to be another reality beneath that which he had seen. The reality was that of the atom with a very small hard core and with a very large, almost empty periphery, the realm of orbital electrons. It was a reality which he could see only with the eyes of the mind, but he held it to be as real as what he could see and touch.

It was this holding fast to reality with the vision of one's mind, a genuinely realistic though equally metaphysical vision of reality beneath, which was the kind of vision from which Mach wanted to liberate physics, as if the vision in question were the worst kind of mental aberration. His crusade of antimetaphysical exorcism reached its dramatic pitch when Rutherford began to conjure up the true vision of the atom, a most dramatic step in man's quest for reality. For it was in 1910, that Mach replied to Planck in a highly emotional tone: "If belief in the reality of atoms is for you essential, I will separate myself from the way of thinking appropriate for physics, I will be no true physicist, I will renounce every scientific claim—such in short is my 'thanks' to the community of believers. Freedom of thought is dearer to me."[21]

The expression "freedom of thought" was rarely more misplaced. Instead of being a champion of freedom of thought, scientific or otherwise, Mach was the sad prisoner of his sensationist philosophy. It ultimately led him to espouse Buddhism which is a form of being confined to sensationist solipsism.[22] Indeed, several members of the Vienna Circle, like Carnap, who consistently carried out Mach's sensationism, ended by advocating solipsism while building the world on the logic of sensationism.[23] Now, if there was a man of science remote from solipsism, it was Rutherford. Such a contrast is not without profound relevance for successful scientific methodology. Indeed, it underlies the contrast to which I now wish to call attention. The clash between Planck and Mach had its origin in Planck's awakening to the threat which Mach's program presented for physics. This was the gist of Planck's famous lecture given in Leiden in 1908 on the unity of the world picture in physics.[24] The lecture should be of particular interest to historians of science because much of Planck's argument rested on an analysis of the history of physics. All great advances in physics, Planck argued, rested on one and the same world picture or world view stretching through the history of physics, a world picture which alone provides a logical basis for a fruitful cultivation of physics. This is why Planck's lecture ended with a reference to the phrase: "by their fruits ye shall know them." As the latest of the fruits, Planck referred to the newly-established reality of atoms. It was this claim, coupled with Planck's reliance on a biblical phrase, which provoked Mach's rejoinder that he did not wish to join the community of believers.

With that Mach, the historian of physics, detached himself from such believers in an objective, coherent world—from all great men of physical science from Copernicus through Galileo and Newton, to Faraday and Maxwell. With the same rejoinder Mach, the physicist, parted company with such creative giants of the physics of his time as Planck, Einstein, and Rutherford. Such is the last contrasts through which I would like to illustrate Rutherford's world view. Mach's separating himself from Einstein, nay, renouncing his theory of relativity—a process in the making since 1909—came into the open when the preface, which Mach wrote in 1913 to his book on physical optics, was published in 1920.[25] Mach rejected Einstein's relativity because he clearly and very early perceived that instead of relativizing everything, special and general relativity implied an objective world independent of observers and their subjective or relative sensations. It is this recognition which shows on the one hand the penetrating power of Mach's intellect, but on the other his being imprisoned in his sensationism which ultimately made everything subjective and stifled his creativity in physics. Had it not been for this, Mach might have become the formulator of relativity, as Einstein himself pointed out.[26] What Mach could have done in radioactivity is not merely a matter of guessing. The Austria of Mach's day was the chief source of radium at a time when Rutherford most needed the precious stuff. With all that radium around, he showed no interest in it, a fact not without supreme irony. While Mach never surrendered to the objective world of relativity, radioactivity made him recognize, shortly before his death, the existence of atoms. On being shown the sparks produced by a speck of radium on a scintillation screen, he could only mutter: "I now believe in the existence of atoms."[27]

It is this kind of reluctant, half-hearted surrender to reality which the progress of science cannot tolerate. For had Mach lived four years longer, he would have paid no attention to Rutherford's Bakerian lecture delivered in 1920, in which Rutherford predicted the existence of neutrons, deuterons, triple hydrogen, and triple helium. Eighteen years later, in writing Rutherford's obituary notice for the Royal Society, Chadwick commented: "A lecture in which the speaker clearly foresees four future discoveries, together with some of the actual properties as later found, is perhaps unique."[28] In 1922, in the thirteenth Kelvin lectures given to the Institution of Electrical Engineers, Rutherford predicted the existence of the positron[29] and did so again in that matter-of-fact style which left no doubt about his sense of reality, be it ordinary, atomic, or subatomic reality.

No sooner had these predictions been made, than it not only became fashionable to dissolve atomic reality into wave packets, but any dissent was considered *lèse majesté*. Rutherford mostly kept aloof from his fashion, and he did so with disdain. He used to refer to its chief spokesmen, namely the protagonists of the Copenhagen interpretation of quantum mechanics, as "those fellows,"[30] without debating with them. But had he reminded them that experimentation with those allegedly unreal wave packets required more and more real money from the taxpayers' pockets, the realism of the reminder would have been very Rutherfordian.[31] Undoubtedly, one of the reasons that kept him from debating with the Copenhagen people was that he was no wizard in mathematical physics, a subject more and more esoteric and forbidding since Schrödinger came forward with his wave mechanics and Heisenberg with his matrix mechanics. But even apart from mathematical physics, debating was not Rutherford's forte. He could go, nonetheless, to the heart of the matter in crucial moments. After Bohr sent him the manuscript of his famous paper on the hydrogen atom in 1913, his reply showed the commonsense realism in Rutherford at its penetrating best. The passage from Rutherford's letter to Bohr is well-known but is worth repeating: "There appears to me one great difficulty in your hypothesis, which I have no doubt you fully realize, namely, how does an electron decide what frequency it is going to vibrate at when it passes from one stationary state to the other? It seems to me that you would have to assume that the electron knows beforehand where it is going to stop."[32]

Fourteen years later in 1927, Rutherford could only muse when he saw Dirac and Heisenberg lock horns at the Solvay Congress on essentially the very same epistemological problem which he had pointed out to Bohr, but which Bohr tried to resolve by ruling out of court all questions concerning ontology and causality. It is this rejection of realism, or rather questions about ontological reality, which is the gist of the Copenhagen interpretation of the quantum theory and also its disastrous pitfall, as can be seen from the manner in which Dirac and Heisenberg tried to cope with the formation of ionization tracks in cloud chambers. Since ontology and causality could not be resorted to as means of explanation, Dirac assumed that somehow *nature* makes a coherent choice out of an infinitely large number of possibilities. This personification of nature was rejected out-of-hand by Heisenberg, but only by a sleight-of-hand which made matters even worse. According to Heisenberg, it was not nature that made the choice but the observer himself that constituted nature by his very choice of observation.[33] Such was the complete subjectivization of nature which Rutherford clearly perceived to be invited by Bohr's procedure, a subjectivization with which Rutherford could not live. Nor for that matter, could the Copenhagen people, except in their non-scientific hours. They filled those hours with a philosophizing which was wholly at variance with that enlightened but robust realism that makes science possible, by elevating it from the level of a clever game with nature to an understanding of nature.

As I said, Rutherford most likely mused, for he did not speak in public on controversial issues of scientific method and philosophy. At most he referred to the marvelous method of science without offering details. One rare exception should, however, be recalled. His Presidential Address of 1923 to the British Association started by calling the first decade of the century the heroic age of science "because never before in the history of physics has there been witnessed such a period of intense activity when discoveries of fundamental importance have followed one another with such bewildering rapidity."[34] The address ended with a warning very appropriate for those swayed today by the fashion of straitjacketing science into incommensurable paradigms. The warning should also be a rude awakening for those who think that it was only recently, namely, in the sixties, that the progress of science began to be pictured as a continual demolition of previous theories. This view, which Rutherford called not only an error, but something "that could not be farther from the truth," was, to quote his words, "far too prevalent today," that is in 1923.[35] Moreover, as if to give more discomfort to future captives of paradigms, he took aim at claims that presented Newton's and Einstein's physics as irreconcilable with one another.[36]

One could only wish that Rutherford had spoken more on the philosophy of science, but, fortunately perhaps, he did not do so. If he had, he might have followed those scientist-philosophers who think that formal speech in philosophy requires formal training in physics but only informal excursions into philosophical literature. Rutherford did not speak in public of philosophy, of politics, and even less of religion. Even in private he was mostly tacit on these matters. He did science with his deeds, and his account of each of those deeds bespoke a world view in which the world was a coherent, inexhaustibly rich, objectively existing, and objectively investigable entity. All his deeds were so many refutations of sophisticated latter-day theories of science. Those theories turn out to be mere sophistries when called to account for the cosmic reality which science is supposed to investigate, to say nothing of the gigantic probings of objective reality by experimental physics, probings upon which theorists invariably must rely in spite of their often solipsistic theorizing about reality.

Rutherford never discussed politics and brooked no such discussions in his laboratory, but again he preferred to be a politician with his deeds. He was one of the first and most active to give refuge and work to scientists threatened by Nazi tyranny.[37] What his thoughts were, when his most appreciated collaborator, Kapitza, was not permitted in 1934 by Communist tyranny to return to England, should not be difficult to guess. He knew all too well that Kapitza referred to a rigidly streamlining government as he wrote in his letter of 1936: "After all we are only small particles of floating matter in a stream which we call Fate. All that we can manage is to deflect slightly our track and keep afloat—the stream governs us."[38]

As to scientific politics, or the politics of science, he took no part in it, nor was he ever gloomy about the potential misuse of his discoveries, or of scientific discoveries in general. He was an optimist, a believer in goodness, honesty, uprightness, hard work, and sense of duty—characteristics which are usually ignored in the vast Rutherford literature. These characteristics he largely brought from his family background, which is worth exploring, however briefly, as it may throw light on the deepest roots of his world view. The basic principles, if not the formalisms of Christian faith, which his grandparents carried with them from Scotland and England to New Zealand, were an integral part of their famed grandchild's character. He hardly ever spoke of religion, but some of his deeds spoke louder than words. A.S. Eve, for many years his co-worker and chief biographer, relates that shortly before the death of W.B. Hardy, a friend of Rutherford, the latter happened to be with the Right Reverend Dr. E.C. Pearce, Bishop of Derby. Soon the conversation turned to the failing health of Hardy, and Rutherford remarked: "Hardy is terribly ill," to which he added in a tone of genuine earnestness: "You will pray for him, Pearce, won't you?"[39]

The request was part of a simple, unpretentious, unarticulated, but earnest view which Rutherford held of reality including the reality beneath the phenomena. His earnest asides about it were as revealing as his somewhat hilarious remarks, though he really did not mean to joke when he said that no physical theory is worth much, if it cannot be explained to a barmaid.[40] Indeed, such had to be the case, though not in a simplistic sense, if the cause of physics was to be safeguarded. That cause is predicated on the simplicity, objectivity, and coherence of nature. Although he was the first to formulate the statistical law of radioactive decay, he never drew the inference that statistics meant the elimination of ontological causality, namely, that on the atomic level events could occur without cause. He did not draw that inference because he held a view which showed nature to be simple, coherent, and objective. This view of nature is the force that gave rise to that intellectual wave which is physics, a wave to which Rutherford gave a new gigantic amplitude and the crest of which he proudly rode. Such a wave is known by the riches which it washes ashore in accordance with the tenet: "by their fruits ye shall know them." Those who produce such waves refute by their very deeds scientists and sundry philosophers and historians of science whose pastime, as Einstein once put it, is to play a dangerous game with reality,[41] and whose sole aim, I might add, is to discourage their fellow men from seeing the reality beneath. This is why they shy away from the gigantic deeds of science such as are embodied in Rutherford, undoubtedly the greatest glory of the McGill Laboratory, about which he wrote: "There is a saying that it is the first step that counts, and it is clear that to McGill belongs whatever credit is due for the early ideas and experiments, which opened up the way into the unknown which all subsequent investigations have followed."[42] The subsequent investigations were the exploration of the nucleus, investigations which he later described with his exuberant love of reality: "I know of no more enthralling adventure than this voyage of discovery into the almost unexplored world of the atomic nucleus."[43] It was his belief that the adventure would last as long as there were men to take the ever new, first, and indispensable step toward reality.

Notes

1. See, for instance, the concluding remarks in L. Badash's article, "Rutherford, Ernest," in *Dictionary of Scientific Biography* (New York: Charles Scribner's Sons, 1970-), vol. XII, pp. 25–36. The view expressed in these statements is not entirely a matter of retrospective evaluation as can be seen in note 11 below.

2. See J. Rowland, *Ernest Rutherford: Atom Pioneer* (New York: Philosophical Library, 1957), p. 129. The passage, which is quoted in *Rutherford: Being the Life and Letters of the Rt. Hon. Lord Rutherford, O.M.* by A.S. Eve (Cambridge: University Press, 1939, p. 374) from the same address of Rutherford to the meeting of the British Association in Leicester in 1933, also contains his emphasis on pure research: "A lot of nonsense has been talked about transmutation. Our interest in the matter is purely scientific, and the experiments which are being carried out will help us to a better understanding of the structure of matter." Rutherford was, however, among the first to note three years later the great possibilities opened up by the extraordinary effectiveness of slow neu-

trons in producing nuclear transformations. It was still necessary, he added, to produce those slow neutrons in large quantities, the prospect of which did not seem to
him to be promising. See E.N. da C. Andrade, *Rutherford and the Nature of the Atom*
(Garden City, N.Y.: Doubleday, 1964), pp. 210–11. In his first book, *Radioactivity*
(1904), Rutherford had already called attention to the enormous quantity of energy
contained in very small quantities of matter, as revealed by radioactivity. At the
height of World War I, in 1916, he not only compared the energy obtainable in principle from one pound of radioactive material with the energy gained from one hundred million pounds of coal, but also expressed his hope that radioactive energy would
not be available until man was living at peace with his neighbours! See M. Oliphant,
Rutherford: Recollections of the Cambridge Days (Amsterdam: Elsevier, 1972), pp. 139–40.

3. In 1909, or more than 60 years before the first soft-landing of a space probe on Mars,
    Sir Charles Darwin took the view that whatever the skill of H.G. Wells's Martians, it
    was unlikely that terrestrial beings would solve the problem of hitting with good accu-
    racy any given spot on Mars "ten thousand years from now." The context of his re-
    mark, which is certainly a classic of poor prognostication of the future course of
    technology, was his discussion of the Chamberlin-Moulton theory of the evolution of
    the solar system, published under the title, "A Theory of the Evolution of the Solar
    System," *Internationale Wochenschrift für Wissenschaft, Kunst und Technik* 3 (1909), cols.
    921–34. See especially col. 930.

4. A remark made to his assistant, H. Geiger, the day before Christmas, 1910. See N.
    Feather, *Lord Rutherford* (new ed.; London: Priory Press, 1973), p. 133.

5. As reported in his essay, "Rutherford," in his *Variety of Men* (Harmondsworth: Pen-
    guin, 1969, p. 17) by C.P. Snow present at the occasion.

6. Cambridge University Press, 1928, p. 327. The phrase quoted is one of the stylistic
    gems that abound in Eddington's writings and can easily distract from their occasional
    superficiality. For regardless of what was left of the physical world by Rutherford's
    investigations, there was nothing left to kick in the world as it emerged in Eddington's
    perspective. Caught in that perspective the physicist could only exclaim at the end of
    his research that he had found his own footprints (*Space, Time and Gravitation: An Outline
    of the General Theory of Relativity* [Cambridge University Press, 1920, p. 201]). Yet all the
    brilliance of Eddington's style was not enough to dispel the shadow cast by the monu-
    mental figures of Planck, Einstein, and Rutherford, about whom Eddington himself
    admitted that "it would scarcely be possible to name a more formidable trio" testi-
    fying on behalf of causality (*New Pathways in Science* [Cambridge University Press,
    1935, p. 296]). Their support of causality was, of course, an integral part of their un-
    swerving advocacy of realism. Planck's and Einstein's epistemological realism is in part
    the topic of the eleventh and twelfth chapters of my Gifford Lectures, *The Road of
    Science and the Ways to God* (Chicago: University of Chicago Press; Edinburgh: Scottish
    Academic Press, 1978).

7. A favorite dictum of J. Robert Oppenheimer. To give the name proton, as Rutherford
    did, to a fundamental particle proved to be just as inappropriate as to christen another
    one omega many years later.

8. See his presidential address, "The Electrical Structure of Matter," to the meeting of
    the British Association in Liverpool in 1923, in its *Report*, p. 1.

9. For details, see my *The Relevance of Physics* (Chicago: University of Chicago Press, 1966),
    pp. 155–57.

10. Quoted in Eve, *Rutherford,* p. 39.

11. See Badash, "Rutherford," pp. 27–28.

12. Account of the incident appeared in print in the *McGill News* as part of an encomium of Rutherford after his death in 1937. In the same account it was also noted that Professor John Cox, head of the physics department at McGill, quickly rose to Rutherford's defense and predicted that his work would one day be valued as high as that of Faraday. See Eve, *Rutherford,* p. 88.

13. The retort was aimed at Eve; see his *Rutherford,* p. 436.

14. An extraordinary feat, if seen in contrast, for example, with Planck's mistaken efforts to refute Boltzman's statistical interpretation of the second law of thermodynamics and to discredit Einstein's view of light as a stream of quanta! Einstein himself repeatedly had to discard apparently good solutions of a unified field theory.

15. He did so in his Bakerian lecture. See *The Collected Papers of Lord Rutherford of Nelson,* published under the scientific direction of Sir James Chadwick (London: George Allen and Unwin, 1962–65), vol. III, p. 34. Without using the word neutron, Rutherford spoke of certain conditions under which "it may be possible for an electron to combine much more closely with the H nucleus, forming a kind of neutral doublet. Such an atom would have very novel properties."

16. See Andrade, *Rutherford and the Nature of the Atom,* 209.
    Andrade was an eyewitness of the incident.

17. For the best account of that influence, see chapter 13 in *Ernst Mach: His Work, Life, and Influence* (Berkeley: University of California Press, 1972).

18. See chapters 13 and 14 in my Gifford Lectures, *The Road of Science and the Ways to God* (Chicago: University of Chicago Press; Edinburgh: Scottish Academic Press, 1978).

19. This "improved and enlarged edition" of the work, *Machs Grundrisz der Physik für die Höheren Schulen des Deutschen Reiches* (Leipzig: G. Freytag; Wien: F. Tempsky, 1908) was, of course, the work not of Mach but of F. Harbordt and M. Fischer, who, however, did it in an unmistakably Machist spirit and undoubtedly in consultation with Mach himself. Thus, while acknowledging the extreme fruitfulness of atomic theory in leading to fundamentally new discoveries, they warned against attributing certainty to it. (See Part II, p. 8.) The few lines on radioactivity (see *ibid.,* pp. 235–36) were largely devoted to the enormous quantities of energy released in radioactive phenomena. The paucity of words on radioactivity should seem all the more revealing as Vienna became a major center on radioactive research shortly after the discoveries made by Becquerel and the Curies. The famed *Jahrbuch für Radioaktivitat und Elektronik* was already in its fourth year in 1908, and among its contributors there were several Viennese physicists. Rutherford's *Radioactivity,* originally published in 1904 was well known to them. Two of them, Stefan Meyer and Egon R. von Schweidler, became co-authors of the classic monograph, *Radioaktivität—* published as if by irony of fate in 1916, the year of Mach's death—a work which not only was full of references to Rutherford's research but for years also rivalled in importance Rutherford's *Radioactive Substances and their Radiation* (1913).

20. "Forty Years of Physics," a lecture delivered in 1936. For its text, see J. Needham and W. Pagel (eds.), *Background to Modern Science* (New York: Macmillan, 1938), especially pp. 67–68.

21. See Mach's account of the leading principles of his scientific epistemology, "Die Leitfaden meiner wissenschaftlichen Erkenntnislehre und ihre Aufnahme durch Zeitgenos-

sen," Scientia, 7 (1910), p. 233. It was Mach's reply to Planck's Leiden address discussed below.

22. The chapter, "Mach and Buddhism," in Blackmore's *Ernst Mach* should be an eye-opener not only on that logically final phase of Mach's intellectual development, but also on the studied care by which this aspect of Mach's life and thought was covered with silence in the countless encomiums heaped on Mach, in speech and in print, by members of the Vienna Circle.

23. The solipsism implied in Carnap's *Der logische Aufbau der Welt* (1928) and in the basic postulates of logical positivism was, however, as a rule, passed over in silence by logical positivists.

24. For an English translation of that lecture, "Die Einheit des physikalischen Welt-bildes," which Planck considered to be one of his best lectures, see *A Survey of Physics: A Collection of Lectures and Essays by Max Planck,* translated by R. Jones and D.H. Williams (London: Methuen, 1925), pp. 1–26.

25. In that preface (see pp. vii–viii in his *The Principles of Physical Optics: An Historical and Philosophical Treatment,* translated by J.S. Anderson and A.F.A. Young [1926; New York: Dover reprint, n.d.]) Mach declined to be seen as a forerunner of relativity which he saw as "a transitory inspiration in the history of science."

26. Einstein did so in his obituary of Mach, "Ernst Mach," *Physikalische Zeitschrift* 17 (1916), p. 103

27. For details and references, see my *The Relevance of Physics,* p. 551.

28. Quoted in Eve, *Rutherford,* p. 281.

29. This prediction, made according to Rutherford's own admission (see Eve, *Rutherford,* p. 290) on an *a priori* basis, shows particularly well that he was not a grim empiricist, but a far-sighted realist not at all adverse to far-fetched theorizing. His prediction was coupled with the remark that at present there was not "the slightest evidence of the existence of such a [positive] counterpart" of the electron. In a remarkable anticipation of the idea of anti-worlds made of antimatter, Rutherford spoke in 1935 of such parts of the universe in which the respective roles of positive and negative electric charges may be reversed.

30. *Ibid.,* p. 394. Snow, who could hardly ever see anything wrong with philosophies and social programs based mainly or entirely on science, tried to create the impression (see his *Variety of Men,* p. 16) that by "those fellows" Rutherford meant not certain scientists and scientist-philosophers, but "logicians, critics, and metaphysicians." Had such been the case, Rutherford's admiration for the success of wave-mechanics would not have been noticeably grudging.

31. At any rate, Rutherford did remark: "They play games with their symbols, but we in the Cavendish, turn out the real solid facts of Nature." See Andrade, *Rutherford and the Nature of the Atom,* p. 210.

32. The quotation is from Rutherford's letter of March 20, 1913, to Bohr. See Eve, *Rutherford,* p. 221.

33. See *Electrons et photons: Rapports et discussions du Cinquième Conseil de physique tenu à Bruxelles du 24 au 29 Octobre 1927 sous les auspices de l'Institut International de Physique Solvay* (Paris: Gauthiers-Villars, 1928), pp. 258–63. The solipsism implied in Heisenberg's position

deserves only the reply, "Cherish it," which Chesterton gave to someone claiming that solipsism was the most reasonable philosophy. Dirac had, of course, to assume that Nature would never go back on her choices, but such a personified and rigorous consistency is best to be ascribed to a personal Creator and not to a nature which for the purposes of science cannot be animate, or else one has to endorse Aristotle, the physicist!

34. See p. 1 of *Report* quoted in note 8 above.

35. *Ibid.,* p. 24.

36. A proof of this alleged irreconcilability is in a sense the culminating point in T.S. Kuhn's *The Structure of Scientific Revolutions* (Chicago: University of Chicago Press, 1962), pp. 100–01. The subjective idealism underlying its theme and many other modern interpretations of the history and philosophy of science as a chain of themata, images, myths, research programs, and so forth explains all too well the almost complete absence there of references to Rutherford and to the enormous part of modern science created by him. Hostility to the metaphysics of realism can only produce escapism from much of that reality of science which is embodied in the creativity of great realist scientists, such as Rutherford, whose greatness prompted none other than Born to consider him the greatest scientist he had ever known, including even Einstein! See Oliphant, *Rutherford,* p. 157.

37. See Eve, *Rutherford,* pp. 375–76 and 380–81.

38. *Ibid.,* p. 400. It is not difficult to guess in this connection the emotions of Rutherford who was found in a "state of explosive indignation" on learning about the treatment of many scientists in Nazi Germany. See Andrade, *Rutherford and the Nature of the Atom,* p. 203.

39. See Eve, *Rutherford,* p. 402.

40. Reported by Sir Cyril Hinshelwood in his presidential address to the British Association, "Science and Scientists," *Nature* 207 (1965), p. 1058.

41. In his letter of December 22, 1950, to Schrödinger. See *Letters on Wave Mechanics: Schrödinger, Planck, Einstein, Lorentz,* edited by K. Przimbram, translated with an introduction by M.J. Klein (New York: Philosophical Library, 1967), p. 36.

42. See Eve, *Rutherford,* p. 352.

43. See Rowland, *Ernest Rutherford,* p. 133.

1900:
The Cavendish Physicists
and the Spirit
of the Age

NEIL CAMERON

Historians of science who set out to analyse and explain the links between scientific thought and practice and the wider cultural and intellectual environment are bound to find it a risky process. Tracing the course of a significant development in science is generally difficult enough; attempts to consider the life and thought of scientists as either causes or consequences of more general factors nearly always require indulgence in speculation, however buttressed with statistics and footnotes. Those who were still willing to make the venture, especially the early makers of sweeping sociological generalizations, were likely to find themselves the object of sharp attacks by the more careful, if more narrow, specialists in the "internal" development of particular scientific disciplines.

It has come to be recognized in recent years that the debate over the relative merits of these two approaches is to a considerable extent one of emphasis and definition. Those writers who are primarily interested in the evolution of concepts and problems have been justifiably sceptical of the amount of enlightenment that can be provided by a consideration of the social, religious, or philosophical *milieu* in which discoveries were made; they would probably prefer to see such studies relegated to intellectual or social history. Yet even they would probably concede a certain debt to those philosophers and philosophers-cum-historians who have cast a wider net, and tried to explain just what it is that scientists do, and what they give to, and receive from, the world in which they act.

These synthesizers and generalists of the history and philosophy of science have turned again and again to the study of certain favourite individuals—Galileo, Newton, Darwin, Einstein—whose names have come to connote entire intellectual revolutions. For Einstein in particular, even specialists in the history of physics have found themselves compelled to give some consideration to philosophical and popular interpretations of his ideas and influence. This has also been true, if less spectacularly, for men like Planck, Bohr, and Heisenberg. The great theorists of relativity, quantum theory, and wave mechanics were often themselves eager to explore the philosophical implications of their work, and their biographies suggested the existence of fascinating, if problematic, interconnections with the general intellectual ferment of Central Europe.[1]

It is partly for this reason that so many more scholars have been attracted to the world of Einstein and Planck than to that of Thomson and Rutherford. The importance of the achievements of the latter *as physicists* has been readily recognized, and the older biographies and memoirs are now being complemented by more detailed and analytical studies of the practice of physics in Britain—for example, of the generally hesitant and unhappy response to relativity theory in the earlier years of the century.[2] But there is still very little that has been published about the Cavendish researchers in relation to more general questions about the nature of European society.[3]

It is now 40 years since the death of Rutherford; this seems an appropriate occasion to give some general consideration to the world that made him and the world he helped make. This essay makes no claim to be more than a preliminary and tentative exploration of such a large topic. It does not aim to provide any new understanding of the theories of atomic structure and radioactivity at the turn of the century but only to give a perspective on the world in 1900.

Let us begin with a man of letters who made one of the most famous, if ultimately unsuccessful, attempts to assimilate the major developments of nineteenth-century scientific thought into a general intellectual synthesis:

Since Bacon and Newton, English thought had gone on impatiently protesting that no one must try to know the unknowable at the same time that every one went on thinking about it. The result was as chaotic as kinetic gas ... but [Adams] sought only its direction. For himself he knew, that, in spite of all the Englishmen that ever lived, he would be forced to enter supersensual chaos if he meant to find out what became of British science—or indeed of any other science.[4]

Henry Adams wrote these lines in 1903, on reading Karl Pearson's *Grammar of Science*. Pearson had dismissed the accounts of force and matter to be found in texts like those of Lord Kelvin as 'hopelessly illogical' and had demanded that they be replaced by a strictly sensationalist description of nature. Adams was at once repelled and fascinated by Pearson's arguments and the similar ones he found in the works of Ernst Mach. But he was not even interested in contesting the presuppositions of the positivist writers; for him, their books were less philosophical expositions than symbols of the intellectual and cultural chaos that he saw as marking the new century.

For he had charted the course of triumphant mechanism and materialism through the previous century and now believed that he was watching the disintegration of even those harsh creeds, as the dynamo continued to turn, faster and faster. He took a gloomy satisfaction in the new scientific developments—Roentgen's rays, and the 'metaphysical bomb' of the Curies' radium—which had contributed to the destruction of the older view of reality. These had appeared in the 1890's, but he chose to call 1900 itself the year that 'continuity snapped'; as his authority, he mockingly cited a British philosopher-statesman: "In 1904, Arthur Balfour announced on the part of British science that the human race without exception had lived and died in a world of illusion until the last year of the century. The date was convenient, and convenience was truth."[5]

British scientists and philosophers had played a particularly important role in all the later acts of the sweeping historical drama that Adams had conceived. Like many interpreters of the nineteenth century, he associated even those of their ideas which he disliked with the most powerful historical currents of the industrial age. Bacon had been the prophet, Newton the legislator; now the combination of overseas expansion and industrialism would cover the world with steam engines, factories, electrical plants, engineers, and utilitarian administrators.

From about the 1870's, those British writers who were to have the most profound impact on their age had begun to take an increasingly pessimistic view of the transformation of thought and society that was being effected by industrialism and modern science. It was a pessimism of a new kind, one based less on fear of the future than on a corrosive scepticism that left none of the institutions of the previous age untouched. The literature of the Romantic and mid-Victorian periods had, of course, included some of the fiercest indictments of the machine age, but those indictments had largely been made by men who still conceived of a cultural ideal against which the actual failings of the new society could be measured. What was characteristic of the newer sensibility was the growing belief that cultural standards were disappearing altogether—even the rather unsatisfactory ones that had been provided by Barbarians, Philistines, and Populace.

For the men of letters, the world of culture had been cut adrift. Neither Victorian religion nor freethought, Romanticism nor utilitarianism, could provide any sort of cultural bedrock, any set of unifying assumptions that could make sense of an emerging chaos. An elderly American Brahmin like Adams might concede that he was a man of another time, that the world was slipping away from him. But his sense of fragmentation and disintegration was shared by a much younger generation of writers in England; a literary historian of the period 1880 to 1914 in that country entitled his book *Journey Through Despair.*[6]

Exceptions can be found: Wells, Shaw, and Bennett come most readily to mind, although even these men recognized that old conventions were disappearing and that new ones had to be created. While the most pessimistic appraisals of the cultural condition came from the writers who combined *avant-garde* literary and artistic experimentalism with conservative or reactionary political convictions, only a small proportion of their criticisms can be attributed to a particular philosophical and political temperament; remarkably similar perceptions could be found in the works of liberals like E.M. Forster.[7]

How different, how very different from the life of our own dear Cavendish scientists. The British research physicists, triumphant exploiters of that very specialization of method and purpose so feared by the cultural critics, worked in an atmosphere of buoyant optimism and intellectual excitement, while outside science their moral and intellectual universe remained almost classically Victorian.

Even from the perspective of the present, in which specialization has reached a level that can only be called pathological, it is still fascinating to contemplate the gulf that separated the physicists from the men of letters, especially in a period when science exercised such a profound effect on the literary imagination. Rutherford probably would have particularly delighted Adams as an appropriate symbol of the new age. Starting with a scholarship to Cambridge that had been financed with the profits of the Great Exhibition of 1851, Rutherford's career was shaped by steamships, telegraphs, electrical generators, radioactive emanations, industrial patronage; his life, as well as his science, highlighted nearly all of Adams' favorite themes.

But this is an outsider's view. There is nothing in Rutherford's correspondence from Cambridge or Montreal to suggest that he saw himself or his science as participants in any sort of general intellectual revolution. Nor do his native English colleagues appear to have viewed matters any differently. At least at first glance, none seem to exemplify the thesis advanced by Lewis Feuer about the great Continental theorists: That theoretical daring can be traced to a more general philosophical and even political radicalism.[8] Adams might regard Balfour as speaking 'on the part of British science,' but the dramatic turn of phrase with which he heralded the new century was stictly his own. It would be duplicated by Eddington, but not by the Cavendish experimentalists, who included

Rayleigh, Balfour's brother-in-law. Even Thomson, who had a broad range of general interests outside physics, took for granted the complete separation of professional work from other areas of thought.

In literature and philosophy, on the other hand, the outlook which most resembled that of the Cavendish men could only be found among late Victorians like Bertrand Russell and H.G. Wells. That kind of temper which is generally identified as 'modern' was completely different, although some of its older representatives had already begun their search for new forms in the Victorian period; it is curious to recall that Joseph Conrad and J.J. Thomson were born about the same time. The generation born in the 1880's included T.E. Hulme, T.S. Eliot, D.H. Lawrence, and James Joyce. These writers were uncompromising in their conviction that the new century was a time of cultural watershed and transformation.

It would be easy enough to show striking antitheses of individual temperament and sensibility between mid-Victorian scientists and men of letters, but what can be discerned by the early 1900's is a general *pattern* of dissociation and mutual incomprehension. How had such a pattern developed? English intellectual life had always been characterized by greater individualism and anarchy than its Continental counterpart, but it had also possessed qualities of social and institutional coherence: the Public School ethos, the dominant position of the major Oxbridge colleges, the network of friendships and intermarriages that helped create what Noel Annan has called the 'intellectual aristocracy.'[9]

Before attempting to answer the question, it may be helpful to consider some of the more common explanations that have been provided for the immense gulf separating most of the scientists from most of the humanists and social critics. All of these explanations contain elements of the truth, but they do not tell the full story.

The first and simplest provides the implicit basis for much of the argument in Lord Snow's famous lectures about the 'two cultures,' and is an argument that was also accepted by many of his harshest critics. It amounts to the assumption that there is a general type of scientific mind. Whether this mind is regarded as mainly a product of nature or nurture, it is assumed to have changed very little throughout the ages, or at least throughout the last four centuries. It is exemplified by William Harvey against both Bacon and Donne, by Rutherford as against both Balfour and Eliot. It is a mind which is generally conceived, by both admirers and detractors, as inquisitive, adventurous yet analytically rigorous, radically innovative in the interpretation of nature but often unreflective and conventional in the realm of human affairs, narrow in focus less by necessity than in consequence of the sheer fascination exercised by particular problems. It may be described as having its origins in Christian, especially Protestant theology, in the Faustian imperatives of capitalism, or in complex Freudian childhood influences, or it may be seen as ultimately inexplicable. It may be held up as a model for general emulation or excoriated as the very *fons et origo* of Philistinism, but in either case, it is assumed to be a readily identifiable type; there is no problem understanding its contempt for speculative metaphysics, its indifference to cultural synthesis, its perennial optimism.

To see this kind of mind as being manifested in the Cavendish is easy enough, but largely because so much of the whole concept is a disguised tautology, a description of observable behaviour masquerading as an analysis of individual psychology. With a little ingenuity, it can be used to explain almost anything, from Maxwell's fondness for doggerel to the spirit-hunting of Lodge and Crookes. Furthermore, unless it can be assumed that the scientific mind and temperament is fully determined at birth, a mere process of labelling does not explain how its possessors came to constitute a separate 'culture.'

A slightly different method of identifying a general British scientific mind puts the emphasis on the 'British,' rather than the 'scientific.' It can be found in its clearest and most uncompromising form in Pierre Duhem's famous survey of physical thought, the French edition of which appeared just after the beginning of the century.[10] Duhem, and his great colleague Poincaré, regarded English physicists with a mixture of admiration and exasperation. They could find in them no trace of their own drive to achieve elegance, consistency, symmetry, and completeness—only a passion for workable hypotheses, mechanical models, demonstrations that could be given a readily comprehensible intuitive meaning. From the French point of view, the English had *no* theory, in the really grand sense of the word, only a kind of inspired thrashing about.

Duhem was far less reluctant than most modern historians would be to attribute this behaviour to a distinctive national genius, one that could be as readily discerned in English literature as in English science. It was a genius that combined great imaginative power with a firm grasp on reality, but which had little capacity for achieving coherence, systematic order, or depth. British scientific thought was to be understood, then, as merely a subcategory of a more general empiricism.

If the latter term is used very broadly, to describe a general intellectual style, then it may be aptly enough applied to the Cavendish tradition. But it must be emphasized that this does not imply that the physicists subscribed to any particular doctrines of Locke, Hume, or Mill.

They seldom made any specific pronouncements about ontology or epistemology, although they did occasionally make explicit their aversion to abstraction and system-building. Rayleigh, for example, at the end of his own term at the Cavendish, gave a presidential address to the British Association which briefly encapsulated this outlook. He paid tribute to Maxwell, not only as a scientist but as a mentor of sound principles:

> The impress of his thoughts may be recognised in much of the best work at the present time. As a teacher and examiner he was well acquainted with the almost universal tendency of uninstructed minds to elevate phrases above things: to refer, for example, to the principle of the conservation of energy for an explanation of the persistent rotation of a fly-wheel . . . Maxwell's endeavour was always to keep the facts in the foreground, and to his influence, in conjunction with that of Thomson and Helmholtz, is largely due that elimination of unnecessary hypothesis which is one of the distinguishing characteristics of the science of the present day.[11]

For all the major institutional, as well as scientific, developments that followed at the Cavendish in the four decades after Rayleigh's departure, it could still be said that the characteristic intellectual style remained largely similar to that found in his presidential address. Since this accompanied an outstanding record of scientific achievement, it has led to a natural tendency to develop a sort of Whig interpretation of the history of physics. The scientists who produced most of the biographies and memoirs of the great Cavendish days commonly took for granted the professionalization, specialization, and concentration of attention on a few objectives that had emerged in experimental physics by the turn of the century. Since Thomson and Rutherford got excellent results by this concentration of attention, it is scarcely surprising that their former students should be relatively uninterested in their metaphysical presuppositions— or unmetaphysical presuppositions—and their general relationship to culture and society. Since the whole subsequent development of university education and science appears as a logical sequel to the direction taken by the Cavendish, it is convenient to treat its entire history as analogous to the history of parliamentary reform, blending tradition and innovation in the sensible British way.

But if the institutional and intellectual history of British physics is to be treated in this way—and there is obviously much to be said for the analogy—why does it show such a completely different pattern from that emerging in the world of general ideas? If the scientists were only expressing a particular form of an enduring national temper, then it would appear that for some reason the traditional guardians of culture were not. It may be recalled that even the academic philosophers of the period were turning toward Hegelian idealism, or at least toward some variant form. British philosophers have sometimes treated this development as a curious aberration; Russell and Moore, especially the latter, would soon lead the errant sheep back into the fold. But what is commonly understood to be the characteristically modern temper in literature can scarcely be treated in the same way—it provided the basis of a permanent schism. We take Lawrence and Eliot as our prophets and cultural geographers, not H.G. Wells.

It will be suggested here that the origins of this division of sensibility can be found largely in the intellectual and institutional changes in British society that took place in response to the economic and demographic pressures of the high-Victorian era. This division may best be understood as the consequence of a loss of control by the cultural and political elite, a breakdown in the attempt to provide a certain amount of synchronism in the intellectual and social development of English society. The central causes of this loss of control were industrial revolution, population expansion, and foreign (especially German) competition; the consequences were generally fortunate for the development of physics, but more questionable for the subsequent general evolution of British society.

It was in the mid-Victorian period that the full impact of the social changes brought about by the industrial revolution began to be felt in education and general culture. The spectacularly rapid increase in population and its concentration in London and the new industrial towns of the north, the rapid growth of the number and size of new fortunes in the same areas, and the corresponding expansion of Dissenting and utilitarian influence had all been taking place for over half a century, but it took considerable time for their force to be felt in such strongly traditionalist institutions as the Oxford and Cambridge colleges.

The major public schools and the older universities had remained committed to the social-cultural ideal of the gentleman-amateur, which attempted to reconcile the competing claims of class, status, and power, but not through the inculcation of a single system of religious or philosophical ideas. Instead, it depended upon a uniform code of manners and behaviour, within which individuality and versatility could be actively encouraged. Wealth alone could not make a gentleman, nor variety of intellectual interests an amateur; a certain degree of cultivation was necessary, and the traditional educational institutions were there to provide this. Conversely, those who had once been admitted to the charmed circle could sometimes maintain their position even in difficult financial circumstances, especially if they could manage to make an advantageous marriage or find a helpful patron.

The maintenance of this ideal required a fairly general deference to its representatives from the rest of the population and could involve a very cruel form of snobbery, especially toward those hopeful unfortunates who were beginning a social climb that could only be completed by their children or grandchildren. A family that began in obscure circumstances could produce a gentleman, but not in a single generation. The emphasis on 'breeding' also meant that young men who could claim the most impressive quarterings could more easily violate the general code of manners without loss of status. The incongruities that resulted were a favourite theme for Victorian novelists; both the individual of ambiguous status and the arrogant, brainless aristocrat could be portrayed as comic or tragic figures in the society of gentlemen.

Nonetheless, it is a social arrangement that has many appealing qualities; that is one of the reasons that bits and pieces of it have survived into modern English life. At his best, the gentleman-amateur tried to keep philosophy, literature, science, personal relationships, and political life within a single universe of discourse, or at least within a series of overlapping circles that possessed a considerable amount of interaction and mutual understanding. He took at least as much of his education from the social circles in which he moved as from what he could obtain from the written word; the results he produced scarcely suggest that this condemned him to superficiality.

Up until the 1850's and 1860's, the Oxford and Cambridge colleges provided an undergraduate education that was designed to meet this ideal. The central university administrations were weak and impecunious. The college fellows held most of the real power, which they generally used to preserve a traditional curriculum that gave a central position to classical studies. It was possible to obtain an extremely rigorous education in mathematics—the famous Cambridge Tripos examination is an indication—for which the students usually obtained private coaching. The mathematics curriculum was very extensive and included problems in mechanics and occasional other branches of applied mathematics bordering on physics. But the final exams were a culmination, at least as often as they were a preparation for further studies. High Wranglers, students who obtained outstanding grades on the Cambridge Tripos, were as likely to find their careers in the Law or the Church as in academic or scientific life, or perhaps merely manage an estate.

Mathematics and theoretical mechanics had a position in the traditional curriculum that was as old and honoured as the teaching of classics itself. Furthermore, mathematical theorems and exercises could be taught as a finished body of knowledge, a background the graduate could draw on for the rest of his life. The laboratory sciences, being in a constant state of evolutionary development, could not make the same claim, and opposition to their introduction as a major part of undergraduate studies came not only from classicists, but from men like William Whewell and Isaac Todhunter.

Furthermore, the traditionalists could argue that the existing system of instruction had not been by any means sterile. The number of Wranglers who had remained in the universities to teach mathematics and carry on their own private investigations in physics might be small, but it included, between 1830 and 1860, George Green, G.G. Stokes, Arthur Cayley, William Thomson, and Clerk Maxwell. These men increased the general prestige of science with their work, and were beginning to see the possibilities that would be provided by the creation of university laboratories, but they were by no means dedicated to a wholesale attack on the traditional curriculum. Maxwell, even when first Director of the Cavendish, was still often heard to say that a classical education, with its attention to clarity and precision of meaning, was as good a training as any for the research physicist.

Research was not encouraged; those who had the inclination and the aptitude could pursue it on their own. It was generally assumed that genuine scientific originality could not be produced to order; it simply turned up from time to time, as a talent of occasional Wranglers or for that matter of men who had not been through a conventional education at all, like Davy and Faraday. The preservation of general quality was more important than bringing about an increase in productivity in specialized fields; a loss to the laboratory might be a gain for the bench or the pulpit.

The small numbers who did choose to devote their entire energies to scientific investigations might find themselves happiest in the company of other scientists, including those who were not products of the Public Schools and Oxbridge colleges. But the still very limited occupational opportunities in science kept the number of men who did original work while depending on it for a living very small. Aristocrats and men of independent means made up a substantial proportion of the whole community of scientists. This was especially true in physics, which had both the strongest links with university mathematics and the smallest prospects for providing professional or industrial employment. The gentlemanly style had its effects, even on those who came from humble origins; Faraday himself regarded the very term 'physicist' as a detestable German importation, always preferring to be regarded as a 'natural philosopher.'

But the transformations that had occurred in British society in the first half of the nineteenth century made it impossible to preserve the existing position of science in the social system of gentlemen and amateurs. Population growth and new money had led to the founding of new colleges and universities in the industrial towns, and for that matter in the colonial possessions of the Empire. Their establishment had coincided with the rise of the new discipline of chemistry, which at once required laboratory instruction, professionalization, large numbers of practitioners, and a degree of compromise between quality and quantity (it was a subject which provided far more scope than physics for the capable plodder). It held out the promise of utilitarian application, and launched as a new subject in new universities, it did not have to face immediate competition from the older universities.

Once this program began, Oxford and Cambridge could no longer exercise their former degree of control over the place of science in culture. If the colleges held fast to their traditional curriculum, the development of science would eventually come under other leadership, in London, Manchester, or elsewhere. Even the alternative—to establish their own undergraduate courses and teaching laboratories—meant a fundamental departure from their previous educational philosophy. The study of the scientific disciplines, instead of remaining a sequel to general education, would become a rival force, drawing in students who had high intelligence but little grounds for attachment to the older cultural ideal, and the establishment of new professorial chairs would reduce the importance of the particular colleges as centres of educational and cultural development. But only movement in this direction could assure that the older universities would maintain their pre-eminent position.

Recognition of this fact was signalled in 1850, with the introduction of several new Honours Schools at Oxford which included natural science. A year later, Cambridge followed with a proliferation of Natural Science Tripos programs. Initially, these courses were often taught by polymaths who also gave instruction in the traditional disciplines, and they attracted only a tiny number of students. Laboratory facilities were still minimal; at Oxford, for example, the first chemistry teacher used the basement of Balliol. The growth in the number of students who made natural sciences their major subjects was painfully slow, not just for the first years of the new régime, but for the next four decades. When C.T.R. Wilson graduated from Cambridge in 1892, he was *the only student* to graduate with physics as his main subject, almost 20 years after Maxwell had begun instruction at the Cavendish.[12]

The Cavendish, it need scarcely be noted, was still successful in attracting capable research students, although the same can not be said of the Clarendon at Oxford, opened a little earlier. The early history of both these laboratories dramatically highlights the way in which aristocratic and gentlemanly influences still shaped the character of British physics. The 1860's had seen a continuance of the pressure from scientists, scientific publicists, and some politicians to expand scientific instruction, a movement given increased urgency by the disastrous showing of British technology at the International Exhibition of 1867 compared to 1851, which brought home the increasing threat of industrial competition from abroad, especially from the Germans. However, neither the Government, the central university administrations, nor the separate colleges were willing to provide the tens of thousands of pounds necessary to build modern physics laboratories with proper facilities. At Oxford, a trust left by the Earl of Clarendon from the proceeds of the sale of his *History of the Great Rebellion,* and originally intended to provide a riding stable, was conveniently turned to the more pressing use; at Cambridge the Duke of Devonshire, who was at once a Whig aristocrat, a metallurgist and capitalist, a Wrangler, and the Chancellor of the University, provided the necessary money. The first Cavendish Director was Maxwell, a Scottish laird; the first Director of the Clarendon was R.B. Clifton, another Cambridge Wrangler who came highly recommended by several leading physicists and a Lincolnshire landowner.

Maxwell and his successor Rayleigh still represented the gentlemanly ideal, while being also brilliantly gifted and energetic physicists; Clifton was satisfied with being a gentleman. He did practically no research, did not encourage his students to do so, and did not seek to attract students who were doing original work. He carried the traditional concept of the proper role of mathematics in undergraduate instruction into physics; he preferred to devote his lectures mainly to optics and acoustics, in which a finished body of proofs could be taught over and over again. He published practically nothing. Yet this lack of activity apparently did not much disturb his contemporaries; he served three times on the Council of the Royal Society, was Vice-President in 1896–1898, and took frequent part in government inquiries on the state of British science and education. Both he and Rayleigh would probably have considered the most important factor in their lives in the 1870's not to be the establishment of laboratory physics, but the great agricultural depression of the period, which had a disastrous effect on their tenants. But while Rayleigh abandoned his Chair after five years to continue a whole series of important researches on his own for another 35 years, Clifton kept his position at the Clarendon throughout that same period.[13] Thus in the 1870's at Cambridge you could find Maxwell, at Oxford, Clifton; in the 1880's at Cambridge, Rayleigh, at Oxford, Clifton; and from then on until the end of the First World War, at Cambridge, J.J. Thomson; at Oxford, Clifton. Oxford had begun to achieve some distinction in chemistry by the turn of the century, but it is easy enough to see why bright, young, would-be physicists would flock to Cambridge.

At the end of the century, three major determinants gave the Cavendish its characteristic style. The first was the remaining influence of the gentleman-amateur tradition; the second, the new opportunities provided for research students who were from outside that tradition after 1895; the third, the example and mediating influence of Thomson himself. All of these were also modified in their effect by the exciting range of experimental possibilities that had been provided by the discovery of radioactivity and the use of electrical discharges to study the properties of matter.

The survival of the older tradition can be seen in the example of H.F. Callendar, who preceded Rutherford in the Macdonald Laboratory at McGill. He had taken a First Class in classics and another in mathematics as an undergraduate, but had done no physics at all before 1885. When Thomson wrote his memoirs, he recalled of him:

> [His] career at the Laboratory was in some respects the most interesting in all my experience....He had never done any practical work in physics, nor read any of the theory except in a very casual way. He had not been in the Laboratory for more than a few weeks when I saw that he possessed to an exceptional degree some of the qualifications which make for success in experimental research....I knew from the ability he had shown as an undergraduate that, whatever the subject might be, he would have no difficulty in mastering the literature about it.[14]

Another of the research students of this period, W. Craig Henderson, became President of the Union and was later a K. C., and other examples could be given.

But the decision of Cambridge to open the university to post-graduate students from elsewhere meant the virtual admission that the idea of graduate research and professionalism had won the day over amateurism. The university had found itself faced with stiff competition from the newer British universities (many now boasting Cavendish graduates as professors) and also from Germany. The Germans had not had educational ideals greatly influenced by the model of general cultivation; they had pushed rapidly ahead with professionalism and highly specialized graduate research. Their universities were far cheaper than their British counterparts and offered the attraction of the Ph.D. Oxford and Cambridge regarded this latter invention with some distaste, as a legitimation of the very narrow pedantry they sought to oppose; they did not introduce it for several years more. But Cambridge was willing to go so far as to provide a B.A. for successful research students from elsewhere; their decision was timed to coincide with a policy change by the Commissioners of the Exhibition of 1851, requiring winners of their scholarships to move immediately to their chosen graduate school for two years. Previously, it had been possible to take the first year stipend at home, and science students were likely to spend the following year in Germany. But the new regulations, plus the attractiveness of a Cambridge degree, brought many gifted but impecunious young scholars to Cambridge. From the standpoint of developing physics at Cambridge, the new policy was an outstanding success. Rutherford was certainly the most famous example, but there were many others; of the 103 scholarships awarded to physicists between 1896 and 1921, 60 went to students who spent a whole or a part of their time at Cambridge.[15]

Thomson was a great physicist and physics teacher; he was also a mediator between Cambridge tradition and single-minded physics. He came from a Manchester bookseller's family, of Scottish origins, and he had studied mathematics at Owens College as an undergraduate, ironically enough because he could not afford the steep apprenticeship fees then required for a career in engineering. But he was also a product of two decades at Cambridge, and he used as much influence as he could to integrate the new arrivals into the social world of the university. The Cavendish workers were usually given residence at Trinity College, dining at the B.A. table. Thomson's biographer, the fourth Lord Rayleigh and a former student, comments:

> [It] was quite natural that they should be regarded at first by some as intruders and 'not Cambridge men.' But J.J.'s action soon removed any feeling of this kind. From the outset he let all Cambridge know how he welcomed these newcomers, and he made the Research Students quick to realise that they were now 'Cambridge men' in the fullest sense and anxious to adapt themselves to Cambridge traditions and habits of life.... The breaking down of all barriers, and the welding of all into one Cambridge school, was the work of J.J.[16]

This judgment should be qualified with the note that harmony among physicists of different background was not the same as equality of status in the eyes of the Trinity Fellows. Just before he made his final decision to take the McGill Chair, Rutherford wrote from Cambridge to his fiancée:

> As far as I can see, my chances for a Fellowship are very slight. All the dons practically and naturally dislike very much the idea of one of us getting a Fellowship, and no matter how good a man is, he will be chucked out. There is a good deal of friction over this research business.... I know perfectly well that if I had gone through the regular Cambridge course, and done a third of the work I have done, I would have got a Fellowship bang off.[17]

This is a very revealing passage: It shows both a degree of deference and a flash of resentment, the resentment of a man who might be said 'practically and naturally to dislike very much' the idea that scientific merit alone would not be the measure by which his prospects were determined. Rutherford, with his generosity and good nature, could understand the attitude of the dons in human terms, but he could scarcely imagine any other criteria of considering scientific achievement than a meritocratic one. But he did not have occasion to dwell bitterly on his situation. The McGill appointment gave him the chance to 'run his own show' and to undertake his famous collaboration with Soddy. During his later triumphant career, he would establish more and more the new image of scientific man.

It should by now be clear that the profound difference in sensibility and intellectual preoccupation that marked off most of the Cavendish physicists from the founders of literary and cultural modernism, however much it owed to individual peculiarities of temperament or existing traditions of scientific and literary thought, had more immediate causes. The interpreters of culture saw the social and demographic forces that were transforming Britain as cataclysmic, discrediting or rendering irrelevant the major premises of thought and behaviour around which Victorian society was constructed. They turned to Continental thinkers for inspiration—to the French Symbolists, to Bergson, Nietzsche, Sorel, and Croce. They sought moral and aesthetic absolutes, and the creation of new elites, either to effect a moral and political regeneration of society or to provide rallying points and refuges for the saving remnant.

Cambridge, on the other hand, had attempted to find a compromise between established conventions and the meritocratic and philistine imperatives of nineteenth-century science. The curriculum changes and the acceptance of students who were intellectually gifted but not seasoned in the traditional way transferred the prestige of the institution to a new figure, more professional scientist than gentleman scholar, but still a 'Cambridge man,' whose conception of culture and behaviour had been at least subtly modified by his experience there. The preservation of tradition and the benevolent feudalism of the Laboratory produced a curious consequence. The physicists, by and large, remained Victorians. Lord Snow is mistaken; it is not the future that they have in their bones, but the past. Perhaps it is just as well.

Notes

1. See, for example, such works as Ronald Clark, *Einstein* (N.Y., World, 1971); Lewis Feuer, *Einstein and the Generations of Science* (N.Y., Basic Books, 1974); Donald Fleming and Bernard Bailyn, eds., *The Intellectual Migration* (Cambridge, Harvard Univ. Press, 1969); Allan Janik and Stephen Toulmin, *Wittgenstein's Vienna* (N.Y., Simon & Schuster, 1973).

2. Stanley Goldberg, 'In Defense of Ether: the British Response to Einstein's Special Theory of Relativity, 1905–1911', in *Historical Studies in the Physical Sciences,* vol. 2, 1970, pp. 89–125.

3. Helpful studies which at least touch on the cultural relations of science include W.H.G. Armytage, *The Rise of the Technocrats* (London, Routledge & Kegan Paul, 1965); Eric Ashby, *Technology and the Academics* (London, Macmillan, 1958); Joseph Ben-David, *The Scientist's Role in Society* (Englewood Cliffs, N.J., Prentice-Hall, 1971); D.S.L. Cardwell, *The Organisation of Science in England* (London, Heinemann, 2nd ed., 1972); G.R. Searle, *The Quest for National Efficiency 1899–1914* (Berkeley, U. Cal. Press, 1971); Romualdas Sviedrys, 'The Rise of Physical Science at Victorian Cambridge', in *Histor. Stud. in the Phys. Sci.,* vol. 2, 1970, pp. 127–151; Sir J.J. Thomson, *Recollections and Reflections* (London, Bell, 1936). The one famous attempt to deal directly with the subject, is of course, C.P. Snow's *Two Cultures* (N.Y., Mentor, 2nd ed. 1964), to which may be added a whole series of polemic replies, most notably that of F.R. Leavis *Two Cultures?* (Cambridge, C.U.P., 1962). But both of these writers do more to manifest a sensibility than explain how it emerged.

4. Henry Adams, *The Education of Henry Adams* (Boston, Houghton Mifflin, 1946 repr. of 1918; privately pub. in 1906), p. 451.

5. *ibid.,* p. 457.

6. John A. Lester, Jr., *Journey Through Despair 1880–1914; Transformations in British Literary Culture* (Princeton, Pr. Univ. Press, 1968); see also such works as Malcolm Bradbury, *The Social Context of Modern English Literature* (Toronto, Copp Clark, 1971) and David S. Thatcher, *Nietzsche in England 1890–1914* (Toronto, U. of Tor. Press, 1970).

7. See especially Forster's *Howard's End* (London, 1910).

8. Feuer, *op. cit.*

9. Noel Annan, 'The Intellectual Aristocracy' in J.H. Plumb, ed., *Studies in Social History* (London, Longmans, 1955), pp. 243–287.

10. Pierre Duhem, *La Théorie Physique: Son Objet, Sa Structure* (Paris, Rivière, 1906); trans. by P. Wiener as *The Aim and Structure of Physical Theory* (Princeton, Pr. Univ. Press, 1954).

11. Lord Rayleigh, 'Presidential Address to the British Association', Montreal, 1884, reprinted in Robert Bruce Lindsay, *Lord Rayleigh; The Man and his Work* (London, Pergamon, 1970), pp. 138–154, p. 152.

Scientific Revolutionaries of 1905: Einstein, Rutherford, Chamberlin, Wilson, Stevens, Binet, Freud

STEPHEN G. BRUSH

In the history of physics, 1905 is celebrated as the year when Albert Einstein published his remarkable papers on relativity, the photon theory of light, and Brownian movement. The previous decade had seen the discovery of X-rays, radioactivity and the electron, Planck's quantum theory, and the Rutherford-Soddy theory of atomic transmutation; these were soon to be followed by the Rutherford-Bohr model of the atom and the development of general relativity, matrix mechanics and wave mechanics. Together these events constituted a revolution in physics.

But radical changes were also occurring in other sciences: a new theory of the origin of the solar system and the formation of the planets and satellites; a new method for estimating the age of rocks (and thus the minimum age of the earth); the revival of Mendelian genetics and the establishment of the role of chromosomes in determining sex and other characteristics; a new method for measuring human intelligence; and a theory of the unconscious sexual basis of behavior. In each case 1905 marks the birth (not the conception or maturity) of a major discovery or theory. In this paper I discuss some aspects of the events in physics, geogony, biology, and psychology, as a tentative effort to identify common themes and interrelations in the late-nineteenth-century context.

Our understanding of revolutions in science is based primarily on the history of physical science; the phrase "second scientific revolution," sometimes applied to the early-twentieth-century developments,[1] assumes that the first revolution was that associated with the Copernican heliocentric theory and the adoption of the mechanical laws of Galileo and Newton. Thomas S. Kuhn's theory of scientific revolutions is a generalization from such examples.[2] Kuhn postulates that scientists tend to adopt a definite conceptual framework or "paradigm" as an unquestioned basis for research, until insuperable difficulties block their progress; then they may switch to a new paradigm without a completely rational justification. Since the set of important problems and the criteria for their satisfactory solution change along with the paradigm, it is difficult to see linear progress toward a single goal of scientific knowledge when one looks back across the discontinuities formed by scientific revolutions. The need for occasional revolutions might be inferred from the view that no single paradigm can guarantee continued success since it depends on one of several equally valid ways of looking at the world, each of which is bound to prove inadequate if pursued to the exclusion of the others. (At this point one might establish a connection between Kuhn's ideas and the otherwise very different "thematic" analysis of Gerald Holton.[3])

Kuhn's theory has come under heavy attack from historians and philosophers of science. Aside from the general complaint that Kuhn uses the terms "paradigm" and "revolution" in an imprecise and inconsistent fashion, philosophical critics object to his giving license to the dogmatic adoption of paradigms that are not subject to objective assessment; this seems to permit a lowering of standards of scientific rigor, especially among behavioral and social scientists who have welcomed Kuhn's conception of science and used it to justify their own pet dogmas.[4,5] Historians protest that Kuhn has not analyzed any single revolution in enough detail to prove that it conforms to his model; the Copernican Revolution, on which Kuhn has written most extensively, lacks his "crisis" stage based on the perception of anomalies which is supposed to lead to the breakdown of the earlier paradigm.[6]

Nevertheless, Kuhn's theory is the most widely known explanation of scientific change *outside* the professions of history and philosophy of science, and some people with experience in scientific research have endorsed the accuracy of his description of how scientists behave.[7] Indeed, if there were not a substantial amount of truth in Kuhn's theory, it could not have survived criticism for so long. Thus, we have a paradox: A philosophical-historical thesis about science has been rejected by philosophers and historians of science but kept alive by others who write about science.

Is it possible to improve Kuhn's theory so as to retain its valid core while removing the objectionable features? The most important attempt so far is Imre Lakatos' "methodology of scientific research programmes." Lakatos provides a retrospective rational justification for changes from one research programme to another, but only at the cost of ignoring how such changes actually occurred.[8] His theory is, therefore, just as unsatisfactory to historians as Kuhn's is to philosophers.[9]

My view is that theories such as those of Kuhn and Lakatos are inadequate to explain major scientific revolutions because they concentrate on theory-change within a single scientific field. I suggest that one should look more carefully for interactions between fields and for historical factors common to developments in several fields. This is not a new approach, but I think that it has not been adequately exploited.[10]

I suspect that no single formula will ever explain all scientific revolutions, but we should be able to understand the major ones better than we do now. Since there have only been two revolutions big enough to be called "Scientific Revolution" (implying changes in several sciences at the same time), perhaps we do not really need to show that they have the same structure. In any case, I am not proposing a general theory of scientific revolution.

1905 ± ?

At first glance one is struck by the different time-scales of the first and second Scientific Revolutions. The first one seems to have been dragged out over two or three centuries, as is suggested by the title of A.R. Hall's book *The Scientific Revolution 1500–1880,* whereas the second one is often limited to 1895–1930. I think this contrast is somewhat misleading, since one can argue that the breakdown of Newtonian mechanical philosophy really began around 1800 and proceeded throughout the nineteenth century, even though scientists at that time did not realize that they were participating in the early stages of a revolution.[11] Moreover, if one includes the impact of science on technology as part of the revolution (as is often done), it is clear that the later stages extend at least into the 1950's. Thus, the "acceleration of history" has only amounted to a factor of two since the seventeenth century, much less than Henry Adams and modern writers on "exponential growth" have estimated.[12]

Yet it is remarkable how many landmark events did happen in a single decade. Even without the discoveries in physics mentioned above, the list is impressive.[13]

Mathematics: David Hilbert announced the agenda for the twentieth century with his famous list of unsolved problems (1900). Henri Lebesgue formulated the modern concepts of length, area, and volume in his "measure theory" (1902, 1903). Bertrand Russell published his first attempt to subsume mathematics under logic (1903). Maurice Frechet generalized functions to functionals (1906).

Astronomy: T.C. Chamberlin and F.R. Moulton threw out the nebular hypothesis for the origin of the solar system in 1900 and replaced it by the planetesimal theory in 1905 (see below). J.C. Kapteyn analyzed stellar motions into two streams, giving the first glimpse into large-scale galactic dynamics (1904). Annie Jump Cannon began publishing her descriptions of stellar spectra in 1901, leading to the massive *Henry Draper Catalogue* and the modern system of spectral classes of stars. Ejnar Hertzsprung, building on this work and on Antonia Maury's discrimination of the sharpness of spectral lines, established the distinction between giant and dwarf stars and proposed the color-magnitude graph (now called the "Hertzsprung-Russell diagram") which is the basis for theories of stellar evolution (1905–1907). George Ellery Hale erected a 60-inch telescope on Mt. Wilson (1908) and had already begun raising funds for a 100-inch telescope, thus opening a new era of galactic research.

Geophysics: B.B. Boltwood and R.J. Strutt, applying Rutherford's discoveries on radioactive transmutation, developed the techniques of radioactive dating and showed that the earth's age is to be reckoned in billions of years rather than only in a few tens of millions as had been believed in the nineteenth century (1905–1910). John Milne, R.D. Oldham, and others developed the new science of seismology to the extent that it became possible to infer details of the internal structure of the earth (1900–1906), and the San Francisco earthquake of 1906 stimulated H.F. Reid to propose his "elastic rebound" theory. Kristian Birkeland and Carl Störmer began their studies of the polar aurora and analyzed the motion of charged particles in the earth's magnetosphere (1902–1903 and the following years).

Chemistry: H.F.W. Siedentopf and Richard Zsigmondy invented the ultramicroscope, opening up colloid chemistry (1902–1903). Walther Nernst introduced the quantum theory to physical chemistry and proposed the third law of thermodynamics (1906). G.N. Lewis conceived his electronic theory of valence (the "cubic atom") in 1902 though he did not publish it until 1916.

Biology: The rediscovery and establishment of Mendel's principles by Hugo de Vries, Carl Correns, and Erich von Tschermak-Seysennegg (1900) began the modern development of genetics. Identification of the role of "chromosomes" in sex determination by Clarence McClung (1902), Correns (1903), Nettie Stevens (1905), E.B. Wilson (1905–1909) and later T.H. Morgan suggested that the inheritance of other traits might also be associated with definite parts of the reproductive cells. The role of specific chemical substances, "hormones," in physiological processes, was established by W.M. Bayliss and E.H. Starling (1904–1905).

Psychology: Alfred Binet and Theodore Simon published their first scale for the measurement of intelligence in 1905; as subsequently revised (1908) it became the basis for the "intelligence quotient" which L.M. Terman popularized as a quantitative method of classifying human minds. Together with the related "Scholastic Aptitude Test," the IQ test has had an enormous impact on American education and race relations. Sigmund Freud's theory of the unconscious mind, developed in a series of major publications from 1898 to 1915, transformed psychiatry and is often supposed to have provoked a revolution in sexual behavior.

Anthropology: Franz Boas was appointed in 1899 to the faculty at Columbia University, where he trained the next generation of anthropologists. Boas and his disciples threw out the nineteenth-century Darwinian preconceptions about primitive and advanced stages of cultural evolution in favor of detailed study of societies on their own terms. The result was a "cultural relativity" that continues to shock many Americans—witness the MACOS controversy[14]—by denying the existence of universal standards of behavior. Boas vigorously attacked the racial theories that had been derived from nineteenth-century evolutionary principles. In 1906, invited by W.E.B. DuBois to speak at Atlanta University, Boas urged Blacks not to accept the inferior status which whites were trying to impose on them and asserted that there is no scientific basis for racism. In a landmark study of the headforms of descendants of immigrants to the United States (1908–1910) Boas showed that the numerical measurements ("cephalic index") previously used by anthropologists to identify racial types did not determine a fixed inherited property; the head form was significantly affected by environmental factors in one or two generations.

Technology: The internal combustion engine powered two new modes of transportation. The Wright brothers achieved the first successful controlled flight of a heavier-than-air device in 1903 and publicly demonstrated the practicality of their aeroplane in 1905. Ransom Olds introduced the first *cheap* automobile in 1901, quickly followed by Henry Ford with his Model A (1903) and Model T(1908); within a few years mass production techniques allowed millions of Americans to buy the new horseless carriages. Guglielmo Marconi obtained a patent for "wireless telegraphy" in 1896, and sent the first radio messages across the Atlantic Ocean in 1901. With J.A. Fleming's diode valve (1904) and Lee de Forest's triode (1906), the Electronic Age was born.

Albert Einstein (1879–1955)

During the past ten years, historians of physics have given considerable attention to Einstein's early work and its relation to contemporary developments in electromagnetism and optics, quantum theory, and Brownian movement.[15] Perhaps the most important conclusion of these studies is that Einstein was not responding to the failure of classical theories to account for specific experimental results, but rather was attempting to find a unified viewpoint and a set of fundamental principles that would lead to satisfactory descriptions of phenomena previously handled in an arbitrary or inconsistent way by existing theories. In 1905 Einstein could not yet point to measurements that agreed with his formulas better than those of his rivals, although such measurements were available a few years later. Nor could he claim that his theories offered comprehensible explanations of physical processes in the sense of the mechanistic science of the seventeenth to nineteenth centuries. His theories introduced a bizarre world in which light behaves like both waves and particles, random molecular motions can reverse the flow of entropy, and clocks run more slowly in speeding vehicles. Behind all this was Einstein's vision of a world governed by a unified set of mathematical laws and formal principles so right and necessary that, once uncovered, they would have to be recognized forever by both God and man.

Since Einstein did not succeed in finding his unified theory, it is difficult for us to discuss its philosophical implications or its intellectual links to the other ideas that were born at the beginning of the twentieth century. Instead, we must be content to examine the consequences of the restricted doctrines he actually published in 1905.

The special theory of relativity denies the existence of absolute space, but that idea had already been sharply cirticized by Leibniz, Mach, and others. More radical was Einstein's rejection of absolute time, and his claim that it is meaningless to say two events occur simultaneously unless they are also at the same place. Previously, time had been conceived as an independent factor, a great river flowing along, almost a *cause* of events. If one could make time stand still, one could imagine the entire universe stopped in its tracks, a cosmic freeze frame. Not only physical processes, but biological evolution and human consciousness were governed by the steady flow of time. Now Einstein was suggesting that time is a dependent variable, influenced by the circumstances of the observer; he was telling his Swiss hosts that the clocks and watches on which they lavished so much painstaking craftsmanship were not universal time-keepers—they could not even be synchronized by owners in different frames of reference. Time was not continuous, uniform, and unique, but contingent, a collection of all the sequences of discrete events in the lives or "world-lines" of all the atoms in the universe.[16]

A few years earlier Ludwig Boltzmann had analyzed the great generalization of nineteenth-century thermodynamics: The entropy of the universe is always increasing as time goes on. If entropy is interpreted as molecular disorder, as Boltzmann proposed, then there may be random fluctuations that cause local decreases in entropy, though he doubted whether these would ever be observed. If the universe goes through long-period cycles, then entropy must decrease as often as it increases in order to return to its initial value. Boltzmann suggested that for biological organisms the direction of time is determined by the direction of entropy increase. Hence, the statement "entropy increases with time" is a tautology: For sentient beings existing during the entropy-decreasing phase of the cosmic cycle, all processes would be running backwards (from our point of view); time itself would be reversed; and they could also conclude that "entropy increases with time."[17]

Probably no one took this idea seriously before 1905, not even Boltzmann himself. But Einstein's theory of Brownian movement pinpointed a physical situation in which atomic fluctuations have visible consequences, so that a statistical interpretation of thermodynamics is inescapable. Einstein himself did not draw the conclusion that time runs backward during such fluctuations, but Boltzmann's views on entropy retained enough respectability during the following decades that the philosopher Hans Reichenbach could elaborate the concept of alternating cosmic time directions in a perfectly serious manner in 1956,[18] and at least a few cosmologists have introduced the concept into theories of the expanding-contracting universe.[19]

According to Einstein the limits on what we can know about time (or anything else) are set by the properties of light signals.[20] But light, he tells us in his "photoelectric effect" paper of 1905, comes in discrete packages, quanta or "photons." Though photons also have some wavelike properties, the old picture of light or radiation as a continuous process must be abandoned when we get to the atomic level. Does this mean that time no longer flows smoothly but jerks along in small bursts? We still do not know whether one can legitimately draw this conclusion or what it would mean if we could.[21]

Ernest Rutherford (1871–1937)

In Einstein's relativity theory, the quantitative difference between space and time dissolves into a mere quantitative distinction between frames of reference, as does that between mass and energy; in his theory of light, the dichotomy between waves and particles is resolved by a mathematical formula that unites both entities ($E = h\nu$); and in his theory of Brownian movement the gap between macroscopic and microscopic realms is bridged by the intermediate realm of colloidal particles in suspension. This remarkable feature—the transformation of quality into quantity—is equally well illustrated in the radioactive transmutation theory of Rutherford and Soddy (1902–1903).[22] The chemical elements, thought to be distinct kinds of substances since the apparent failure of Prout's hypothesis, could now be transformed into each other according to the "new alchemy." It was soon recognized that different elements were simply different ways of organizing the same basic raw material, the building blocks being protons and electrons, plus—as was later found—neutrons. With the help of the theories worked out by Bohr, Pauli, Heisenberg, and Schrödinger, one could deduce "in principle" all chemical properties of an atom from the number of positive charges in its nucleus.

In 1905 Rutherford showed that one could use the experimentally determined rates of radioactive decay of radium and uranium to estimate the ages of rocks. J.W. Strutt, building on Rutherford's earlier work, succeeded in obtaining similar results at about the same time.[23] Thus, with the help of the notion of radioactivity as a random series of discrete events—made explicit as a statistical theory in 1905 by Egon von Schweidler—geological time could now be measured.[24]

To understand the historical significance of the determination of the age of the earth by radioactive dating, we must go back to the mid-nineteenth century.[25] At that time geologists were attempting to estimate the times of past events by measuring the rates of slow processes like weathering and erosion, assuming that these processes had been going on at about the same rate for as long as was necessary to produce the observed effects. Darwin relied on such estimates when he suggested in the first edition of the *Origin of Species* in 1859 that something like 300 million years of geological history might be available for evolution by natural selection.

The geologists' habit of postulating time scales of several million years (or indefinitely longer) was denounced in the 1860's by William Thomson (later Lord Kelvin), one of the giants of nineteenth-century science. Thomson adopted the prevalent theory that the earth had gradually cooled down from a hot molten ball, in line with the nebular hypothesis for the origin of the solar system. Assuming that no internal sources generated new heat, and that all heat transfer within the earth took place by conduction, he estimated that no more than 100 million years and probably no more than 20 million years had elapsed since the solidification of the earth. Whatever the numbers might turn out to be, Thomson was sure that at some finite time in the past the earth had been too hot, and at some finite time in the future would be too cold, for human habitation.

Although Darwin deleted the 300-million-year estimate from later editions of the *Origin of Species* and his theory did not really depend on any particular time scale, Thomson's low estimate of the age of the earth was generally regarded as an objection to evolution as well as a criticism of geological theory. One way of avoiding this objection was to postulate that environmental effects might accelerate evolution so that it could produce the desired effects in a shorter time. Such postulates were examples of the "neo-Lamarckian" versions of evolution popular at the end of the nineteenth century.

Thomson's theory of the cooling of the earth was closely connected with his principle of the dissipation of energy (1852), later incorporated by Clausius into the generalized second law of thermodynamics: entropy increases with time. Since high entropy means disorder (Boltzmann) and reduced availability of energy for doing useful work (Thomson and Clausius), one could interpret the Second Law as an assertion that things must go from bad to worse. Why should this be so? Blame it on the steady flow of time which causes all things to decay.

The discovery of radioactivity at once suggested that the age of the earth need not be limited in the way Thomson had claimed. With a previously unknown source of energy to balance the heat lost from the original store, the hot initial state could be pushed into the distant past, while the cold final state receded into the indefinite future. "Doomsday Postponed!" was the first public reaction to such suggestions. Radioactive dating quickly stretched the geological time scale by two orders of magnitude, from Thomson's 20 million years, past Darwin's 300 million years, to the immense figure of three to five *billion* years.

Thomas Chrowder Chamberlin (1843–1928)

Thomson shared with nineteenth-century geologists the assumption that the earth cooled down from a hot liquid ball, though they differed on the length of time occupied by the cooling process. An offshoot of this assumption was the idea that there was once a dense atmosphere rich in carbon dioxide which absorbed the sun's radiation; then, when the carbon dioxide disappeared from the atmosphere, there was an abrupt drop in temperature, precipitating the Ice Age.[26]

Chamberlin, a Wisconsin geologist, specialized in the study of glacial rock formations. Curiosity about the cause of ice ages led him to examine theories of ancient climates and the composition of the earth's original atmosphere. In 1892 the Irish physicist G. Johnstone Stoney (the origina-tor of the term "electron") pointed out that the absence of hydrogen from the earth's atmosphere and the apparent lack of any atmosphere on the moon could be explained by the kinetic theory of gases: A significant frac-tion of the lighter molecules would be expected to have speeds exceeding that needed to escape the gravitational field of the earth or moon, and over a long period of time these gases would leak out into space. Accord-ing to Maxwell's velocity distribution law, the number of molecules hav-ing such high velocities should increase with temperature. Chamberlin realized that Stoney's arguments invalidated the concept of a hot primi-tive earth with a dense atmosphere; at temperatures high enough to melt rocks, not only carbon dioxide but oxygen and nitrogen would be quickly dissipated into space. Thus the nebular hypothesis, in so far as it attrib-uted the formation of the earth to condensation from a hot gas, was re-futed by the fact that the earth still retains the gases in its present atmosphere.[27]

Chamberlin recruited Forest Ray Moulton, a young astronomer at the University of Chicago, to help him analyze the quantitative details of existing theories and develop a satisfactory alternative scheme for the ori-gin of the earth. In 1900 Chamberlin and Moulton published comprehen-sive critiques of the nebular hypothesis, bringing together old and new objections in a way that persuaded many astronomers of the inadequacy of Laplace's theory. One of the major discrepancies was that most of the angular momentum in the solar system is carried by Jupiter and the other great planets, whereas according to the nebular hypothesis angular mo-mentum should be concentrated in a rapidly spinning sun.[28]

Chamberlin and Moulton proposed a two-stage theory of the origin of the solar system, published in full in 1905: In the first stage, another star passed near the sun and drew gaseous material from it by tidal forces. (In the original version of the theory this stage was described as the for-mation of a spiral nebula, but subsequent work in astronomy showed that the spiral nebulae have a much greater size than could be associated with a single solar system.) In the second stage, the gaseous material has cooled and condensed into solid particles of various sizes—the planetesimals—which then collect together to form the planets and satellites.

The nebular hypothesis was based on a gradual process of cooling and condensation, with only the *minimum* amount of discontinuity needed to explain the formation of discrete bodies in the solar system; but the

Chamberlin-Moulton theory began with a single catastrophic event (encounter of two stars), and then attributed the formation of planets to a random sequence of discrete, inelastic collisions of the planetesimals. Moreover, Chamberlin rejected the doctrine of monotonic cooling of the earth, arguing instead that cold planetesimals would generate heat by their infall and rearrangement, allowing the possibility that the earth could warm up and later cool down.[29]

Since cosmogonists subsequently rejected stellar encounter and returned to something like a nebular hypothesis for the origin of the solar system after 1945, the Chamberlin-Moulton theory is sometimes considered obsolete, though its second stage—formation of the planets by accretion of planetesimals—survives in many modern theories.[30] Chamberlin does not now seem to be as important a revolutionary as Einstein and Rutherford, but that is partly because we tend to judge past scientists on the basis of present theories. In his own time Chamberlin played a pivotal role in the breakdown of a simplistic evolutionary cosmology; some of his ideas were rejected, but others have been incorporated in a more sophisticated, modern version of evolutionary cosmology.

Edmund Beecher Wilson (1856–1939)

At the end of the nineteenth century, Darwin's theory of evolution was in sad shape. The notion that natural selection, simply by acting on random variables, could explain the transformation and development of all biological species, no longer seemed plausible. Instead, biologists found it necessary to assume that the environment somehow acts directly on the process of inheritance, somewhat as Lamarck had suggested.[31] In psychiatry and criminology, the theory of "degeneration" proposed by Benedict Augustin Morel in 1857 gained considerable popularity.[32] According to Morel and his followers, the vices and misfortunes of parents affect the hereditary endowment of the offspring, causing insanity, physical debility, moral weakness, and many other stigmata of degeneracy. The offspring will be even more vulnerable to the temptations and degradations that afflicted their parents, and so the following generation will decay even further. (This process is imaginatively portrayed in Emile Zola's Rougon-Macquart series of novels, written when the theory of degeneration was in vogue.)[33]

In 1900 the doctrine that biological evolution is a gradual, inexorable process, pushed either up or down by environmental circumstances, was assaulted by the revival of Mendel's theory of heredity. As for the Chamberlin-Moulton theory, we must not let hindsight distort our assessment of the impact of this innovation. Since the 1940's we know that Darwinism and Mendelism can be combined into a consistent "synthetic" theory of evolution, but that was not at all evident in 1900. Mendelian genetics appeared to be quite inconsistent with Darwinian evolution—as it was then understood. In focussing on the transmission of characteristics from one generation to the next, Mendel's theory appeared to deny any role to the environment and set aside the question of long-term change. Heredity was atomized: The chromosomes (and later their constituent genes) were independent units that could be shuffled around almost randomly at each mating, and they determined traits in a mathematically precise fashion regardless of any external factors that might act on the developing embryo (at least that was how it seemed in 1900).[34]

When E.B. Wilson began his career in the 1880's, some of the groundwork for this discrete, hereditarian viewpoint was being laid by the German biologists August Weismann and Theodor Boveri. Weismann argued that the "germ plasm" is isolated from the rest of the organism and claimed that his experiments proved the *non*-inheritance of acquired characteristics (if you cut off the tails of three blind mice they can still produce offspring with tails and good eyesight). Boveri (in whose laboratory Wilson worked in 1891-1892) established the individuality of chromosomes as identifiable parts of cells and found evidence that each chromosome may be responsible for a definite part of the hereditary endowment of an organism. In the first edition of his influential book on *The Cell in Development and Inheritance* (1896), Wilson, therefore, placed the seat of heredity in the chromosomes in the cell nucleus. This work helped prepare American biologists to receive Mendel's work when it was independently rediscovered and confirmed four years later by de Vries, Correns, and Tschermak-Seysenegg.

For Wilson the central problem of biology was to explain how the individual organism develops from the fertilized egg and how that egg arises from the parental organisms. A synthesis of genetics and embryology was needed, and for this purpose Wilson concentrated on cytology, the study of the cell. The cell nucleus carries the chromosomes that determine the hereditary endowment of the organism and guide the development of the embryo into the adult.

Since the seventeenth century, biologists had debated whether the development of an organism is merely the "unfolding" ("evolution" in its original sense) of a performed miniature carried by the egg or sperm, or instead involves the sequential appearance of new and more complex structures from an undifferentiated ovum. This battle—"preformation" versus "epigenesis"— had apparently been won by the epigenesists in the nineteenth century on purely empirical grounds: The most detailed microscopic observations showed that the egg lacks the structure of the adult. But epigenesis lacked any theoretical explanation of how this structure developed, unless one postulated "vital forces" of some kind.

In his presidential address to the New York Academy of Sciences published in 1905, Wilson argued that recent research offered a solution to the problem. Embryology had established epigenesis as a fact; Mendelian genetics and cytology now provided a physical basis for the assumption that there is a particular *substance* "peculiar to each species of plant or animal that is transmitted in the germ-cells and has the power to determine the development of the egg according to its nature.... This physical basis is represented by a substance contained within the nucleus." But the nucleus itself has a complex structure, "apparently one that must be conceived as a kind of primary or original preformation."[35]

Thus, Wilson introduced a viewpoint that could be characterized, in earlier terminology, as a synthesis of epigenesis and preformation, the former describing development, the latter heredity.[36] The implication of his viewpoint for twentieth century biology is that neither epigenesis, with its overtones of vitalism, nor preformation, with its connotations of determinism, is an appropriate fundamental principle; and indeed, one rarely finds either word in the contemporary literature. Both heredity and development can be seen as random processes[37] controlled in very specific ways by molecular entities.

Nettie Maria Stevens (1861–1912)

One of the first major achievements of twentieth-century biology, linking embryology to the new genetics, was the discovery of the mechanism of sex determination by chromosomes. Previously it was thought that environmental factors such as nutrition played a major role in determining the sex of the developing embryo.[38] Wilson expressed the prevailing nineteenth-century view in the 1900 edition of *The Cell:*

> We are not yet able to state whether there is any one causal element common to all known cases of sex-determination. The observations cited above, as well as a multitude of others that cannot here be reviewed, render it certain, however, that sex as such is not inherited. What is inherited is the capacity to develop into either male or female, the actual result being determined by the combined effect of conditions external to the primordial germ-cell.[39]

Wilson himself helped to establish the opposite conclusion during the next two decades: The sex of the embryo is fixed at conception by the combination of two particular chromosomes, known as X and Y. In most species, including humans, the combination XX produces a female while XY produces a male. The Y chromosome acts like a Mendelian dominant unit (for maleness) and the X like a recessive (for femaleness). The simplest version of Mendelian theory then predicts a 50-50 male-female ratio.[40]

According to most textbooks on genetics or its history, the discovery of the chromosome mechanism for sex determination was primarily due to Wilson and Nettie M. Stevens, who found in 1905 that several species of insects produced two kinds of sperm, clearly distinguishable by size. The larger was shown to produce females on fertilization, the smaller to produce males. Microscopic examination also showed that the difference in sperm size was due to the presence or absence of an extra "X" chromosome; in some cases, where it was absent, a smaller "Y" chromosome took its place. The Mendelian theory was then applied (as indicated above) by Wilson and T.H. Morgan, so that sex was the first trait whose inheritance could be directly associated with a simple identifiable set of genetic particles.

The textbook account is misleading in two ways: first, in ignoring the historical fact that the discovery involved the work of several other biologists (especially C.E. McClung and Carll Correns) and did not occur all at once in 1905; second, in creating the impression that Wilson did most of the crucial work. It is usually stated that the 1905 contributions of Wilson and Stevens were "independent," but since Wilson was much better known and published more extensively on the subject, he tends to accrue more credit through the operation of the "Matthew effect" as described by Robert Merton.[41]

A comprehensive account of the discovery of chromosomal sex determination cannot be given here, but it is appropriate to say something about the neglected contribution of Nettie Stevens. It appears that few people have ever heard of her work, not even those who are now trying to publicize female scientists as "role models" to encourage girls to have scientific careers.

Stevens was born in Vermont, worked for some time as a librarian, and entered Stanford University at age 31. In 1900, having obtained a B.A. and an M.A. in physiology from Stanford, she transferred to Bryn Mawr where she did doctoral research under the direction of T.H. Morgan. It is interesting to note that Bryn Mawr, a small women's college, was one of the best places in the United States to do graduate work in biology at that time; E.B. Wilson taught there before he went to Columbia in 1891, and he was succeeded by Morgan (now regarded as the leading geneticist of the early twentieth century) who followed Wilson to Columbia in 1904. Stevens received her Ph.D. from Bryn Mawr in 1903 and stayed on as a research associate with a grant from the Carnegie Institution of Washington.

Morgan supported Stevens' grant application with a letter describing what was originally intended as a joint project on the factors determining sex in aphids and other insects. The letter makes it clear that he was looking for the effects of factors such as nutrition on the developing embryo; it was her idea to investigate the role of chromosomes. Wilson also wrote a letter of recommendation for Stevens, calling her "not only the best of the women investigators, but one whose work will hold its own with that of any of the men of the same degree of advancement."[42]

Stevens first succeeded in establishing the function of sex chromosomes in *Tenebrio mollitor,* the common meal worm:

> Since the somatic cells of the female contain 20 large chromosomes, while those of the male contain 19 large ones and 1 small one, this seems to be a clear case of sex-determination... the spermatozoa which contain the small chromosome determining the male sex, while those that contain 10 chromosomes of equal size determine the female sex. This result suggests that there may be in many cases some intrinsic difference affecting sex, in the character of the chromatin of one-half of the spermatozoa, though it may not usually be indicated by such an external difference in form or size of the chromosomes as in Tenebrio.[43]

Her manuscript containing this result was submitted to the Carnegie Institution on May 23, 1905, and was sent on May 29 to Wilson, as a member of the Institution's advisory committee, for review. He returned it on June 13 with a highly favorable recommendation, and it was published in the Carnegie monograph series in September 1905.

On May 5 Wilson had sent his own paper on chromosomes to the *Journal of Experimental Zoology.* He had chosen a species of insect *(Anasa tristis)* in which the male has one less chromosome than the female, rather than a smaller chromosome as is usually the case. In a note added in proof, he stated that he had "determined beyond the possibility of doubt" that the male has only 21 chromosomes while the female has 22; this result was not explicitly given in the original text of the paper. Moreover, he acknowledged that he had learned about Stevens' results in the meantime. His paper was published in the August 1905 issue of the *Journal of Experimental Zoology,* and thus it may appear that he gained priority over Stevens. However, one must take account of the following facts:

1. Wilson probably did not arrive at a firm conclusion regarding the nature of sex determination before he had seen the manuscript of Stevens'

paper, thus his discovery cannot really be called "independent" of hers. 2. He was a member of the editorial board of the *Journal of Experimental Zoology*, which may account for the relatively prompt publication of his paper—the same issue contained a paper by Stevens that had been submitted in December 1904, a delay of eighth months compared to three for Wilson! 3. The actual publication of Wilson's paper may not have been earlier than that of Stevens', since at least one biologist, Ross G. Harrison, *received* Stevens' paper a day before Wilson's.[44] 4. Wilson and Stevens were not discovering exactly the same thing, since the Y chromosome, which is essential in determining maleness in many species, is absent in Wilson's *Anasa tristis*. 5. In an article published later in 1905, Wilson expressed grave doubts that sex could be completely determined by chromosomes, and seemed to revert to a semi-environmental theory.[45] Stevens, perhaps because her knowledge of the subject was less extensive, was more certain that the role of the chromosomes is decisive.

According to Nettie Stevens (which was not generally accepted by other biologists for two or three more decades), sex is determined by a single random event rather than by a gradual process involving the environment. And, of course, the mechanism for creating an organism requires the encounter of two parents, just as Chamberlin's mechanism for creating a family of planets requires the encounter of two stars. By contrast, Rutherford's mechanism for the creation of a "daughter" element, while based on a random event independent of the environment, is a form of nonsexual reproduction; creation of elements by fusion, Prout's dream, was not yet realized.

Alfred Binet (1857–1911)

The proposition that human traits are determined primarily by heredity rather than environment gained strong support from the introduction of the "intelligence test" by Binet and Simon in 1905. But it would be a serious mistake to interpret their work only in terms of today's controversies about the correlation of IQ with race and socio-economic background. Binet did emphasize the use of a numerical scale—mental age—as an appropriate measure of intelligence at any given chronological age. But he never claimed that the ratio of these ages was a constant, fixed at birth for each person, and his colleague Simon lived long enough to denounce the subsequent abuse of the IQ concept as a betrayal of Binet's real contribution to psychology.[46] Binet was an anti-environmentalist only in the limited sense that he opposed certain extreme environmentalist theories popular in his own day—association psychologies that attributed the entire content of the mind to outside sources, and the degeneration theory (mentioned above) that postulated environmental effects on the process of inheritance itself.[47]

Binet developed his intelligence test at least partly as a response to the social demand that special education be provided for children who seemed incapable of learning in a "normal" fashion, yet were not completely helpless. Educators and public officials wanted a method for identifying and classfying children according to varying degrees of deviation from the norm—"idiots," "imbeciles," etc.—so that they could be assigned to curricula designed for their limited capacities. As a consequence of Binet's work, we now define this as the problem of the diagnosis and treatment of "mental retardation."

In his early studies Binet encountered the prevailing doctrine that almost any kind of mental or physical abnormality is to be ascribed—in the absence of an obvious, specific cause—to hereditary degeneration. He attended the lectures and hypnotic demonstrations of the famous Paris psychiatrist J.M. Charcot, an advocate of the degeneration theory. But Binet gradually became skeptical about the validity of organic explanations of mental disturbance.

One premise of the degeneration theory was common to other psychological doctrines of the late nineteenth century: that mental capacity can be measured by physical examination or simple physiological tests. Binet devoted considerable effort to trying out mental tests based on this premise and eventually rejected them. He found that neither the "stigmata of degeneracy" such as physical deformity nor the efficiency of sensory perception could give any reliable indication of the intelligence of a subject. He was especially struck by the example of Helen Keller, who was obviously intelligent although blind, deaf, and mute. Binet proposed to *define* intelligence in terms of complex mental processes—judgment, understanding, and memory—and to *measure* it using those processes.[48]

In order to design a reliable intelligence test for defective children, Binet had to study the intelligence of normal children, to find out what intellectual tasks they could perform at different ages. He discovered that abnormal children could be roughly equated, in intelligence, to normal children who are much younger; in other words one often cannot tell from the answers to test questions whether the child is normal or abnormal unless the age is known. Thus, Binet's test eventually yielded a "mental age," not based simply on the number of right answers but on the subject's approximate level of mental functioning. A child who could successfully perform all the tasks at the five-year level was then given the six-year tasks, and so on until the limit of failure was reached. Inherent in this scheme is the assumption (on which Jean Piaget later built his theory of child development) that each child goes through the same well-defined sequence of qualitatively different mental stages.

For Binet, mental growth is a series of discrete steps taken at times which are unpredictable—and perhaps socially influenced—for each individual, though statistically regular in a population. Some children are "retarded" in the sense that they take longer than average to reach a given mental age and may never reach the normal adult stage; others are advanced. Nowhere in his writings did Binet claim that each person makes continuous progress at a constant rate (mental age/chronological age); he did not structure psychological time that way.

Nevertheless Binet's test was quickly adopted and exploited by those who believed that intelligence is a hereditary trait, like sex determined at conception by a combination of chromosomes. In 1916 Lewis M. Terman at Stanford University published an American version, the "Stanford-Binet" intelligence test. Following a suggestion by W. Stern, Terman defined the "intelligence quotient" as 100 times the ratio of mental age to chronological age. The Stanford-Binet was standardized on 1,000 white California children (excluding all foreign-born), in such a way that the average IQ of the population was 100 by *definition* from ages three to sixteen.[49]

Terman suggested that the IQ test could save money for society by early identification of those most likely to become criminals—he argued that the criminal is a person too stupid to learn that crime does not pay. Industry could also economize by weeding out applicants not smart enough to do the job.

The issue of racial differences in IQ was first raised when an early version of Binet's test was given to 1,700,000 U.S. soldiers during World War I; it was found that whites scored significantly higher than blacks, on the average. The controversy about whether this difference is due to heredity or environment (or some combination of both) continues to the present day.[50]

In contrast to the violent disagreements about white and black intelligence resulting from the IQ test, Binet's work has indirectly led to a consensus on the issue of sex differences in mental ability. Earlier, it was generally believed that males are intellectually superior to females, though a few are greatly inferior. But Terman's early results indicated that girls score a little bit *higher* than boys on the Binet test. Naturally, he did not conclude from this fact that females are really more intelligent than males; instead, the test had to be adjusted by eliminating those questions that seemed "unfair" to boys. (I suppose one could argue that the test contained a "cultural bias" against boys—Binet developed many of his test questions by trying them out on his two daughters.) Thus in the later "standardized" Stanford-Binet IQ tests, boys and girls have the same average IQ at every age—but this is part of the *definition* of IQ, not a *result* of the test.[51] Psychologists were willing to abandon the presupposition of inherent male supriority and support the axiom that general intelligence is the same for both sexes (on the average), although research continues on sex differences in special mental abilities. They were not willing to accept the result that females may have slightly higher general intelligence than males; this seems to be one of those cases in which an anomaly is not allowed to refute the theory but is removed by minor adjustments. Compare the result that whites have higher intelligence than blacks, which was perfectly acceptable (to white, male psychologists) and thus did not call for any adjustment of the test!

Terman also refuted the long-held opinion that the *variability* of intelligence is less among females than males, this being a supposed explanation for the alleged fact that both geniuses and idiots are more frequent among males. His conclusion that the statistical distribution of IQ is about the same in both sexes implied that social factors are responsible for the paucity of great women scientists and philosophers, and thus provided an argument for improving educational opportunities for women and encouraging them to enter professional careers.[52]

Finally, it should be noted that Terman, in his "longitudinal" study with Melita Oden of 1,000 gifted children, starting in 1921, dispelled the stigma attached to those who display intellectual precocity. Degeneration theorists such as Cesare Lombroso had emphasized the similarity between genius and insanity, assuming that a large deviation from the norm in *either* direction is bound to produce instability of the personality. Terman and Oden showed that gifted children do not grow up to be less healthy, or sexually maladjusted compared to normal children.[53]

Sigmund Freud (1856–1939)

Revolutions are sometimes started by people who only want to perfect an existing structure by sanding down its rough spots and scraping away encrusted dirt, but reveal in this process unexpected cracks in the foundation. Their followers tear down the whole thing and construct a new system based on the master's ideas, but which he may find it hard to accept. Einstein rejected quantum indeterminism though he had in effect invented it himself.[54] Binet did not live long enough to see his intelligence test transformed into the IQ test, but he certainly would not have believed that every child should be tagged for life with a single number that determines his or her educational and career opportunities (and even marriage partner, if one went along with some of the "eugenic" schemes proposed in the early twentieth century). The absurdity of a one-dimensional quantification of the human mind is perhaps nowhere more evident than in the assignment of IQs to historical "Men of Eminence" by Terman's colleague Catherine Cox.[55] Some sample ratings: Goethe 210, Leibniz 205, Newton and Voltaire each 200, Napoleon 145. Surely the most important characteristics of these minds fail to be captured by such numbers!

Sigmund Freud did not wait for his relatively timid followers to push his doctrines to a ridiculous extreme—he did that himself. Because of his reckless habit of applying his speculative theories everywhere despite missing or contrary evidence, Freud is the only one of the seven revolutionaries of 1905 who is not generally acknowledged to be a true scientist. The recent posthumously-published biography of Woodrow Wilson was the final proof, for many otherwise sympathetic readers, that Freud had no compunctions about using his psychoanalytic method as a hatchet to dismember personalities he disliked, rather than as the therapeutic surgeon's knife he claimed it to be.[56] To reduce the greatest achievements of the human race to the products of anal-neurotic compulsion or frustrated incestuous desires seems even more detestable than to certify a person as a genius or a potential criminal on the basis of an IQ score assigned at age seven.

But we cannot understand a scientific revolution by conducting a post mortem on the corpse 70 years later; we must return to its conception, birth, and early development, to see what circumstances allowed or encouraged it to burst forth on the world. It is not the present scientific status of Freud's theory that concerns us, or even its influence on contemporary human sexual behavior, but its historical role in the transition from nineteenth-century to twentieth-century psychology. It is appropriate to focus on the "birth trauma" associated with Freud's *Three Contributions to the Theory of Sex*, published in 1905.[57]

The leading psychiatrists of the late nineteenth century—Charcot, Valentine Magnan, Paul Mobius, Charles Féré, and Richard von Krafft-Ebing—had been struck by the bizarre sexual perversions practiced by their patients, but refused to admit any connection between such behavior and that of "normal" people. Instead, they ascribed perversions, along with idiocy, insanity, and criminality, to the effects of hereditary degeneration. This diagnosis implied that nothing could be done to bring the patient back to a normal human state; one could only protect society by incarcerating and sterilizing degenerate persons, or by allowing the rigors of natural selection to weed out these "unfit" members of the race. For those like Max Nordau who attributed all the ills of society—including modern art—to degeneration,[58] the notion that abnormal behavior might be caused by a conflict between human nature and the mores of civilized society would have been as unacceptable as the proposal that productive citizens be taxed to support those who could not take care of themselves.

Freud asserted that sexual perversions are not due to degeneration but to "normal" tendencies pushed in certain directions by early experiences. (He credited Binet with the observation that fetishes result from early sexual impressions.)[59] He was an environmentalist insofar as he believed that mental disturbances are caused by the patient's previous interactions with other people, especially parents and siblings. At the same time he maintained that sexuality is a universal driving force, and that its channeling in the ordinary European family situation leads almost inevitably to certain psychodynamic structures or "complexes" found in adult men and women.[60] Neuroses, psychoses, and perversions can be understood as smaller or larger deviations from the normal state, and their symptoms can be alleviated—if not completely eliminated—by uncovering the repressed subconscious memory of the traumatic experience that triggered the deviation.

The differences between Binet's and Freud's psychological theories are obvious, but there are also similarities. Both were led from a concern with abnormal people to a general theory of the human mind, placing abnormals on a continuum with normals rather than isolating them as helpless or dangerous degenerates. Both postulated a discrete series of stages in the psychic development of the child, though for Binet these were small steps (marked by the ability to succeed in specific test items), whereas for Freud they were major transitions affecting the entire personality (the oral, anal, and genital stages). Both argued that as the human mind matures, it develops a distinct structure that deals with complex mental processes (including judgment, reasoning, and conscious memory), and this structure must be studied on its own terms apart from the physical, organic, or subconscious factors that may appear to influence it. The ego, the intelligent mind, is not reducible to a collection of reflexes, drives, and instincts.

Just as mental age for Binet does not coincide with chronological age but may run ahead or crawl behind in a jerky fashion, Freud's unconscious mind has its own peculiar clock whose hands move in response to events rather than to the mere passage of time.[61] In some respects the final outcome is determined because the external events must eventually occur in all but the most extreme cases. Binet's children sooner or later learn to speak a language and to perform the necessary tasks of daily life. Freud's little girl and Freud's little boy see and compare each other's naked bodies; the girl develops penis envy, the boy a castration complex. "Anatomy is destiny" for Freud means that women must develop a different (and ultimately inferior) kind of mind as a result of learning about the differences of their bodies from men's.[62] "IQ is inherited" means (not for Binet but for some of his followers) that American blacks, on the whole, cannot escape intellectual inferiority and a low socioeconomic status except by being adopted by white families and educated in predominantly white schools.[63]

Conclusions

The single common factor that appears to link the scientific revolutions of 1905 is a change in the perception of *time,* from an absolute, uniformly-flowing, independent variable to a contingent, discrete variable dependent on random events. More concisely, the transition was from an evolutionary world view infected by physical dissipation and biological degeneration, to a stochastic world view shaken and possible rejuvenated by collisions and catastrophes.[64] Others have commented on this kind of connection between theories in different sciences—e.g., the analogy between Freud's psychodynamics and catastrophic interpretations of the earth's early history—but more historical research on the interactions of the sciences at the beginning of the twentieth century is needed in order to establish its significance.[65]

Other factors give deeper insight into the nature of particular theories. *Atomism,* in the general sense of a particular view of substances or phenomena previously thought to be continuous, is involved not only in the new concept of time, but in Einstein's theories of Brownian movement and of light, Rutherford's theory of radioactivity, Chamberlin's concept of the material from which the earth formed, and the Boveri-Wilson-

Stevens-Morgan concept of the chromosomes as carriers of heredity. An emphasis on mathematical formulations or *quantification* of concepts previously described in qualitative or crudely mechanistic ways can be found in Einstein's relativity, Mendelian genetics applied to sex determination by chromosomes, and Binet's intelligence scale. *Dualism,* the description of phenomena in terms of the interaction of two opposing entities, is characteristic of Einstein's theory of light (retaining wave and particle aspects), Chamberlin's postulated stellar encounter leading to the formation of the solar system, Wilson's sex chromosome theory, and Freud's psychodynamics (including both male and female aspects within each single mind).

Yet in many ways these ideas were reversions to earlier doctrines. While Einstein, Binet, and Freud were not part of the academic establishment in 1905, the others did have university positions, and the three Americans—Chamberlin, Wilson, and Stevens—were receiving substantial financial support from the Carnegie Institution. All of them were working in scientific communities that expected new ideas to be generated as a matter of course. Despite the dogmatism of disciples, they were often cautious in advancing their theories: Einstein called his photon theory a "heuristic viewpoint," and Chamberlin initially advanced his planetesimal theory as only one of several working hypotheses rather than a permanent replacement for the existing theory.[66] All of them perhaps *should* have been cautious for some of the revolutionary ideas of 1905 were destined to be rejected by later generations.[67]

Anyone who proposes a new theory presumably thinks there is something unsatisfactory about the previous ones, yet it is often difficult for other scientists to see anything fundamentally wrong with the ideas until new ones have been developed. Thus, the notion that a scientific revolution requires a period of "crises" brought on by perceived failures of a dominant paradigm is inadequate, as long as one looks only at the situation within a single discipline. It is often difficult to identify exactly which paradigm is being overthrown by the revolution; for example, in the recent shift to Chomskyian linguistics, what was being replaced was not a specific doctrine in linguistics, but rather a more general attitude of positivism or behaviorism.[68] A satisfactory account of scientific revolutions in general or—if that is too much to expect—of a particular scientific revolution must take account of theories and viewpoints that cut across several disciplines, such as the monotonic evolutionary doctrine based on the nebular hypothesis or the theory of heredity degeneration. Such an account may also offer an explanation of the connections between scientific, philosophical, and cultural movements, all of which seem to have reached a turning point in 1905.[69]

Acknowledgments

This article owes much to the writings of Gerald Holton, although he was not in any way involved in its preparation. For useful comments and criticism I am indebted to Michael Gardner, Francis Haber, Paul Hanle, George Kauffman, Mary Matossian, and Thaddeus Trenn, none of whom should be held responsible for the gross errors and oversimplifications which any knowledgeable reader will undoubtedly detect.

The article is based on research supported by the National Science Foundation's History and Philosophy of Science Program.

Notes

1. M. Capek, "The Second Scientific Revolution," *Diogenes,* 1968, *63*:114–133. L. Badash, *Rutherford and Boltwood* (New Haven: Yale University Press, 1969), p. 1. I. Asimov, *Asimov's Biographical Encyclopedia of Science and Technology* (Garden City, N.Y.: Doubleday, 1964), p. 306. J.J. Beer and W.D. Lewis, in K.S. Lynn *et al., ed., The Professions in America* (Boston: Houghton Mifflin, 1965), pp. 110–130. J.D. Bernal, *Science in History* (Cambridge, Mass.: MIT Press, 1971), vol. 3, pp. 703, 993.

2. T.S. Kuhn, *The Structure of Scientific Revolutions* (Chicago: University of Chicago Press, 1962). Kuhn has revised his views in the second edition of this book (1970), pp. 174–210, and in F. Suppe, ed., *The Structure of Scientific Theories* (Urbana: University of Illinois Press, 1974), pp. 459–482.

3. G. Holton, *Thematic Origins of Scientific Thought: Kepler to Einstein* (Cambridge, Mass: Harvard University Press, 1973); "On the Role of Themata in *Scientific Thought,"* *Science,* 1975, *188*:328–338. An example of a Holtonian use of Kuhnian terms is Donna Haraway, *Crystals, Fabrics and Fields: Metaphors of Organicism in Twentieth-Century Developmental Biology* (New Haven: Yale University Press, 1976).

4. Philosophical critiques of Kuhn's theory: D. Shapere, "The Structure of Scientific Revolutions," *Philosophical Review,* 1964, *73*:383–394. J.W.N. Watkins, S.E. Toulmin, K.R. Popper, and M. Masterman, in I. Lakatos & A. Musgrave, eds., *Criticism and the Growth of Knowledge* (London: Cambridge University Press, 1970), pp. 25–37, 39–47, 51–58, 59–89. I. Scheffler, *Science and Subjectivity* (Indianapolis: Bobbs-Merrill, 1967). C.R. Kordig, *The Justification of Scientific Change* (Dordrecht: Reidel, 1971). D. Shapere, "The Paradigm Concept," *Science,* 1971, *172*:706–709. W. Berkson, "Some practical issues in the recent controversy on the nature of scientific revolutions," *Boston Studies in the Philosophy of Science,* 1974, *14*:197–209. R.L. Purtill, "Kuhn on Scientific Revolutions," *Philosophy of Science,* 1967, *34*:53–58. F. Suppe, in F. Suppe, ed., *The Structure of Scientific Theories* (Urbana: University of Illinois Press, 1974), pp. 135–151, 483–499. D. Böhler, "Paradigmawechsel in analytischer Wissenschaftstheorie?" *Zeitschrift für allgemeine Wissenschaftstheorie,* 1972, *3*:219–242. K. Tribe, "On the Production and Structuring of Scientific Knowledge," *Economy and Society,* 1973, *2*:465–478. A. Shimony, "Comments on two epistemological theses of Thomas Kuhn," *Boston Studies in the Philosophy of Science,* 1976, *39*:569–588. W.H. Austin, "Paradigms, Rationality, and partial Communication," *Zeitschrift für allgemeine Wissenschaftstheorie,* 1972, *3*:203–218.

5. Use of Kuhn's theory in behavioral and social sciences: Benjamin N. Ward, *What's Wrong with Economics?* (New York: Basic Books, 1972). D.A. Hollinger, "T.S. Kuhn's Theory of Science and its Implications for History," *American Historical Review,* 1973, *78:*370–393. Robert W. Friedrichs, *A Sociology of Sociology* (New York: Free Press, 1970). S.B. Barnes, "Sociological Explanations and Natural Science: A Kuhnian Reappraisal," *Archives of European Sociology,* 1972, *13:*373–393. J. Stephens, "The Kuhnian Paradigm and Political Inquiry: An Appraisal," *American Journal of Political Science,* 1973, *17:*467–488. M. de Vroey, "La Structure des Revolutions Scientifiques et les Sciences Economiques," *Revue des Questions Scientifiques,* 1974, *145:*57–70. H. Martins, "The Kuhnian 'Revolution' and its Implications for Sociology," in *Imagination and Precision in the Social Sciences: Essays in Memory of Peter Nettl* (London: Faber & Faber, 1972), pp. 13–58. E.M. Segal and R. Lachman, "Complex Behavior or Higher Mental Process: Is there a Paradigm Shift?" *American Psychologist,* 1972, *27:*46–55. L.B. Briskman, "Is a Kuhnian Analysis applicable to Psychology?" *Science Studies,* 1972, *2:*87–97. C.G.A. Bryant, "Kuhn, Paradigms and Sociology," *British Journal of Sociology, 1975, 26:*354–359. E.L. McDonagh, "Attitude Changes and Paradigm Shifts; Social Psychological Foundations of the Kuhnian Thesis," *Social Studies of Science,* 1976, *6:*51–76. D.S. Palermo, "Is a Scientific Revolution taking place in Psychology?" *Science Studies,* 1971, *1:*135–155. C.-J. Bailey, "Trying to Talk in the New Paradigm," *Papers in Linguistics,* October 1971, *4* (no. 2):312–338. J.B. Lodahl and G. Gordon, "The Structure of Scientific Fields and the Functioning of University Graduate Departments," *American Sociological Review,* 1972, *37:*57–72. H. Kuklick, "A 'Scientific Revolution': Sociological Theory in the United States, 1930–1945," *Sociological Inquiry,* 1973, *43:*3–22. George Ritzer, *Sociology: A Multiple Paradigm Science* (Boston: Allyn & Bacon, 1975). A.W. Imershein, "Organizational Change as a Paradigm Shift," *Sociological Quarterly,* 1977, *18:*33–43. J.D. Novak, *A Theory of Education* (Ithaca: Cornell University Press, 1977). T. Thoresen, "Art, Evolution, and History: A Case Study of Paradifm Change in Anthropology," *Journal for the History of the Behavioral Sciences,* 1977, *13:*107–125.

6. Historical critiques of Kuhn's theory: N. Koertge, *A Study of Relations between Scientific Theories: A Test of the General Correspondence Principle,* Ph.D. Thesis, University of London, 1969 (Ann Arbor, Mich.: University Microfilms, order no 76-8180). R.J. Hall, "Kuhn and the Copernican Revolution," *British Journal for the Philosophy of Science,* 1970, *21:*196–197. J.C. Greene, "The Kuhnian Paradigm and the Darwinian Revolution in Natural History," in D.H.D. Roller, ed., *Perspectives in the History of Science and Technology* (Norman: University of Oklahoma Press, 1971), pp. 3–25. Stephen Toulmin, *Human Understanding,* vol. 1 (Princeton: Princeton University Press, 1972), p. 103. K. Meyer, "Das Kuhnsche Modell wissenschaftlicher Revolutionen und die Planetentheorie des Copernicus," *Sudhoffs Archiv,* 1974, *58:*25–45. O. Gingerich, "Crisis versus Aesthetic in the Copernican Revolution," *Vistas in Astronomy, 1975, 17:*85–93. D.O. Edge and M.J. Mulkay, *Astronomy Transformed: The Emergence of Radio Astronomy in Britain* (New York: Wiley, 1976), pp. 386–394. H. Mehrtens, "T. S. Kuhn's Theories and Mathematics: A Discussion Paper on the "New Historiography" of Mathematics," *Historia Mathematica,* 1976, *3:*297–320. Numerous private communications.

7. N. Wade, "Thomas S. Kuhn: Revolutionary Theorist of Science," *Science,* 1977, *197:*143–145. M. Ruse, Review of Lakatos & Musgrave, eds., *Criticism and the Growth of Knowledge,* in *Theory and Decision,* 1972, *3:*187–190. T.P. Swetman, "The Response to Crisis—A Contemporary Case Study," *American Journal of Physics,* 1971, *39:*1320–1328. B. Jones, "Plate tectonics: A Kuhnian Case?" *New Scientist,* 1974, *63:*536–538. W.J.

Fraser, "On Paradigms," *Science,* 1971, *173*:868–870. A Hallam, *A Revolution in the Earth Sciences* (New York: Oxford University Press, 1973), p. 108.

8. I. Lakatos, "Falsification and the Methodology of Scientific Research Programmes," in I. Lakatos and A. Musgrave, eds., *Criticism and the Growth of Knowledge* (London: Cambridge University Press, 1970), pp. 91–195 (see p. 138 for an admission that the actual history is ignored in applications of the methodology). I. Lakatos, "History of Science and its Rational Reconstructions," *Boston Studies in the Philosophy of Science,* 1971, *8*:91–136 (see p. 107 for an argument that the philosopher should *improve* history rather than be governed by it). E. Zahar, "Why did Einstein's Programme supersede Lorentz's?" *British Journal for the Philosophy of Science,* 1973, *24*:95–123, 223–262. P. Urbach, "Progress and Degeneration in the 'IQ Debate,'" *British Journal for the Philosophy of Science,* 1974, *25*:99–135, 235–259. A. Elzinga, *On A Research Program in Early Modern Physics* (New York: Humanities Press, 1972). Y. Elkana, "Boltzmann's Scientific Research Programme and its Alternatives," in Y. Elkana, ed., *The Interaction between Science and Philosophy* (Atlantic Highlands, N.J.: Humanities Press, 1974), pp. 243–279. C. Howson, ed., *Method and Appraisal in the Physical Sciences* (New York: Cambridge University Press, 1976).

9. A.I. Miller, "On Lorentz's Methodology," *British Journal for the Philosophy of Science,* 1974, *25*:29–45. M.A.B. Deakin, "On Urbach's Analysis of the 'IQ Debate,'" *British Journal for the Philosophy of Science,* 1976, *27*:60–65. T.S. Kuhn, "Notes on Lakatos," *Boston Studies in the Philosophy of Science,* 1971, *8*:137–146. R.J. Hall, "Can we use the History of Science to Decide between competing Methodologies?" *Boston Studies in the Philosophy of Science,* 1971, *8*:151–159. K.F. Schaffner, "Einstein versus Lorentz: Research Programmes and the Logic of Comparative Theory Evaluation," *British Journal for the Philosophy of Science,* 1974, *25*:45–76. P. Feyerabend, "On the Critique of Scientific Reason," in C. Howson, ed., *Method and Appraisal in the Physical Sciences* (New York: Cambridge University Press, 1976), pp. 309–339. N. Koertge, "Rational Reconstructions," *Boston Studies in the Philosophy of Science,* 1976, *39*:359–369. S.G. Brush, "A Geologist among Astronomers: The Rise and Fall of the Chamberlin-Moulton Cosmogony," *Journal for the History of Astronomy* (in press).

10. In a recent essay, T.S. Kuhn argues that rather than study the history of the separate disciplines as they are now defined or the history of science as a whole at a given period, it is more fruitful to look at "clusters" of fields that were closely related for several centuries. Thus, the First Scientific Revolution involved primarily the "classical physical sciences" (astronomy, statics, optics) rather than the empirical Baconian sciences. By the late nineteenth century, the separation was no longer clear-cut, but other clusters had begun to form. "Mathematical vs. Experimental Traditions in the Development of Physical Science," *Journal of Interdisciplinary History,* 1976, *7*:1–31.

11. S.G. Brush, *The Kind of Motion We Call Heat* (Amsterdam: North-Holland, 1976), pp. 35–51. Also, see note 10 above.

12. Henry Adams, *The Degradation of the Democratic Dogma* (New York: Macmillan, 1919; reprint, New York: Capricorn Books, 1958), pp. 261–305; *The Education of Henry Adams* (reprint, Boston: Houghton Mifflin, 1961), chaps. XXXIII & XXXIV. D.J. de Solla Price, *Little Science, Big Science* (New York: Columbia University Press, 1963), pp. 1–32. Gerard Piel, *The Acceleration of History* (New York: Knopf, 1972), pp. 21–41.

13. Further information may be found in the following reference works: C.C. Gillispie, ed., *Dictionary of Scientific Biography* (New York: Scribner, 1970–1976). R. Taton, ed., *Science in the Twentieth Century* (New York: Basic Books, 1966).

14. J. Walsh, "NSF: Congress takes hard look at behavioral science course," *Science*, 1975, *188*:426–428.

15. J. Neu, ed., "One Hundred Second Critical Bibliography of the History of Science and its Cultural Influences (to January 1977)," *Isis*, 1977, *68*:Part 5, Index, and earlier bibliographies in this series.

16. Einstein's impact on the concept of time: M. Capek, *Philosophical Impact of Contemporary Physics* (Princeton, N.J.: Van Nostrand, 1961), Chapters III, VIII, XI, XII, XIII. Gerald Holton, "The Metaphor of Space-Time Events in Science," *Eranos-Jahrbuch*, 1965, *34*:33–78. J.D. North, "The Time Coordinate in Einstein's Restricted Theory of Relativity," in J.T. Fraser, F.C. Haber and G.H. Müller, eds., *The Study of Time* (New York: Springer-Verlag, 1972), 12–32.

17. L. Boltzmann, "Zu Hrn. Zermelo's Abhandlung über die mechanische Erklärung irreversibler Vorgange," *Annalen der Physik*, ser. 3, 1897, *60*:392–398; English translation in S.G. Brush, *Kinetic Theory*, vol. 2 (New York: Pergamon Press, 1966), pp. 238–245. See also L. Boltzmann, *Lectures on Gas Theory*, translated by S.G. Brush from the 1896–1898 edition (Berkeley: University of California Press, 1964), pp. 443–448.

18. H. Reichenbach, *The Direction of Time* (Berkeley: University of California Press, 1956).

19. See the references given in S.G. Brush, *The Kind of Motion We Call Heat* (Amsterdam: North-Holland, 1976), pp. 639–640 (note 29).

20. For clarification of Einstein's position on this point see C. Scribner, Jr., "Mistranslation of a Passage in Einstein's Original Paper on Relativity," *American Journal of Physics*, 1963, *31*:398.

21. Quantization of time: M. Capek, *op. cit.* (note 16), Chapter XIII; *Bergson and Modern Physics* (Dordrecht, Holland: Reidel, 1971), pp. 133–151, 198–207, 343.

22. E. Rutherford and F. Soddy, "The Radioactivity of Thorium Compounds," *Journal of the Chemical Society*, 1902, *81*:321–350, 837–850; "The Cause and Nature of Radioactivity, Part II, Section IX. Further Theoretical Considerations," *Philosophical Magazine*, ser. 6, 1902, *4*:584–585; "Radioactive Change," *Philosophical Magazine*, ser. 6, 1903, *5*:576–591. E. Rutherford, "The Succession of Changes in Radioactive Bodies," *Philosophical Transactions of the Royal Society of London*, A, 1905, *204*:169–219; all reprinted with commentary in A. Romer, ed., *The Discovery of Radioactivity and Transmutation* (New York: Dover, 1964).

     For the views of W. Crookes and others on the significance of this discovery, see L. Badash, "How the 'Newer Alchemy' was Received," *Scientific American*, 1966, *215*, no. 2:88–95.

23. Rutherford's estimate in 1904 (announced at the St. Louis Congress of Arts and Science) was 40 million years for a sample of fergusonite; this was not much longer than Lord Kelvin's earlier estimates of the age of the earth. In a section added to the second edition of his book *Radio-Activity* (Cambridge: Cambridge University Press, 1905), pp. 485–486, he boosted this to 140 million years and hinted that another mineral would turn out to be even older. At the end of a popular article on "Radium—The Cause of the Earth's Heat," *Harper's Magazine*, February 1905, pp. 390–396, he stated that the heat of atomic disintegration would be sufficient to maintain the sun's output of energy for 500 million years. A similar estimate for the age of rocks was given in his Silliman Lectures at Yale in March, 1905, published as *Radioactive Transformations* (New York: Scribner's Sons, 1906). R.J. Strutt's result of 2,400 million years was announced

slightly earlier ["On the radio-active minerals," *Proceedings of the Royal Society of London,* May 24, 1905, A76:88-101, recd. Feb. 28, read March 2], but there was some doubt about its validity; see L. Badash, ed., *Rutherford and Boltwood, Letters on Radioactivity* (New Haven: Yale University Press, 1969), pp. 56, 58-59, 64. For a general survey of this subject see L. Badash, "Rutherford, Boltwood, and the Age of the Earth: The Origin of Radioactive Dating Techniques," *Proceedings of the American Philosophical Society,* 1968, *112*:157-169. A recent historical article states flatly that Rutherford in 1905 was the first to determine the age of a geological object by radioactive methods: H.G. Fabian, "Zur Geschichte der Kalium-Argonu und der Rubidium-Strontium-Methode für die geologische Alterbestimmung," *NTM Zeitschrift für Geschichte der Naturwissenschaft, Technik und Medizin,* 1974, 11 (2):69-81. Most of the fundamental papers on radioactive dating are reprinted in C.T. Harper, ed., *Geochronology* (Stroudsburg, Pa.: Dowden, Hutchinson & Ross, 1973).

24. E. v. Schweidler, "Über Schwankungen der radioaktiven Umwandlung," *Premier Congrès International pour l'Étude de la Radiologie et de l'Ionisation tenu à Liège du 12 au Septembre, 1905,* Comptes Rendus (Bruxelles, 1906), Section de Physique, Langue Allemande, pp. 1-3; reprinted in T.J. Trenn, *The Self-Splitting Atom* (London: Taylor & Francis, 1977), pp. 156-159.

25. For details and references see S.G. Brush, "Thermodynamics and History," *The Graduate Journal* (University of Texas), 1967, 7:477-565; *The Temperature of History* (New York: Franklin, 1977), Chapter III. J.D. Burchfield, *Lord Kelvin and the Age of the Earth* (New York: Science History Pubs., 1975).

26. J. Tyndall, "On the Absorption and Radiation of Heat by Gases and Vapours, and on the Physical Connexion of Radiation, Absorption, and Conduction," *Philosophical Transactions of the Royal Society of London,* 1861, 1-36. S. Arrhenius, "Ueber die Erklärung von Klimaschwankungen in geologischen Epochen (Eiszeit, Eocaenzeit) durch gleichzeitige Veränderung des Gehaltes der Luft an Kohlensäure," *Verhandlungen der Gesellschaft Deutscher Naturforscher und Aerzte,* 1895, Th. 2, Hälfte 1, p. 41; "On the Influence of Carbonic Acid in the Air upon the Temperature of the Ground," *Philosophical Magazine,* ser. 5, 1896, *41*:237-276.

27. T.C. Chamberlin, "A Group of Hypotheses bearing on Climatic Changes," *Journal of Geology,* 1897, 5:653-683. Susan Schultz, *Thomas C. Chamberlin: An Intellectual Biography of a Geologist and Educator,* Ph.D. Dissertation, University of Wisconsin-Madison, 1976.

28. T.C. Chamberlin, "An Attempt to Test the Nebular Hypothesis by the Relations of Masses and Momenta," *Journal of Geology,* 1900, 8:58-73. F.R. Moulton, "An Attempt to Test the Nebular Hypothesis by an Appeal to the Laws of Dynamics," *Astrophysical Journal,* 1900, *11*:103-130. This discrepancy had been pointed out earlier by Babinet, though not as a fatal objection to Laplace's theory. J. Babinet, "Note sur un point de la Cosmogonie de Laplace," *Comptes Rendus Hebdomadaires des Séances de l'Academie des Sciences, Paris,* 1861, 52:481-484.

29. T.C. Chamberlin, "On Lord Kelvin's Address on the Age of the Earth as an Abode fitted for Life," *Science,* new ser., 1899, 9:889-901, *10*:11-18.

30. D. ter Haar and A.G.W. Cameron, "Historical Review of Theories of the Origin of the Solar System," in R. Jastrow and A.G.W. Cameron, eds., *Origin of the Solar System* (New York: Academic Press, 1963), pp. 1-37. W. Metz, "Exploring the Solar System (II): Models of the Origin," *Science,* 1974, *186*:814-818.

31. V.L. Kellogg, *Darwinism Today* (New York: Holt, 1907), pp. 1–9, 25–128. E. Radl, *Geschichte der Biologischen Theorien*, II. Teil (Leipzig: Engelmann, 1909), pp. 439–459, 539–565. E. Nordenskiöld, *The History of Biology* (New York: Knopf, 1928), pp. 562–571. P.J. Vorzimmer, "Darwin's 'Lamarckism' and the 'Flat-fish Controversy' (1863–1871)," *Lychnos, 1969–1970:* 121–170. T.H. Morgan, *Evolution and Adaptation* (New York: Macmillan, 1903), pp. 240ff. G. Allen, "Thomas Hunt Morgan and the Problem of Natural Selection," *Journal of the History of Biology*, 1968, *1*:113–139; "Hugo de Vries and the Reception of the 'Mutation Theory,'" *Journal of the History of Biology*, 1969, *2*:55–87.

32. B.A. Morel, *Traité des Degénérescences Physiques, Intellectuelles et Morales de l'Espece Humaine, et des Causes qui Produisent ces Variétés Maladives* (Paris: Bailliere, 1857).

33. S.G. Brush, *The Temperature of History* (New York: Franklin, 1977), Chapter VII.

34. History of Mendelian genetics: Hans Stubbe, *History of Genetics* (Cambridge, Mass.: MIT Press, 1973); Elof Axel Carlson, *The Gene: A Critical History* (Philadelphia: Saunders, 1966); J.S. Wilkie, "Some Reasons for the Rediscovery and Appreciation of Mendel's Work in the first years of the present century," *British Journal for the History of Science*, 1962, 1:5–18; E. Mayr, "The recent Historiography of Genetics," *Journal of the History of Biology*, 1973, *6*:125–154; P. Sentis, "La Naissance de la Génétique au Début du XXe Siècle," in *De la Méthode en Biologie* (Paris: Lethielleux, 1970), part 2, pp. 1–85.

35. E.B. Wilson, "The Problem of Development," *Science*, 1905, *21*:281–294.

36. Alice Levine Baxter, *Edmund Beecher Wilson and the Problem of Development*, Ph.D. Dissertation, Yale University, 1974, pp. 343–344; "Edmund B. Wilson as a Preformationist: Some Reasons for his Acceptance of the Chromosome Theory," *Journal of the History of Biology*, 1976, *9*:29–57.

37. This was not Wilson's own opinion; see G.E. Allen, "Wilson, Edmund Beecher," *Dictionary of Scientific Biography*, 1976, *14*:434.

38. History of ideas about sex determination: Scott F. Gilbert, *Sex Determination and the Embryological Origins of the Gene Theory*, M.A. Essay, Johns Hopkins University, 1975; G.E. Allen, "Thomas Hunt Morgan and the Problem of Sex Determination, 1903–1910," *Proceedings of the American Philosophical Society*, 1966, *110*:48–57. T.H. Morgan, "Recent Theories in Regard to the Determination of Sex," *Popular Science Monthly*, 1903, *64*:97–116.

39. Edmund B. Wilson, *The Cell in Development and Inheritance* (New York: Macmillan, second ed., 1900), p. 145. Wilson allowed this statement to remain in reprints of the book as late as 1919 (copy in University of Maryland library).

40. E.B. Wilson, "The Chromosomes in Relation to the Determination of Sex in Insects," *Science*, 1905, *22*:500–502; "Studies on Chromosomes. III. The Sexual Differences of the Chromosome Groups in Hemiptera, with some Considerations on the Determination and Inheritance of Sex," *Journal of Experimental Zoology*, 1906, *3*:1–40; "Sex Determination in Relation to Fertilization and Parthenogenesis," *Science*, 1907, *25*:376–379; "Recent Researches on the Determination and Heredity of Sex," *Science*, 1909, *29*:53–70. H.J. Muller, "Edmund B. Wilson—An Appreciation," *American Naturalist*, 1943, *77*:5–37, 142–172.

41. Some authors give the impression that T.H. Morgan made the discovery, without mentioning either Wilson or Stevens; this is extremely unfair since Morgan did not even accept the theory of "internal" (chromosome) determination of sex until 1910

despite the evidence of Stevens and Wilson. For further discussion and references see S.G. Brush, "Nettie M. Stevens and the Discovery of Sex Determination by Chromosomes," *Isis* (in press). For the general theory of the Matthew effect see R.K. Merton, "The Matthew Effect in Science," *Science,* 1968, *159*:56–63.

42. Quoted by permission of the Carnegie Institution of Washington; see Brush, *op. cit.* (note 41) for further details of the grant application.

43. N.M. Stevens, *Studies in Spermatogenesis* (Washington, D.C.: Carnegie Institution of Washington, Publication No. 36, 1905), p. 13. See also *Studies on the Germ Cells of Aphids* (Washington, D.C.: Carnegie Institution of Washington, Publication No. 51, 1906), pp. 15–19.

44. Baxter, *op. cit.* (note 36), p. 308.

45. E.B. Wilson, "The Chromosomes in Relation to the Determination of Sex in Insects," *Science,* 1905, *22*:500–502.

46. Theta H. Wolf, *Alfred Binet* (Chicago: University of Chicago Press, 1973), p. 203.

47. Wolf, *op. cit.,* pp. 5, 41–71, 172, 234.

48. Wolf, *op. cit.,* pp. 154–178. A. Binet and T. Simon, "Sur la Necessité d'etablir un diagnostic scientifique des États inférieurs de l'Intelligence," *L'Année Psychologique,* 1905, *11*:245–336; "Méthodes nouvelles pour le Diagnostic du Niveau Intellectuel des Anormaux, *ibid.* 191–244; "Application des Méthodes Nouvelles au Diagnostic du Niveau Intellectual chez des Enfants Normaux et Anormaux d'Hospice et d'École Primaire," *ibid.* 245–336; "Le Développement de l'Intelligence chex les Enfants," *L'Annee Psychologique,* 1908, *14*:1–94; English translations by E.S. Kite, in A. Binet and T. Simon, *The Development of Intelligence in Children* (Baltimore: Williams & Wilkins, 1916; reprint, New York: Arno Press, 1973), pp. 9–273. English translations of other works may be found in *The Experimental Psychology of Alfred Binet,* ed. R.H. Pollack & M.W. Brenner (New York: Springer, 1969). See also R.S. Lerner, *Dr. Alfred Binet's Contribution to Experimental Education,* Ph.D. Thesis, New York University, 1933.

49. Lewis M. Terman, *The Measurement of Intelligence* (Boston: Houghton Mifflin, 1916). On the early history of the IQ test see: K. Young, "The History of Mental Testing," *Pedagogical Seminary,* 1924, *31*:1–48; F.N. Freeman, *Mental Tests: Their History, Principles and Applications* (Boston: Houghton Mifflin, revised edition 1939); P.H. Dubois, *A History of Psychological Testing* (Boston: Allyn & Bacon, 1970). T.P. Weinland, *A History of the I.Q. in America, 1890–1941,* Ph.D. Dissertation, Columbia University, 1970. Russell Marks, *Testers, Trackers and Trustees: The Ideology, of the Intelligence Testing Movement in America, 1900–1954,* Ph.D. Dissertation, University of Illinois, 1972; Hamilton Cravens, *The Discovery of Man: American Scientists and the Heredity-Environment Controversy 1900–1941* (in press).

50. Race differences in intelligence, other applications of the IQ test: Claude Moore Fuess, *The College Board, its First Fifty Years* (New York: Columbia University Press, 1950). Mark H. Haller, *Eugenics: Hereditarian Attitudes in American Thought* (New Brunswick, N.J.: Rutgers University Press, 1963), pp. 115ff. D.J. Kevles, "Testing the Army's Intelligence: Psychologists and the Military in World War I," *Journal of American History,* 1968, *55*:565–581. C. Loring Brace *et al.,* eds., *Race and Intelligence* (Washington, D.C.: American Anthropological Association, 1971). Robert Cancro, ed., *Intelligence: Genetic and Environmental Influences* (New York: Grune & Stratton, 1971). Ken Richardson and

David Spears, eds., *Race and Intelligence* (Baltimore, Md.: Penguin Books, 1972). H.J. Eysenck, *The IQ Argument* (New York: Library Press, 1971). Evelyn Sharp, *The IQ Cult,* (New York: Coward, McCann & Geoghegan, 1972). Arthur R. Jensen, *Educability and Group Differences* (New York: Harper & Row, 1973). Carl Senna, ed., *The Fallacy of IQ* (New York: Third Press, Joseph Okpakum 1973). P. Urbach, *op. cit.* (note 8). Alan Gartner *et al.,* eds., *The New Assault on Equality: I.Q. and Social Stratification* (New York: Harper & Row, 1974). John C. Loehlin, Gardner Lindzey and J.N. Spuhler, *Race Differences in Intelligence* (San Francisco: Freeman, 1975).

51.   *L.M. Terman, op. cit.* (note 49), pp. 68–72. L.M. Terman and M.A. Merrill, *Measuring Intelligence* (Boston: Houghton Mifflin, 1937), pp. 22, 34. For a comprehensive review of research on this subject see Eleanor Maccoby and Carol Jacklin, *The Psychology of Sex Differences* (Stanford: Stanford University Press, 1974), Chapter 3.

52.   Cf. Charles Darwin, *The Descent of Man and Selection in Relation to Sex* (London, 1871), Chapter XIX; Havelock Ellis, *Man and Woman* (London: Scott, fifth edition, 1914), pp. 485–491. It is claimed that recent evidence does support greater variability in men, and that major genes relating to intelligence may therefore be located on the X-chromosome. See Robert Lehre, "A Theory of X-linkage of Major Intellectual Traits," *American Journal of Mental Deficiency,"* 1972, *76*:611–619.

53.   Lewis M. Terman and Melita H. Oden, *The Gifted Child Grows Up* (Stanford: Stanford University Press, 1947). Cesare Lombroso, *Genio e Degenerazione* (Palermo: Sandron, 1897). William Hirsch, *Genius and Degeneration, a Psychological Study* (New York: Appleton, 1896, trans. from German). John Ferguson Nisbet, *The Insanity of Genius* (London: Ward & Downey, 1891).

54.   S.G. Brush, "Irreversibility and Indeterminism: Fourier to Heisenberg," *Journal of the History of Ideas,* 1976, *37*:603-630. For a Freudian explanation see H.M. Schey, "Einstein's Rejection of Quantum Theory: A Personal Motive," *American Imago,* 1971, *28*:187-190.

55.   Catherine M. Cox, *The Early Mental Traits of Three Hundred Geniuses* (Stanford: Stanford University Press, 1926).

56.   Sigmund Freud and W.C. Bullitt, *Thomas Woodrow Wilson, Twenty-eighth President of the United States, A Psychological Study* (Boston: Houghton Mifflin, 1967).

57.   Sigmund Freud, *Drei Abhandlungen zur Sexualtheorie* (Leipzig: Deuticke, 1905). There are several English translations.

58.   Max Nordau, *Entartung* (Berlin: Duncker, 1892): English translation, *Degeneration* (New York: Fertig, reprint, 1968).

59.   Sigmund Freud, *Three Contributions to the Theory of Sex,* translated by A.A. Brill (New York: Dutton, 1962), p. 19.

60.   Freud's reluctance to deal with the impact of "external reality" in any more than a schematic fashion has created difficulties for psychohistory. See F. Weinstein and G.M. Platt, "The Coming Crisis in Psychohistory," *Journal of Modern History,* 1975, *47*:202-228.
      On the relations between Freud's theory and the late-19th century ideas about instincts, heredity, and degeneration, see: J.C. Burnham, "The Medical Origins and Cultural Use of Freud's Instinctual Drive Theory," *Psychoanalytic Quarterly,* 1974, *43*:193-217. L.B. Ritvo, "Darwin as the Source of Freud's neo-Lamarckism," *Journal of*

the American Psychoanalytic Association, 1965, *13*:499–517. *The Standard Edition of the Complete Psychological Works of Sigmund Freud*, vol. III (1893–1899) (London: Hogarth, 1962), pp. 143–156.

61. A. Bass, *MLN*, 1976, *91*:871–912.

62. Sigmund Freud, "Über die allgemeinste Erniedrigung des Liebeslebens," *Jahrbuch für Psychoanalytischer und Psychopathologische Forschung*, 1912, *4*(1):40–50; "Der Untergang des Ödipuskomplexes," *Internationale Zeitschrift für Psychoanalyse*, 1924, *10*:245–252. *The Standard Edition of the Complete Psychological Works of Sigmund Freud*, vol. 11, pp. 179–190 [see p. 189]; vol. 19, pp. 173–179 [see p. 178] (London: Hogarth Press, 1957, 1961).

63. S. Scarr and R.A. Weinberg, "IQ Test Performance of Black Children adopted by White Families," *American Psychologist*, 1976, *31*:726–739.
    For recent criticisms of the experimental evidence for inheritance of IQ, see N. Wade, "IQ and Heredity: Suspicion of Fraud beclouds classic Experiment," *Science*, 1976, *194*:916–919; L.J. Kamin, *The Science and Politics of IQ* (New York: Wiley/Halsted Press, 1974).

64. As early as 1908 one perceptive observer noted that scientific theories were no longer based on laws that led inevitably to a final state, but rather on self-propagating processes characterized by an "interval of instability and transition between initial cause and definite effect," and lacking a definite final state. Thorstein Veblen, *The Place of Science in Modern Civilization* (New York: Huebsch, 1919), pp. 36–37.

65. R.J. Weber, "Contributions to the History of Psychology: XV. Uniformitarianism in Geology and Behavior Modification," *Psychological Reports*, 1974, *34*:439–444. Gerald Holton, *Thematic Origins of Scientific Thought* (Cambridge: Harvard University Press, 1973), pp. 32–36. F.C. Haber, "The Darwinian Revolution in the Concept of Time," in J.T. Fraser, F.C. Haber and G.H. Müller, eds., *The Study of Time* (New York: Springer-Verlag, 1972), pp. 383–401.

66. Chamberlin's paper, arguing that a scientist should retain several different working hypotheses rather than committing himself to a single one, became so widely known that it was reprinted nearly 70 years after its first publication. "The Methods of Multiple Working Hypotheses," *Journal of Geology*, 1897, *5*:837–848; *Science*, 1965, *148*:754–7.

67. Einstein himself thought his photon hypothesis, but not his relativity theory, was "revolutionary—see Carl Seelig, *Albert Einstein, A Documentary Biography* (London: Staples Press, 1956), pp. 74, 82. Chamberlin called his own theory "revolutionary" in a letter to R.S. Woodward, February 11, 1910, p. 9 (in the Chamberlin file at the Carnegie Institution of Washington).

68. M.E. Winston, "Did a (Kuhnian) Scientific Revolution occur in Linguistics?" in Frederick Suppe & P.D. Asquith, eds., *PSA 1976*, vol. 1 (East Lansing, Michigan: Philosophy of Science Association, 1976), pp. 25–33.

69. S.G. Brush, *The Temperature of History* (New York: Franklin, 1977), Chapter 8.

Astrophysics at the Turn of the Century

GUGLIELMO RIGHINI

Sir Edward Appleton, in his introductory article to the first volume of the *Collected Papers of Lord Rutherford of Nelson,* states that when Rutherford left Cambridge to occupy his first chair of physics at McGill University, he "took the subject of radioactivity with him to Montreal," which in the words of Rutherford "...is a grand subject because there is so much in it that we don't know."

How Rutherford approached and developed a logical and rigorous line of research in all aspects of the radioactive phenomena is well known; less known perhaps is that, well in advance of the scientific thought of his time, he tried to investigate the cosmical aspects of radioactivity. In a lecture delivered before the Royal Astronomical Society of Canada on April 3, 1907, he discussed the radioactive state of the atmosphere, concluding that the amount of radium emanation present in the air was equal to that liberated from 200 tons of radium bromide in equilibrium. Since it was impossible to admit that much solid radium in the form of fine particles existed in the air, Rutherford, collecting data about the radioactivity of several type of rocks, concluded that the amount of radioactive material in the earth's crusts was so large that not only the radioactivity of the atmosphere was amply justified, but also that the internal heat of our planet can be explained by invoking the thermal emission which accompanies radioactive transformations. With some additional hypotheses, he was able to justify the rise of temperature in the depths of the crust to $1500°K$ at 45 miles of depth, a result, which with slight changes is still valid today. To reinforce his firm conviction, Rutherford added: "I hope that I have made clear to you how the study of radioactivity has profoundly altered our view on the earth's internal heat."

Rutherford tried to evaluate the age of some minerals to obtain the age of the earth; his results were too low—between 500 and 1,000 million years. But 30 years later, when discussing the origin of actinium, he concluded that "the earth cannot be older than 3.4 billions of years."

What is more important, from the point of view of the astrophysicist, are the questions that Rutherford posed in concluding his lecture to the Royal Astronomical Society from which it appears that he was well aware that the contraction theory of Kelvin and Helmoltz was completely insufficient to explain the energy output of the sun: "At the enormous temperature of the sun it is possible that ordinary matter may become radioactive, i.e., it may break up into simple forms, with the emission of a great quantity of heat.... This is only a speculation, but one that must be taken seriously into consideration in coming to a decision of the probable duration of the sun's heat, and consequently of the time for habitation of our globe."

It has to be remembered that these words were pronounced 70 years ago when the constitution of the atom was still very controversial, and when the nucleus was a sort of ghost which had not yet acquired the citizenship of the physical world. At that time the α particles were classified "either a charged hydrogen or an helium atom" and the β-rays were "similar to the electrons produced in the cathode ray discharge of a vacuum tube."

Although the explanation of the heat production inside the sun is not correct (we know that the energy is produced by fusion of protons and not by radioactive disintegrations of high structured atoms), Rutherford's ideas were well advanced compared with astrophysics which was still in its infancy. Of course, the concept of energy derived from the radioactivity of naturally occurring elements was important because it freed physicists and astronomers from the radicated concepts of the old chemistry. It became possible to think in terms of transformations of all manner of atoms. That the ideas so well expressed by Rutherford were not applicable to the sun and the stars became clear when it was found that the relative abundance of any element heavier than lead was too low for any appreciable quantity of energy to be generated by radioactive decay, but it was only in 1920 that Eddington suggested the possibility that the fusion of four protons in an helium nucleus could release an adequate amount of energy to keep the sun and the stars shining.

I mentioned that when Rutherford was teaching physics at McGill, astrophysics was still in its infancy or, to be more precise, was still developing the technical tools to investigate the physical nature of the celestial bodies. I mean "tools" in a wide sense because every advance in astrophysics is conditioned by a previous development of some branches of physics and of its applications.

In this line, for example, the Galilean discoveries of the nature of the moon, the structure of the Milky Way and of the Jupiter system were conditioned by a previous improvement in lens-making, in the production of pure and clean glass discs, and in the technique of observation.

The last decade of the nineteenth century saw the triumph of the refractor telescope with the inauguration in 1897 of the 40-inch instrument at Yerkes. But this triumph also marked the decline of this type of instrument, since the difficulty of obtaining larger, optically perfect, transparent glass discs was unsurmountable. Besides, the cost of the optical working of four surfaces was also very large. The controversy between astronomers in favor of refractors and those preferring the reflecting instrument—started by Joseph Fraunhofer with the construction of the Dorpat refractor of 9.6 inches of diameter in 1824 and followed by Giovan Battista Amici who designed and constructed a 28-centimeter acromat still in use at the Arcetri Observatory—died out. There was a general agreement to construct reflecting telescopes since Steinheil in Munich and Foucault in Paris had independently discovered how to deposit a reflecting thin silver layer on glass. The old system of constructing mirrors invented by Newton was then superseded by the new one, with great advantages in reflecting power. We see, therefore, a rapid flourishing of reflectors in several countries, telescopes that we would now classify as "medium-size instruments" with apertures between 75 and 125 centimeters. This was a premise to further developments in astrophysics, since a reflector is strictly achromatic and well suited for spectroscopic research.

The second half of the nineteenth century brought the astronomer another important means of research—photography. In the granducal library of Florence, now in the Institute of the History of Science, there is a small book of a little-known writer of the seventeenth century whose name is Silvano Belli. He entitled this booklet *Del misurar con la vista* which can be loosely translated *Of visual measurements.* In the introduction the author states that "Certamente è cosa meravigliosa il misurar con la vista ..." ("it is certainly a marvellous thing to measure with the sight"), and he explains how it is possible to measure visually the distance between two towns without going there. This is, in fact, how astronomers since early times have measured angular distances between stars or between planets and stars to find the positions of planets. To refine the measurements in the system of Jupiter, Galileo invented a simple form of micrometer, which was later improved and made practical by Gasgoigne and Azout. But, unfortunately, the human eye is not an impersonal and objective receiver, and we know that in the mechanism of vision there is always a psychological component. The well-known statement that "man sees with the brain not with the eyes" is, in fact, partially true, mainly when the eye has to work near the threshold of its sensitivity; the story of the Mars canals is a clear demonstration of this. Photography was the only means to avoid considerable trouble: the possibility of integrating the effect for long periods, the averaging of atmospheric fluctuations, and the production of a valid document of the observations are the main advantages of the photographic process.

History records a first attempt by the Frenchman Daguerre who obtained a "daguerreotype" of a partial solar eclipse in 1840, and perhaps in the same year, Draper in the United States, exposing for 20 minutes, had success with the full moon. For ten years, apart from some marginal improvements, the process invented by Daguerre was the only one available, and the Bonds at the Harvard Observatory in 1850 made a further step when they obtained images of the bright stars Vega and Castor. The other process, which employed a thin layer of collodion on a glass plate, was developed later, and although very cumbersome (requiring an elaborate preparation, on the spot, of a wet plate), it had several advantages over the daguerreotype. It seems that Warren de la Rue was the first astronomer to use this new process for the 1860 solar eclipse. Photographs of the moon and of the Donati comet were also obtained some years later, always with collodion plates which had a fairly good sensitivity and also a particularly good resolving power. But already in 1850, some photographer had substituted the wet collodion with dry eggwhite, making the photographic plate much more practical; finally around 1870 dry silver bromide gelatine allowed astronomers to photograph faint and even telescopic stars in a fairly short exposure. Thus, a new astronomical practice appeared: using the telescope to take photographs and then measuring them at leisure by day.

Besides increased accuracy, the photographic method allowed one to see, at the same time, all the stars in the field, so that favourable nights might be exploited to the full. The advent of photography and the trend to innumerable measurements of stellar positions was a revenge of the lens over the mirror. In fact, the reflecting telescope at that time had a very small field often limited to less than 1° (the Schmidt-telescope was invented more than 30 years later). But a multi-lens photographic objective could photograph a portion of the sky of 5° in diameter, covering therefore an area 25 times larger than the reflector. This great progress was the consequence of elaborate studies carried on by Seidel, Petzval, and realized practically by constructors like Chevalier, Steinheil, and Zeiss. Objectives of six or eight lenses were constructed for stars down to the fourteenth magnitude with very little measurable distortions in the field.

The success obtained by the brothers Paul and Prosper Henry, who realized excellent objectives for astronomical photography, was so remarkable that an International Conference in Paris in 1889 resolved to construct, by international cooperation, an atlas of the entire sky and a catalogue of exactly-measured star places down to the twelfth magnitude. This was the so-called "Carte du Ciel" enterprise which, unfortunately, took several decades. A similar enterprise of better quality has been realized in recent years thanks to the large Schmidt camera of Mount Palomar. A more practical presentation of a handy catalogue and atlas is the Smithsonian Astrophysical Catalogue published in 1966 which contains 260,000 stars and which has been elaborated with the aid of video-tapes and computers.

Except for the telescope and photography, no discovery has given so great an impetus to astronomy as the spectroscope. After Newton, who observed the colors which compose sunlight, Wollaston was able to see dark lines across the spectrum. But it was Fraunhofer in the second decade of the nineteenth century who mapped the position of more than 300 lines of the solar spectrum. The spectra of the moon, Venus, and Mars were similar to that of sunlight, while the spectra of some bright stars displayed only one line in common. This line given the letter D was later identified as the doublet of Sodium. The big advance in spectroscopy due to Kirchhoff in 1859 opened the important field of qualitative analysis of celestial bodies, which is more or less the beginning of modern astrophysics. Also remarkable in this first period of spectroscopy is the discovery of the Doppler effect (1842) which enabled astronomers to measure the radial velocity of all celestial bodies.

The first to apply the spectroscope to the stars, apart from Fraunhofer's early work, was Giovanni Battista Donati the astronomer who founded the Arcetri Astrophysical Observatory. Donati had the advantage of a good spectroscope constructed for this research by the optician Giovan Battista Amici, who was at that time the Director of the Observatory of Florence. The telescope used by Donati had a rather strange aspect since it was conical. At one end Donati used the famous burning glass (a thick lens of 30-cm diameter) which Benedetto Breganz gave as a present to the Grand Duke Cosimo III. Donati made drawings of the spectra of some stars noting the position of prominent lines. He was also the first to observe the spectra of some comets and made schematic drawings recording the most prominent molecular bands.

But the real founders of stellar spectroscopy were the Jesuit Father Angelo Secchi in Italy and Sir William Huggins in England. Secchi, who was Director of the Observatory of the Roman College located on the roof of the Church of Sant' Ignazio, examined the Spectra of more than 4,000 stars and classified them in four classes following the aspect of their spectra. In the first class he put the bluish-white or white stars like Sirius and Vega; the second class contained the yellow stars like the Sun, Cappella, and Arcturus; the third was the class of the red stars like Antares and Betelgeuse, and in the fourth class he included the red stars with a different kind of absorption band. Later a fifth class for stars showing bright lines or bands was added by Wolf and Rayet of Paris, the so called Wolf-Rayet stars.

The Secchi classification was the starting point for work with a new instrument for mass production of spectra: the "objective prism" telescope, whose invention is in part due to Angelo Secchi. This is a photographic telescope with a prism of a small angle in front of the objective: The point-like image of the star acts as a slit and one has a succession of monochromatic images which constitute the spectrum. With this instrument the Harvard College Observatory produced, in 1890, the famous "Draper Catalogue" in which 19,000 stars were classified in eight spectral classes. This catalogue was the basis for all studies on formation and evolution of the stars.

In the meantime Huggins in England succeeded in photographing the spectra of some bright stars using the dry plate process. He also made a first attempt to analyze the problems connected with the motion of the stars along the line of sight. Applying the Doppler effect to the spectrum of Sirius, he was able to find distinct evidence of a motion of recession. Following the pioneering work of Huggins and Vogel, Keeler and Campbell accumulated data about the line of sight velocity of 300 stars which enabled the astronomers to deduce the speed and direction of the movement of our sun among the stars. This was predicted by Bradley in 1748, but the full explanation was found only around 1930 by Lindblad, Oort, and others who, studying proper motions and line of sight velocities of a large number of objects, discovered the rotation of our Galaxy.

A by-product of the studies on the line of sight velocity of the stars was the discovery of spectroscopic binaries. Pickering at Harvard noted that in the spectrum of the star Ursae Majoris some lines appeared doubled. This was interpreted to mean that the star was double and that the two components were revolving around the center of gravity of the system. Later it was found that in some stars only one spectrum was visible, but that the radial velocity showed periodic variations. This is the case when in the double system only one star is bright and well visible. These systems were, therefore, double stars which the telescope was insufficient to resolve.

Huggins was also the first to study the spectra of nebulae. His work is limited to galactic nebulae since the galaxies were not well known although

Lord Rosse, with his large and famous telescope, had observed around 1850 fourteen spiral nebulae. Huggins found bright lines in the spectrum of diffuse nebulae, which was interpreted as the presence of gases in these objects. Some nebulae observed by him gave only a continuous spectrum indicating that they were probably unresolved star clusters.

Meanwhile the spectroscopic studies of the stars quickly adopted photography as a mean of investigation. Photometric researches, which sought to establish a scale of brightness or "magnitude" for all the stars and to study the variability of some of them, were more closely connected to the visual technique. This is well understandable if we consider that the photographic plate is not a linear detector but has peculiar properties which depend on several parameters like exposure time, temperature during the processing, and so on.

The systematic measurements of stellar brightness, initiated by the Herschels was continued in 1879 by Gould, who in his *Uranometria Argentina* estimated the magnitudes of 8,000 stars visible from Cordoba (Argentina). Several other catalogues of stars' magnitude were published in the last 20 years of the nineteenth century; the most conspicuous of them was the *Potsdamer Photometrische Durchmusterung* issued in 1894 which gave the magnitudes of 14,000 stars from the north pole to the celestial equator down to 7.5 magnitude. This catalogue is fundamental since it establishes the scale of magnitudes, taking the ratio of the brightness of the stars belonging to successive classes of magnitude, as 2.512 to 1, the so-called "Pogson Ratio" proposed by Pogson but based on Herschel's observations.

The photometric scale also had a favorable influence on the observations of variable stars, since results obtained from different observers could be compared and averaged.

Unfortunately, the knowledge of the distances of the stars at the end of the nineteenth century was very poor. The first parallax was measured by Bessel in 1838 for the star 61 Cygni; two years later Struve measured the parallax of Vega, but the measurements were difficult and not precise. The number of stars whose distance was known was 20 in 1880 and 60 at the beginning of the new century. But this small number of stellar distances was sufficient for Hertzsprung to compute the absolute magnitude and to trace in 1901 the famous diagram which is now known as the Hertzsprung-Russell diagram, after Henry Noris Russell developed and perfected the original idea of Hertzsprung.

But also the "meter" of the universe, i.e., the distance between the earth and the sun, was not well known at that time although the astronomer tried to profit of any favorable astronomical event for organizing international enterprises to measure the solar parallax.

In the second half of the century, the study of the sun advanced with rapid strides, although at first restricted chiefly to observation of the sunspots. In 1826 Schwabe, a chemist at Dessau in Germany, began to notice and register the sunspots regularly. After many years, comparing his notes he found that the number of sunspots showed a periodic variation: the maxima and minima returned after nearly ten years. Rudolf Wolf at Bern and Zurich investigated all the historical data about sunspots and traced the periodicity through the centuries. The mean value of the period was eleven and one-ninth years, but with large irregularities between seven and seventeen years.

Still more remarkable was a discovery by Lamont, at Munich, that the irregular perturbations of the magnetic instruments and the earth's magnetic field, also in a ten-year period, were alternately stronger and smaller. The aurorae connected with them showed the same periodicity. Sabine in England and Wolf in Switzerland immediately pointed out that the magnetic perturbations and the aurorae followed the sunspots not only in their periodicity, but also in all their irregular variations. Thus, a most remarkable and mysterious effect of solar disturbances upon terrestrial phenomena came to light.

More important than the simple counting of sunspots was determining their position and motion. The first object was to find the rotation period of the sun. One of the foremost workers in this field was Carrington, at Redhill, who determined the positions of sunspots in 1853–1861. He found that the period of rotation increased with the distance from the solar equator; his results were confirmed by similar work by Spoerer, a German amateur.

Photography, of course, was used to make pictures, and the abundance of light made it possible in a split second of exposure to register all the details of the sun's surface—the spots, faculae, and other markings—so that afterwards their number, their total surface, their shapes and movements, could be studied. A spectacular effect was obtained by combining two pictures in a stereoscope, one taken shortly after the other, when the sun had rotated to a small extent; in this way the sun was seen as a globe, with the dark spots as pits and the faculae floating at high level.

Besides this work, which was used chiefly for statistical purposes, there were refined technical methods for the study of the minute details in the structure of the spots and of the fine granulation of the undisturbed, photospheric surface. Here, it was the French astronomer, P. Jules C. Janssen, at Meudon, who excelled in his enlarged photographs of the granulation and the sunspots. Through a careful comparison of several photographs taken in rapid sequence, Hansky at Pulkovo in 1905 was able to determine the average lifetime of the separate granulae at two to five minutes; then they dissolved and were replaced by others.

When spectrum analysis arose in 1859–1862, chiefly through the work of Kirchhoff and Bunsen, the significance of the dark lines which Fraunhofer had observed in the spectrum of the sun at once became clear and enabled the solar physicist to perform a very careful qualitative analysis of the solar composition. Among the pioneers in solar spectroscopy, was Ångstrom, who in 1868 replaced Kirchhoff's arbitrary scale by the natural scale of wavelengths, expressing them in units of a ten-millionth of a millimeter, units which were later named after him.

A prominent achievement in the development of more powerful instruments to obtain better solar spectra was the construction of concave gratings in 1887 by Henry A. Rowland at Baltimore. Rowland perfected an engraving machine capable of automatically cutting fine grooves at exactly equal distances. The reward of his painstaking work was spectra which remained unequalled for dozens of years. With these gratings Rowland photographed the solar spectrum and published it in 1888 as an atlas of maps, on a constant scale of $1\text{Å} = 3$ mm., so that the entire spectrum between 3,000 and 6,900Å forms a 40-foot-long band. It contains more than 20,000 Fraunhofer lines in all intensities, from barely visible traces up to heavy, dark bands. By measuring the original photographs, Rowland was able to publish in 1896 a catalogue of all these lines, with their wavelengths given to three decimals (hence in seven figures) and their estimated numerical intensities, a standard work used henceforth by every astrophysicist. From the lines he could ascertain the presence of 36 terrestrial elements in the sun.

The first total eclipse after the introduction of spectrum analysis as a current technique in astrophysics was on August 18, 1868 in India, where numerous observers with spectral equipment witnessed the phenomenon. They all agreed, with only small differences in detail, that the spectrum of the prominences consisted in some few bright lines, and that, therefore, the prominences were glowing masses of gas. The brightest lines were the red and green emission lines of hydrogen (designated $H\alpha$ and $H\beta$) coinciding with Fraunhofer's C and F, and a yellow line, first taken for the sodium line D, afterwards seen to be different and denoted D_3. It was not known from any terrestrial spectrum and was, thus, ascribed to an element present only on the sun and called "helium."

The observed emission lines were so brilliant that one of the observers, Janssen from Meudon, immediately understood that the darkness of an eclipse was not needed to make them visible. The next day he placed the slit of his spectroscope just outside the sun's limb and could observe without difficulty the emission lines in full daylight. For some weeks he could study the sun "during a period equivalent to an eclipse of 17 days," as he reported to the Paris Academy. The same result was obtained by Lockyer in England.

At the eclipse of 1870 in Spain, Young discovered in the faint, continuous spectrum of the corona a narrow, green emission line; as it did not occur in any known spectrum, a second unknown solar element was assumed, called "coronium." Another important discovery was made by Young: Having set the slit of his spectroscope nearly tangent to the sun's limb, he saw at the moment of the eclipse, as in a flash, the flaring-up of an innumerable number of emission lines. After one or two seconds they disappeared, when the moon covered the thin layer of only one-inch-width (representing 700 km) that emitted them. It seemed as if all the Fraunhofer lines were for a moment reversed into bright lines because the gas layer absorbing them was seen sideways without the background of the sun; this outer layer was called the "reversing layer."

For the purpose of photographic observation of solar eclipses, an appropriate instrument was devised and constructed by Lockyer. He constructed the "prismatic camera" simply by placing a prism before the camera lens. A self-luminous object can then be pictured in as many images as it emits separate wavelengths, each image showing by its shape the distribution of its atoms emitting this line. A photograph taken at the exact moment of the "flash" shows all the metal lines of the reversing layer as short, narrow arcs, whereas the hydrogen lines and the H and K lines of ionized calcium present the prominences in their true form; the green corona line is pictured as a faint and broad luminous ring, sharply cut off at the inner edge by the limb of the dark moon. In 1893 the first imperfect photographs had been obtained showing, because the exact moment of the flash was missed, only the arcs of hydrogen, helium, H and K. After 1896 prismatic cameras were in regular use at every eclipse because of the vast amount of information they afforded. Mitchell in 1905 perfected the method by using a Rowland grating instead of a prism.

The mysterious coronal lines remained an important object of study at solar eclipses because all attempts to make them visible in full daylight had failed. Curiously, different observers at different eclipses reported new and different coronal lines not perceived before. A few of the brightest lines appeared regularly—besides the green line, a red and a violet line— but for the others there remained doubt as to whether they were real and whether the coronal spectrum were variable. For all these lines, the origin was unknown; perhaps there were more "coronium" elements.

In 1890–1891 Deslandres at Paris and George E. Hale at Chicago, independently and in somewhat different ways, constructed an instrument, called a "spectroheliograph," to obtain monochromatic pictures of the sun. The slit of a spectrograph was made to slide over the sun's image; a firmly connected second slit behind the prism, allowing only the narrow emission line to pass, slid over the photographic plate. Pictures of the sun in the light of one wavelength were made in Chicago and at the Yerkes Observatory. To conduct a more profound study, Hale founded the "Solar Observatory" at Mount Wilson, where later the restricting word "solar" was dropped. The regular study of these pictures, most in the light of the calcium K line and the hydrogen Hα or Hγ, revealed an abundance of remarkable structures.

The spectrum of the sunspots was also the object of many researches since most metallic lines in the spot spectrum with great dispersion show a reversal in their center, a bright line separating the dark line into two components. They were considered to be of the same character as the bright emissions in the center of the hydrogen and H and K lines, i.e., as the result of high layers of hot gases. In 1908, however, Hale discovered at Mount Wilson that their origin was entirely different, *viz.*, the magnetic doubling of the lines through the Zeeman effect. The two components were circularly polarized in opposite directions, showing that strong magnetic fields were acting in the sunspots. It was remarkable that pairs of spots following one another in the solar rotation, which in the Hα light often show opposite directions in the vortex structure, also showed opposite magnetic fields. More remarkable was that the sequence of polarity in such a pair in the northern hemisphere was opposite to the sequence in the southern hemisphere. It suggested the opposite direction of rotation of tornadoes on earth at both sides of the equator. When the whirling charged particles in the two spots forming a pair had opposite directions, Hale considered them as opposite ends of one vortex tube situated in the deeper parts and producing spot phenomena where it ended at the surface. The many new ideas and problems raised by these phenomena acquired a still more curious and mysterious aspect when, after the sunspot minimum of 1912, it appeared that the polarities of the northern and southern hemispheres had interchanged. After the minimum of 1922, a new change took place. It might thus be said that the real period of the sunspots, especially in their magnetic and rotational phenomena, was not eleven but twenty-two years.

Astrophysics could not become a real science until physics itself had developed the phenomena of radiation into a full theory at the beginning of the twentieth century. This development began with the establishment of the general laws of radiation. In 1870 they were so unknown that Secchi put the temperature of the sun's surface at some millions of degrees, whereas the physicist Pouillet found 2,000°. Both results were based on almost the same experimental value of the sun's amount of radiation, but in the one case the radiation was assumed to increase proportionally, in the other exponentially, with the temperature. In 1879 the Austrian physicist Stefan, from accurate measurements over a large range of temperatures, deduced that the total radiation was proportional to the fourth power of the absolute temperature. In 1884 Boltzmann gave a rigid theoretical demonstration of this law. Following along the same paths, Wien in 1893 deduced that the radiation of a perfectly black body was given by one single function of the wavelength, which with changing temperature shifted in such a way that the wavelength of its maximum was inversely proportional to the temperature. These two laws, applied to observational data, established that the temperature of the sun's surface was nearly 6,000°. In 1906 they found their final completion in the radiation formula of Max Planck.

Although Niels Bohr's atomic model, constructed on the basis of the structure devised by Rutherford from his experiments, was not yet developed at that time, it was already clear that the absorption lines observed in the spectra of the sun and the stars could give information on the interchange of energy of the atoms and hence on the physical conditions of the stellar atmosphere. In 1905 Karl Schwarzschild gave a theory of the sun's atmosphere based on the principle of radiative equilibrium according to which the temperature at any point is determined by the radiation interchange. This work, developed later by Milne and Eddington, satisfactorily explained the continuous spectrum and the Fraunhofer lines; it was also the beginning of theoretical research on the physics of stellar atmospheres.

More than a period of progress and conquest, the end of the nineteenth century and the first years of the twentieth, can be considered a preparation for the marvellous developments of the new astrophysics.

In fact, the astronomical instruments of this period, mainly reflectors, were more or less the prototypes of the giants of Mts. Wilson and Palomar which allowed the astronomers to understand the structure and dynamic of our Galaxy, confirmed the existence of a large number of other Galaxies similar to our own, and later discovered the red shift and thus the expansion of the universe. But on a smaller scale, we also see that the spectral classification and the measurement of the stellar parallax lead to the famous H-R diagram produced by the imagination and skill of astronomers like Hertzsprung and Russell. This diagram interpreted according to modern thermonuclear reactions explains almost completely the evolution of the stars. The same can be said about the, sometime tedious, observations of the variable stars. The δ Cephei type, or Cepheids, in the hands of Harlow Shapley and Miss Leavitt produced the famous period-luminosity relationship which became a powerful tool for estimating the distances of clusters and galaxies, once a Cepheid variable was discovered in each group. And we cannot forget the criteria for luminosity discovered simply by evaluating the relative intensity of some lines in the spectra of the stars. From this criteria originated the so-called "spectroscopic parallaxes," which filled the gap left from the method of the trigonometric parallaxes and which allowed astronomers to establish the correct dimensions of our Galaxy.

And, last but not least, solar studies received a strong impulse from the invention of the spectroheliograph; which in turn led to the invention of the spectrohelioscope by Hale, the coronograph by Lyot, and the monochromatic filter by Öhman and Lyot. All of these instruments have contributed to a better knowledge of the solar phenomena and a better understanding of the structure of our sun. The progress made by spectroscopy has helped solve the enigma of the spectrum of the solar corona, thus eliminating the existence of two ghost elements: "the coronium," which was invented to explain the anomalous line of the corona, and "nebulium," which had been invoked to explain the spectrum of the gaseous nubulae.

Opposite: Rutherford's Laboratory Notebooks (see pages 98-99).